ATLAS OF
THE
MIDDLE EAST

ATLAS OF THE MIDDLE EAST

Edited by
MOSHE BRAWER
Tel Aviv University

Prepared by
CARTA, JERUSALEM

MACMILLAN PUBLISHING COMPANY
NEW YORK

COLLIER MACMILLAN PUBLISHERS
LONDON

Editors: Moshe Brawer
Amnon Kartin

Zeev Stössel
Barbara Ball
Sarah Postavsky

Art Director: Eli Kellerman

Copyright © 1988 by Carta, The Israel Map and Publishing Company Ltd.

Macmillan Publishing Company
866 Third Avenue, New York, NY 10022
Collier Macmillan Canada, Inc.

Library of Congress Catalog Number: 88-675435

Printed in the United States of America

printing number
1 2 3 4 5 6 7 8 9 10

Library of Congress Cataloging-in-Publication Data
Karta (Firm)
  Atlas of the Middle East.

  Bibliography: p.
  1. Middle East--Maps. I. Brawer, Moshe, 1919–
II. Title.
G2205.K33 1988   912´.56   88-675435
ISBN 0-02-905271-8

CONTENTS

Abbreviations

° C.	degree Celsius
° F.	degree Fahrenheit
ft	feet
GDP	gross domestic product
in	inches
km	kilometers
mm	millimeters
sq.	square
sq.km	square kilometers

Common geographical abbreviations

I.	Island
J.	Jabal (mountain)
Mt., Mts.	Mount, Mountains
W.	Wādī (watercourse)

Flag color symbols

black   white   yellow   red   blue   brown   green

THE
REGION

The Middle East

There is no agreed definition as to the extent of the
Middle East. There is, however, a wide consensus
that Turkey, Cyprus, Iran, Iraq, Syria, Lebanon,
Jordan, Israel, Egypt, and the Arabian Peninsula
states must be included by all definitions.

To these countries, Sudan was added because
of the importance of the Nile valley, which runs
the length of the country, and Libya because of
the oilfields, which are a continuation of those in
Egypt and the Gulf of Suez.

Since World War II, after having achieved independence, these two countries have been closely
associated with other Middle Eastern states, and
they are part of the political reality of the region.

The total area of the countries surveyed in this
Atlas is 4,425,901 square miles (11,463,094 sq.km),
some 8 percent of the earth's land surface.

The population in the late 1980s was estimated
at 230,000,000 people, about 4.6 percent of the
world's population.

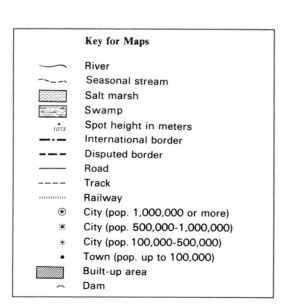

Key for Maps	
⌇	River
⌇	Seasonal stream
▦	Salt marsh
▦	Swamp
▲ 1073	Spot height in meters
–·–·–	International border
– – –	Disputed border
———	Road
– – – –	Track
··········	Railway
✴	City (pop. 1,000,000 or more)
▣	City (pop. 500,000-1,000,000)
◉	City (pop. 100,000-500,000)
•	Town (pop. up to 100,000)
▨	Built-up area
⌒	Dam

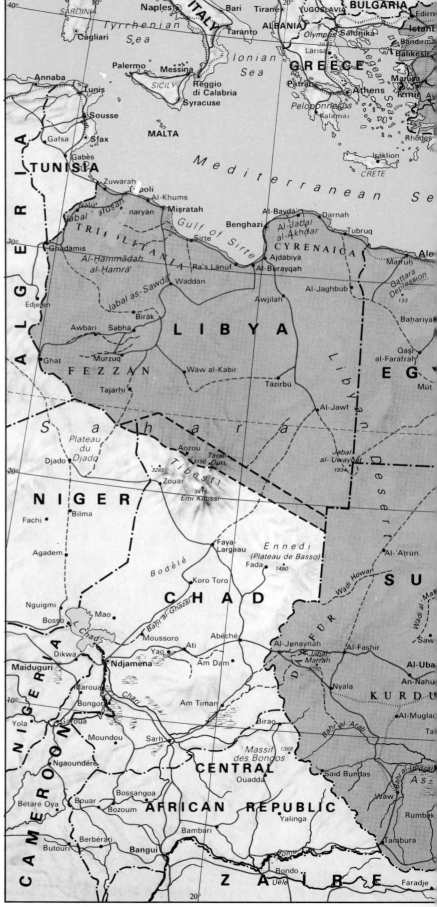

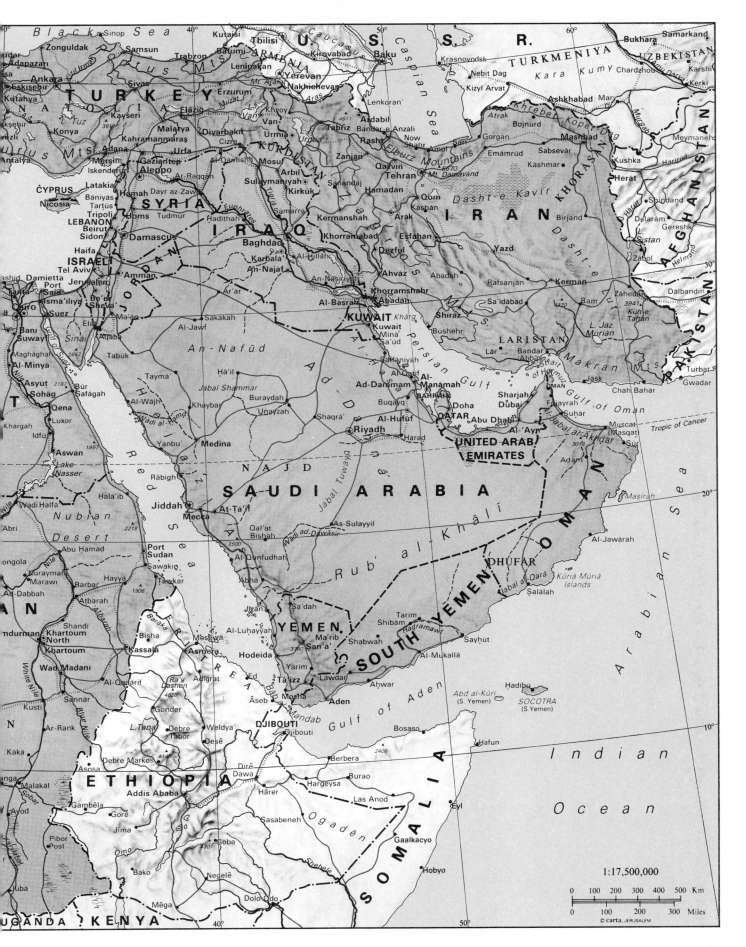

9

Geology

The geological structure of the Middle East to a large extent resulted from the gradual breakup of the ancient "Gondwana" continent, which extended over the earth's southern hemisphere. During this process, which began more than 200 million years ago, the detached fragments were drawn toward the ancient northern continent of "Laurasia." This continental drift, which extended over much of the Cretaceous period (some 70 million years ago), caused the earth's crust to fold in the area between the two continents. The bed of the Tethys Sea, which separated these continents, was covered by thick layers of marine sediments. These were folded and lifted to form the main mountain systems of the Middle East.

These events left the Middle East with three principal geological features: the Arabo-Nubian Massif, the Alpine mountain systems, and an intermediary zone.

In the geological past, the Arabo-Nubian Massif was part of the "Gondwana" continent. The massif is built mainly of crystalline and metamorphic rock, which is exposed in the central part of the massif — in the western part of the Arabian Peninsula, in southern Sinai, and in the eastern regions of Egypt and the Sudan. Much of the eastern and western parts of the massif are overlaid by thick beds of continental sediments (sandstone) and marine sediments (limestone). The former is a product of erosion of the massif itself, and the latter results from the submergence under the Tethys Sea, which during some periods flooded sections of the massif. Another tectonic activity in the region is the faulting and uplifting of the areas consisting of hard, igneous rock. This is most prominently expressed in the Syrian-African Rift, which cuts the massif into two parts in the Red Sea.

The Alpine mountain systems formed as a result of the convergence between the ancient continent of "Laurasia" and those blocks of the "Gondwana" continent that drifted northward. This convergence brought about the folding of the marine sediments embedded in the Tethys Sea, and formed the high mountain chains in Turkey, Iran, and Oman.

Part of these mountains were formed around ancient massifs built of hard igneous rock, which withstood the waves of folding. Examples are the mountain chains that surround the plateaus of Iran and Anatolia, built in part from ancient massifs. A secondary wave of folding lifted the eastern margins of the Mediterranean Sea. Because of this area's proximity to the ancient massif, this folding process was less intense, resulting in the lower elevations and simpler structures of the mountains along the eastern coast of the Mediterranean.

The Arabo-Nubian Massif and the region of the Alpine mountain systems are separated by a large depression which includes north Syria, the Tigris and Euphrates river valleys, and the northern part of the Arabian Peninsula. This region is built of thick beds of marine sediments that were deposited primarily in the Tethys Sea and underwent only light folding. This geological structure produced in some areas the conditions that brought about the formation and accumulation of the huge petroleum reservoirs of the Middle East.

An important geological process was the formation of the Syrian-African Rift at the end of the Tertiary period, about 25 million years ago. This process resulted in breaking up the Arabo-Nubian Massif into two parts separated by the Red Sea

— the Arabian Peninsula and northeast Africa. The widening of the Red Sea has been going on to this day, and the Arabian Peninsula continues to drift away from Africa. The formation of the rift was accompanied by volcanic eruptions along its margins, leading to the presence of volcanic rock over large areas. The extensive basalt-covered regions in Yemen and south Syria are prominent examples of this feature.

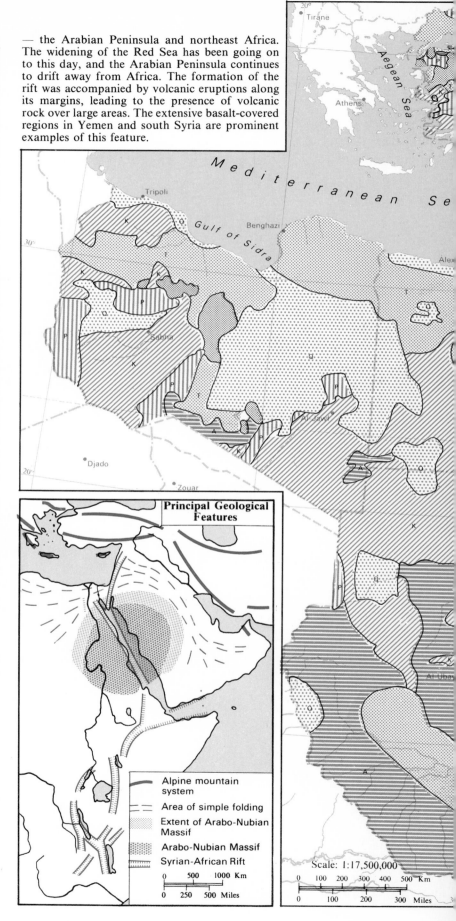

Principal Geological Features

— Alpine mountain system
- - - Area of simple folding
Extent of Arabo-Nubian Massif
Arabo-Nubian Massif
Syrian-African Rift

0   500   1000 Km
0   250   500 Miles

Scale: 1:17,500,000

0   100 200 300 400 500 Km
0   100   200   300 Miles

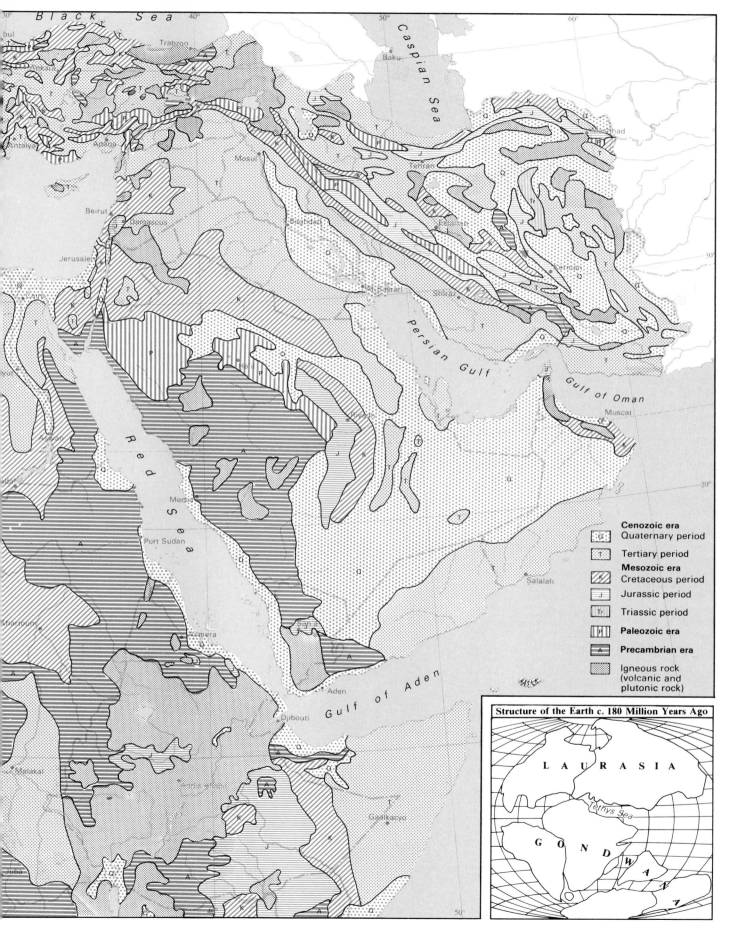

Black Sea

Caspian Sea

Trabzon

Baku

Ankara

Mosul

Tehran

Mashhad

Antalya

Adana

Beirut

Damascus

Jerusalem

Baghdad

Isfahan

Kerman

Al Basrah

Shiraz

Persian Gulf

Gulf of Oman

Muscat

Aswan

Red Sea

Medina

Port Sudan

Khartoum

Kassala

Salalah

Gaalkacyo

Aden

Gulf of Aden

Djibouti

Malakal

Juba

Cenozoic era
Quaternary period

Tertiary period

Mesozoic era
Cretaceous period

Jurassic period

Triassic period

Paleozoic era

Precambrian era

Igneous rock
(volcanic and
plutonic rock)

Structure of the Earth c. 180 Million Years Ago

L A U R A S I A

Tethys Sea

G O N D W A N A

Climate

The Middle East region extends over the belt between latitudes 4° and 42° N. The principal climatic factor affecting the region is the subtropical high barometric pressure. This high pressure is formed as a result of descending dry tropical air from the upper layers of the atmosphere which becomes warmer and dryer along the way. Accordingly, a stable climatic regime prevails in regions with a subtropical high pressure system, characterized by high temperatures and no precipitation. This is the reason behind the formation of the deserts in latitudes 20–28° N, where a subtropical high pressure system prevails year around.

The extent of the area subject to the subtropical high undergoes seasonal changes. In summer the high moves northward and is found over latitudes 20–40° N, and in winter it moves southward to latitudes 10–28° N.

Summer Conditions !n summer, warm and dry tropical air prevails over most of the Middle East, and, together with the strong solar radiation, high temperatures result. It becomes particularly warm in the regions of the Persian Gulf and southern Sudan, over which low-pressure centers form. The low centers, developing over the Persian Gulf, extend from Iraq to Cyprus via northern Syria. Similarly, the barometric low over the southern Sudan extends through Ethiopia to the southern Arabian Peninsula. In the region over which this latter low center extends, precipitation falls in summer.

In the hottest months (July and August), the mean temperature along the Persian Gulf coast reaches 96.8° F. (36° C.). In most of the Middle East regions in Africa, the Arabian Peninsula and on the Iranian Plateau, the mean temperature exceeds 86° F. (30° C.). In the mountainous regions in Turkey and western Iran with altitudes of more than 4,920 ft (1,500 meters), elevation moderates temperatures, although here, too, most mean temperatures exceed 68° F. (20° C.). In areas of increasing distance from the seas, there are marked differences between daily high and low temperatures.

Winter Conditions In winter, the subtropical high moves southward to latitudes 10–28° N. In the northern part of the Middle East (in Iran, Turkey, and sometimes as far as the northern part of the Arabian Peninsula and eastern Mediterranean), an extension of the Siberian high develops, the center of which lies over Siberia and central Asia. Over the Mediterranean lands between the two high-pressure centers there is less cooling than on the continental areas of Europe and Asia, and troughs of low pressure form. Through these troughs, cold and dry airstreams from central Asia and cold and humid airstreams from the Atlantic penetrate the Middle East. The cold air causes a drop in temperatures, and the meeting of the cold air with the humid and relatively warm air of the Mediterranean region results in the formation of fronts that cause precipitation.

South of latitude 28° N, the winter climate is different; here the subtropical high causes stability, resulting in relatively high temperatures and no rainfall.

Rainfall Regimes The Middle East has a number of distinct rainfall regimes:

1. Summer rainfall occurs in the southern parts of the Arabian Peninsula, in central and southern Sudan, and in regions adjoining the Black Sea and the Caspian Sea. The rainfall in the first two regions results from a northward movement of convective precipitation. The rainfall in areas around the Black Sea and Caspian Sea is a result of cyclones (depressions) reaching the region from the west and north.

2. A region with hardly any precipitation between latitudes 20° and 28° N. This belt is dominated by the subtropical high extended throughout the year, which prevents precipitation.

3. Winter rainfall occurs in areas north of latitude 28° N and in the southernmost part of Sudan. In the northern regions of the Middle East, rainfall is the result of the formation of cold fronts along

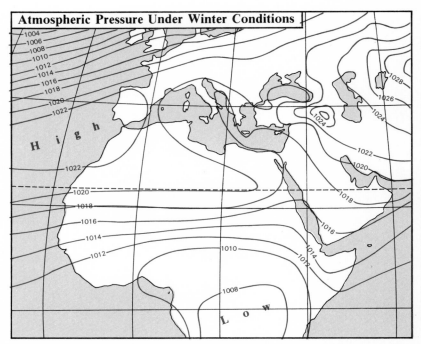

Atmospheric Pressure Under Winter Conditions

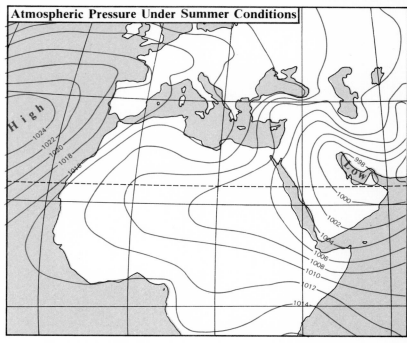

Atmospheric Pressure Under Summer Conditions

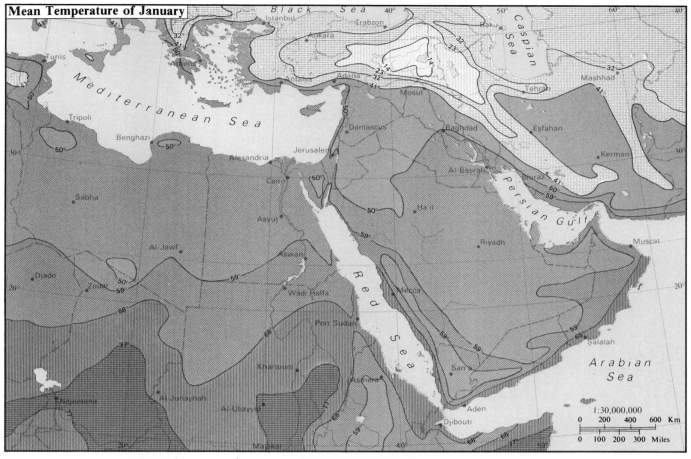

Mean Temperature of January

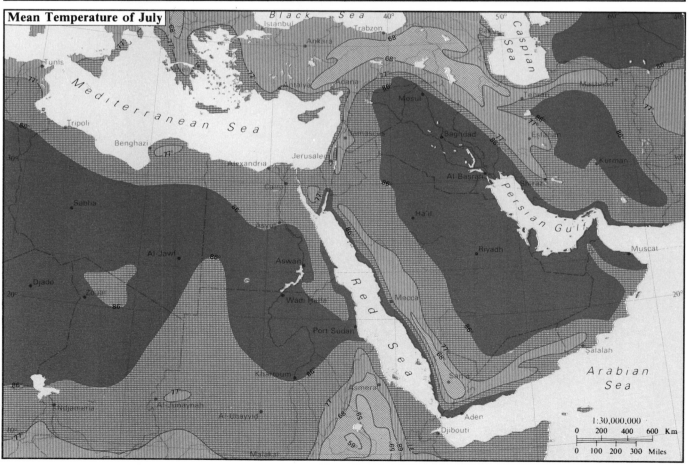

Mean Temperature of July

13

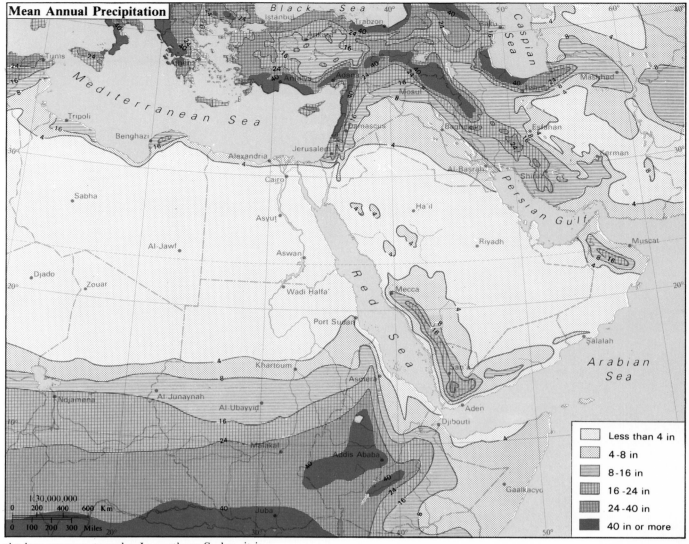

Mean Annual Precipitation

Legend:
- Less than 4 in
- 4-8 in
- 8-16 in
- 16-24 in
- 24-40 in
- 40 in or more

1:30,000,000

0 200 400 600 Km
0 100 200 300 Miles

the low-pressure troughs. In southern Sudan, it is convective precipitation.

In all parts of the Middle East, and mainly north of latitude 30° N, the region's topography has much influence on climatic conditions and especially on the extent and nature of precipitation. The high mountains along the Mediterranean Sea, the Black Sea, and the Caspian Sea receive large amounts of precipitation. Conversely, many inland areas, situated in a "rain shadow" formed by high mountains — the Anatolian Plateau, the Iranian Plateau, and the Syrian-African Rift valley — receive only small amounts of rain.

Average Summer Precipitation, June-September

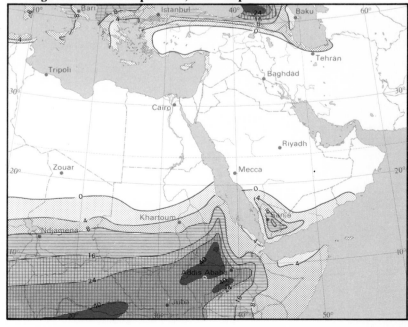

Fauna and Flora

The Middle East contains a great and rich diversity of both plants and animals whose origins stem from all over the old world — Africa, Europe, and Asia. Their appearance in the Middle East came about because of geological and climatic changes in the area since the Miocene epoch.

Until that time, 20 to 24 million years ago, the southern part of Mesopotamia and the Arabian Peninsula were an integral part of the African continent. Turkey, Cyprus, and Iran were attached to the Eurasian landmass, which was separated from the African Plate by the Tethys Sea. This sea isolated the tropical species, which dominated the regions of the African Plate, from the northern species prevailing in parts of Eurasia.

At the beginning of the Miocene epoch, the Tethys Sea receded and began to form the first land bridge between the African Plate and Eurasia. Northern species dispersed south and tropical species north over this land bridge. This process continued intermittently and underwent changes throughout the Miocene and partly during the Pliocene epochs.

This time also saw two additional events. The Syrian-African Rift began to form, resulting in the separation of the Arabian Peninsula from Africa by the Red Sea. Only in northern Sinai did there remain a land bridge connecting Africa with Asia. The second event was the creation of a desert belt between latitudes 10° and 30° N. In this belt communities of plants and animals developed that had adapted to desert conditions (the Saharo-Arabian region).

These developments created two biogeographical barriers: the Red Sea, which left northern Sinai as the single corridor for the various species; and the desert belt, which prevented the tropical species in north Africa and the Levant from moving to the tropical region of Africa.

During the Pliocene but mainly in the Pleistocene, there was a global decrease in temperature in the Levant and north Africa. This resulted in the penetration of many northern plants and animals, in the extinction of some tropical species, and in others being concentrated in special habitats where hot and humid conditions prevailed, such as desert oases and swamp areas. Such habitats are prevalent in the Sudanese region.

The Middle East can be divided into the following biogeographical regions:

The Saharo-Arabian region includes the desert belts of the Sahara, the Arabian Peninsula, and part of Iraq, where a typical desert climate prevails. Annual precipitation never exceeds 5.9 in (150 mm) and is usually less than 2.0 in (50 mm), with marked differences in rainfall each year. The differences between high and low diurnal temperatures are also pronounced, as are those of summer and winter. Humidity is generally low.

Both plants and animals have adapted to these desert conditions. The vegetation is mostly annual and completes its life cycle in the short rainy season. Some of the perennial plants change foliage each year — broad leaves in winter and thin leaves in summer. The variety of species is limited when compared to more humid climates. Among the perennial shrubs, the desert broom, desert anabasis, monospermous wormwood, and the zygophyllum shrub deserve mention, and among the wildlife, the Arabian gazelle, Persian gazelle, and the Arabian oryx.

The Mediterranean region includes all areas close to the northern Mediterranean shores and eastward, as well as part of the north African coast. This region has a temperate and rainy climate in winter, with 15.8–47.3 in (400–1,200 mm) of rainfall, and a hot and dry summer with no precipitation. During the glacial periods, the Mediterranean region was much more extensive than today. We can therefore find remnants of Mediterranean fauna and flora in parts of the Sahara and on Arabian mountain peaks. In these locations, prevailing climatic conditions permit the continued existence of such life.

The Mediterranean flora consists of forests, evergreens, wasteland, and scrubland. Characteristic arboreal species of the region are the Jerusalem pine, the mastic tree, the bay laurel, and the carob. In the eastern Mediterranean region, there are many varieties of geophytes (plants with bulbs or rhizomes) and trees such as the Tabor oak, hanging oak, Syrian maple, and the oriental plane tree. Among the animals, wild boars and the Carmel gazelle can be found.

The Irano-Turanian region covers parts of Iran, Turkey, Iraq, and Syria. The climate of this region is steppe–desert, with rains in winter and sometimes snow. The average annual precipitation is between 5.9 and 13.8 in (150 and 350 mm). Differences in diurnal temperatures and those between winter and summer are extreme.

The vegetation of this region consists mainly of annual grasses and dwarf-shrubs such as the desert wormwood and, in isolated spots, trees such as the Atlantic terebinth. The blossoming season is limited to spring and early summer.

There are no animal species characteristic of this region. Most of the existing wildlife migrated from the north mainly during the Quaternary, and acclimatized to conditions of desert life, among them the long-eared hedgehog, the fat jird, and the onager.

The Sudanese region stretches mainly across the part of Africa just south of the Sahara desert. This region has relatively high temperatures year around, with two rainy seasons in spring and fall.

Jackal

Leopard

Ibex

Average annual rainfall is 9.9–19.7 in (250–500 mm). Sudanese vegetation can also be found in those regions of the Middle East that have similar climatic conditions.

Vegetation and wildlife consist of the remnants of tropical plants and animals that were indigenous to extensive areas in the Middle East until the glacial periods in the Quaternary. When the climate became colder, these species continued to exist only in areas that remained fairly warm and humid, such as in the Syrian-African Rift valley, the coastal regions of Arabia and the Persian Gulf, the desert oases, and some lakes and swamps.

Savannah vegetation characteristic of the Sudanese region includes perennial grasses (mainly from the grain family) and the acacia tree, the tooth-brush (salvadora) tree, and the doom palm. Among the tropical wildlife are the leopard and caracal.

The Irano-Siberian region covers northern Turkey and northern Iran, which experience cold winters with snowfall and hot rainy summers. The main growing season is summer. Deciduous and coniferous forests are typical of the region, while the wildlife here, such as the brown bear, red deer, and Persian squirrel, stems from Europe and northern Asia.

Retama

Bird Migration In fall birds of the northern hemisphere migrate to the south, the majority to the African continent. They return in spring along the same route. Important routes cross the Middle East and millions of birds belonging to hundreds of species pass over the region each year.

The most important route is across Turkey, down the Syrian-African Rift, across the Red Sea and along the Nile to central Africa. This route is identical to the one taken millennia before, when, in the eastern Levant, a land bridge connected the northern continent ("Laurasia") with Africa.

This route allows the birds to fly overland instead of having to cross large bodies of water such as the Mediterranean. Good wind conditions for flights and landings along the Syrian-African Rift, as well as distinct routes, are additional advantages.

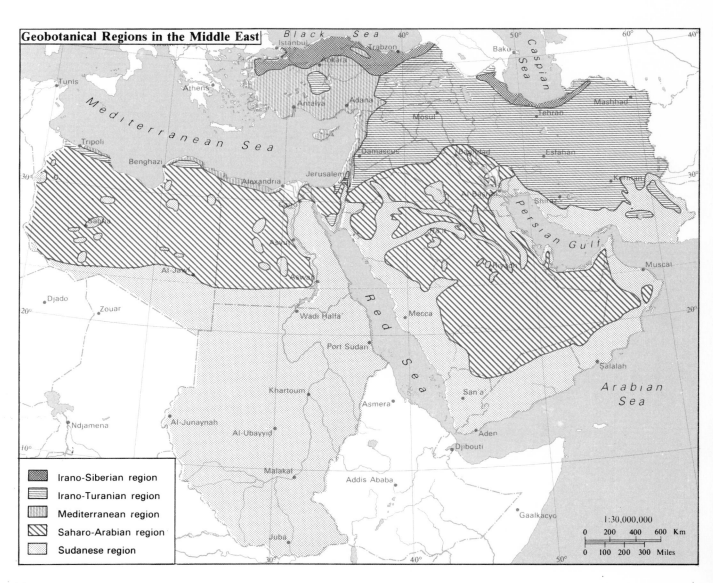

Geobotanical Regions in the Middle East

Irano-Siberian region
Irano-Turanian region
Mediterranean region
Saharo-Arabian region
Sudanese region

1:30,000,000

0 200 400 600 Km

0 100 200 300 Miles

Red-backed shrike

Yellow wagtail

Redstart

Swallow

Black kite

White stork

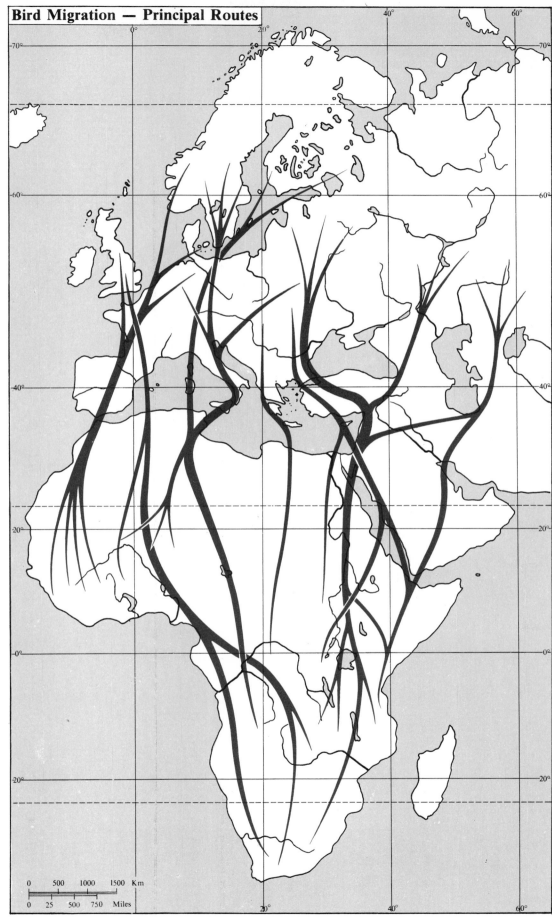

Bird Migration — Principal Routes

Population

The population of the Middle East is mainly Arab in terms of culture and language, and Muslim by religion. There are, however, other races, nationalities, and religions.

For millennia, the Middle East has been a focal point for migration and rule by many nations, some having entered the region from outside. These people left their ethnic and cultural impact on the Middle East.

The Middle East is the cradle of the world's three great monotheistic religions — Judaism, Christianity, and Islam. These religions, mainly Christianity and Islam, are divided into several sects or streams, hence producing a great variety of religious communities in the Middle East. Until the early twentieth century, the mountainous regions were to a great extent isolated from other areas. This enabled the minorities living in these regions to preserve their individual character.

The following races are represented in the population of the Middle East: Mongoloids (Turks, Azerbaijanis, and a number of ethnic groups in north Iran), Indo-Europeans (Iranians, Kurds, Greeks, and Armenians), Semites (Arabs and Jews), Hamites (parts of the population of Egypt and Sudan), and Negroids (Sudanese and Nylotic tribes). The Mongoloids and the Semites are the largest racial groups in the region.

The principal languages in the Middle East are: Arabic, spoken in Egypt, north Sudan, Libya, the Arabian Peninsula, Jordan, Syria, Lebanon, and Iraq; Turkish, current in Asia Minor and in some areas of north Iran; various Iranian languages, spoken by approximately 75 percent of Iran's populace; Greek, spoken in Cyprus; and Hebrew, in Israel. Kurdish and Armenian are spoken by minorities in some of the Middle East countries.

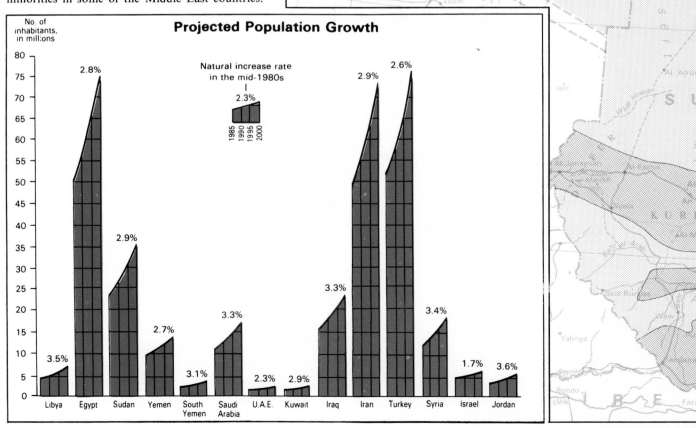

Projected Population Growth

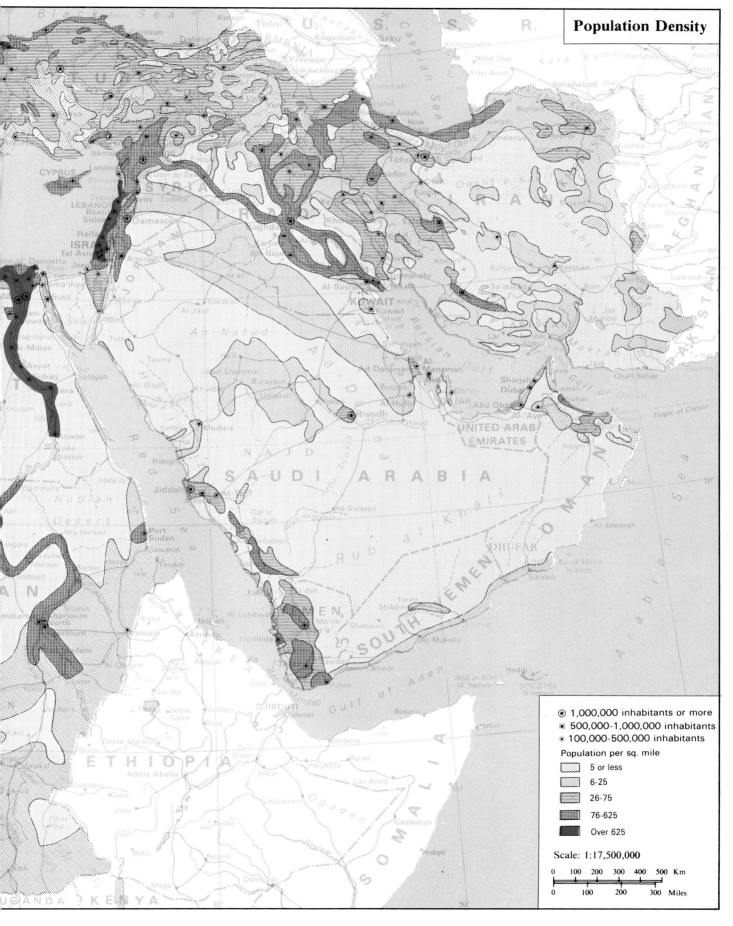

Population Density

⊛ 1,000,000 inhabitants or more
▣ 500,000-1,000,000 inhabitants
◉ 100,000-500,000 inhabitants

Population per sq. mile

5 or less
6-25
26-75
76-625
Over 625

Scale: 1:17,500,000

0   100   200   300   400   500 Km

0   100   200   300 Miles

Most of the Middle Eastern languages have a number of different dialects.

The principal religion in the Middle East is Islam, which is divided into two large sects — the Sunni and the Shiite sect. The Sunnis live all over the Middle East. The entire Muslim population of Turkey, Egypt, Saudi Arabia, Jordan, Israel, and Sudan, as well as a large proportion of Muslims in Qatar, Kuwait, the United Arab Emirates, South Yemen, and Libya, belong to the Sunni sect. The Shiite sect and its various subsects are a large majority in Iran and comprise approximately half of the population in Iraq, Yemen, Oman, and Bahrain. In Lebanon, 27 percent of the population are Shiites, and are known as Metawalis.

In Syria, about 12 percent of the population belong to the Alawite sect, whose origin stems from Shiite Islam. The Druze, a unique religious community also derived from Shiite Islam, live in Lebanon, Syria, and Israel.

Christianity in the Middle East is made up of several churches, the most prominent of which is the Coptic Church. Copts are the great majority of Christians in Egypt and Sudan. The Greek Orthodox form the second largest community; they are found mainly in Turkey, Cyprus, Syria, Lebanon, Jordan, Egypt, and Israel. Next is the Maronite Church whose followers are concentrated in Lebanon, where they constitute about 25 percent of the population.

The Armenian Christians are concentrated in Syria, Iraq, Lebanon, and Iran. Greek Catholics are mostly found in Syria, Lebanon, Jordan, and Israel. The other churches account for small minorities spread largely throughout Lebanon, Syria, Iraq, and Israel.

The majority of Jews in the Middle East live in Israel. There are a number of Jewish communities in Iran and Turkey, and very small communities in Syria, Iraq, Egypt, and Yemen. There are no Jews in Jordan or in Saudi Arabia.

Most of the Middle East population live in villages and subsist on agriculture. However, from the 1930s on, a process of rapid urbanization has taken place, encompassing much of the region. In

Israel, Lebanon, the Persian Gulf emirates, and Libya, the urban population accounts for more than 80 percent of the total population.

Some nomad communities live in the states with desert regions. Their numbers are gradually diminishing as a result of central government policies to settle them in permanent villages.

In many of the Middle East regions, population is sparse, mainly because of the large desert areas, which are very poor in water resources. Relatively dense settlement exists in the central part of the Tigris and Euphrates river valleys (around Baghdād), in northern and western Turkey, and in parts of the coastal region of Libya (near Tripoli and Benghazi). The most densely inhabited areas are in Egypt — along the Nile river and its delta — and in the coastal regions of Israel and Lebanon.

Gross Domestic Product Per Capita, 1983-1985

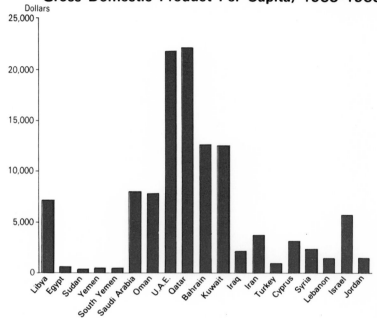

Rate of Urbanization

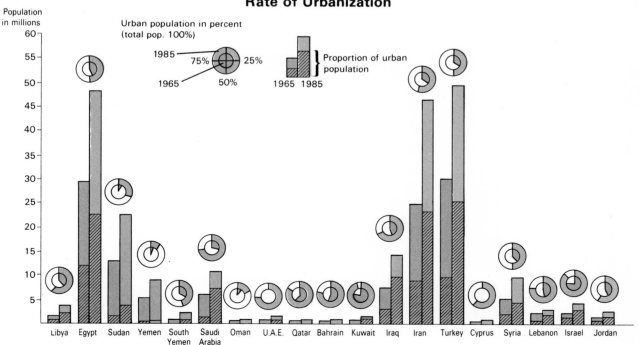

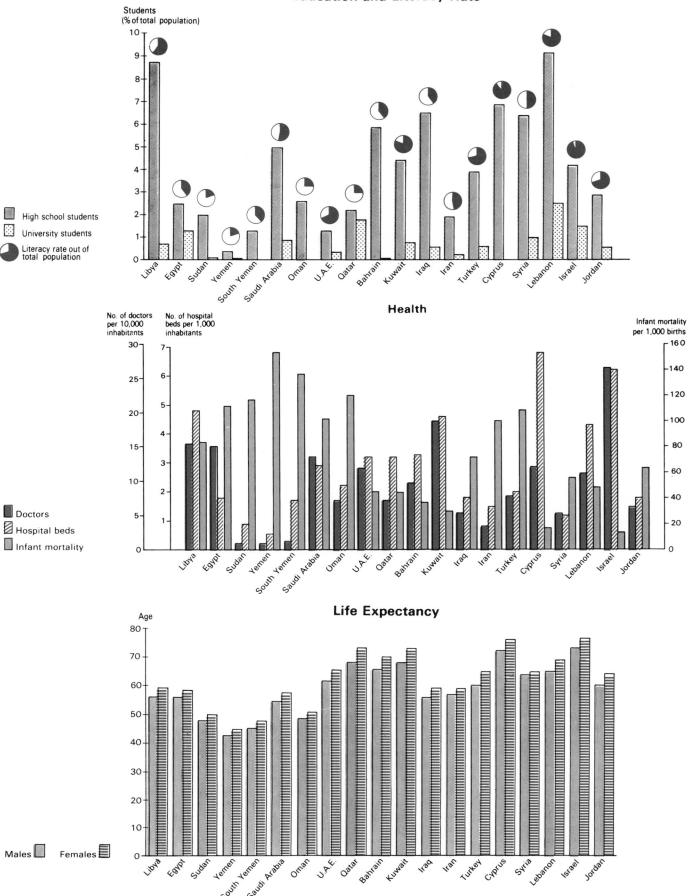

Education and Literacy Rate

Students
(% of total population)

- High school students
- University students
- Literacy rate out of total population

Health

No. of doctors per 10,000 inhabitants

No. of hospital beds per 1,000 inhabitants

Infant mortality per 1,000 births

- Doctors
- Hospital beds
- Infant mortality

Life Expectancy

Age

Males Females

Oil

Oil is a dominant factor in the economy of the Middle East, with a conspicuous impact on other aspects of the life of many inhabitants of the region.

Most of the rich oilfields in the Middle East were discovered after 1940. They are situated mainly in the Persian Gulf region, northeast Iraq, the Gulf of Suez, and Libya. These fields are estimated to hold approximately 54,500 million tons of crude oil, which in 1985 constituted about 57 percent of the world's proven reserves.

Commercial exploitation of oil started in Iran (then Persia) and on the shores of the Gulf of Suez at the turn of the century. Output was comparatively small — 4.7 percent of world production in 1939 — up to World War II. Only after World War II did oil become the dominant source of energy by rapidly replacing coal. This process called for accelerated production of oil in the Middle East. The region provided 16 percent of world production in 1950, 28 percent in 1965, and close to 36 percent in 1972.

After 1972 this percentage fell. In 1985 the Middle East produced 533 million tons of crude oil, or 19.3 percent of world production. Most of the oil is exported in its crude form. In the same year, the Middle East produced about 200 million tons of refined products, or 5.6 percent of world production.

Most of the oil is carried by tankers to its various destinations. To supply and service these tankers, modern and efficient terminals were built, connected by a network of pipelines to the oilfields. One such oil terminal, the largest in the

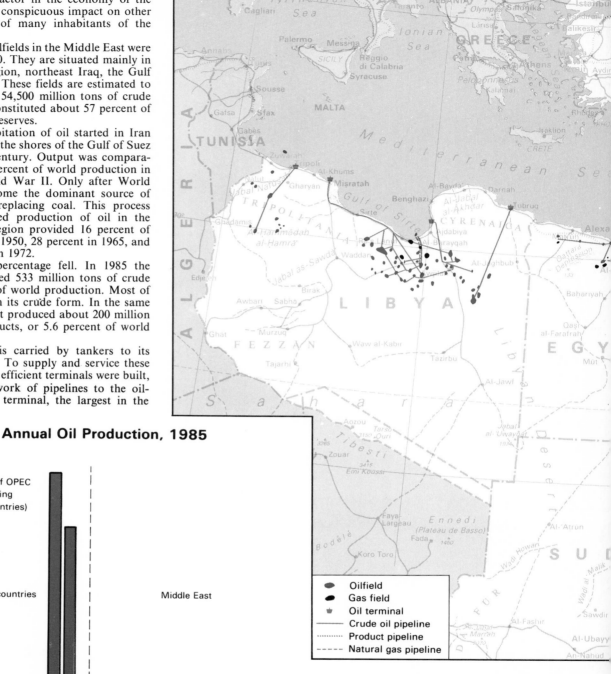

Annual Oil Production, 1985

Millions of tons

Members of OPEC
(Oil Producing
Export Countries)

Other selected countries

Middle East

Legend:
- Oilfield
- Gas field
- Oil terminal
- Crude oil pipeline
- Product pipeline
- Natural gas pipeline

world, was situated on Khārg Island off the coast of Iran. It ceased operating as a result of the Iraq–Iran war which started in 1980.

The rapid expansion of oil production from 1940 onward resulted in huge revenues for the oil-rich countries of the Middle East. The steep rises in the price of oil during the period 1973–1982 and the transfer of ownership from the international oil companies to the local governments contributed greatly to the enrichment of the oil-producing countries.

The steepest increase in oil prices occurred in 1973, when the major producers, mainly the Middle Eastern countries, reduced output drastically and raised prices by some 70 percent. This was made possible because of the high energy demand of

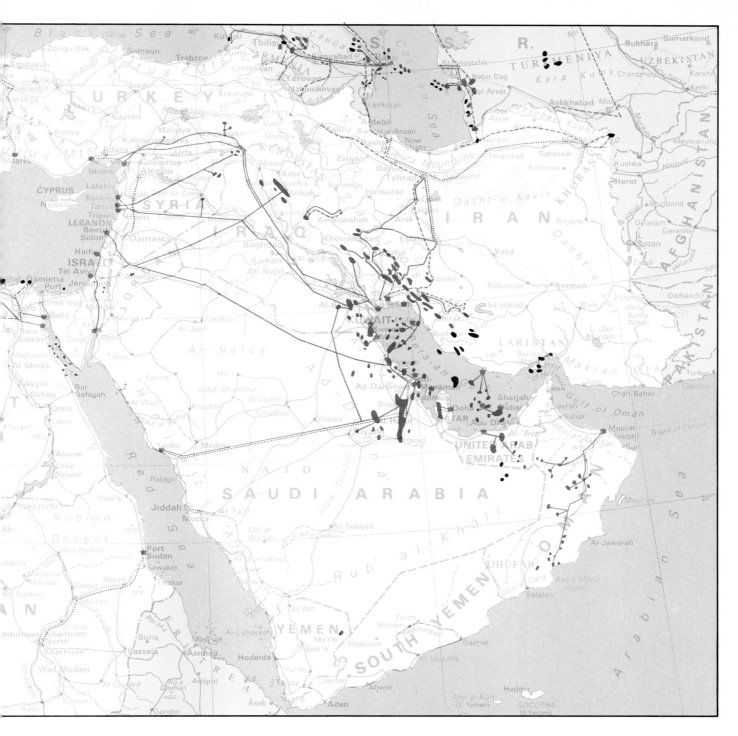

the period and because the industrial countries, all of them oil importers, had no short-term alternative. The resulting oil shortage caused hardships and diminished economic performance in these countries.

During the Yom Kippur War in October 1973 the Arab nations used the oil crisis as a political weapon, pressing the West to discontinue support of Israel.

Oil prices remained high through the 1970s. The huge income generated by the export of oil helped the producing countries to develop new economic projects and modern social services, which greatly improved the standard of living of their population. With the assistance of the oil-rich nations, the poorer countries of the region also enjoyed some progress, though to a lesser extent.

The economic process was accompanied by emigration from the poorer to the richer countries of the region. It is estimated that within the region some five million people migrated during the years 1973–1982.

Beginning in the early 1980s, demand for oil decreased. This was the direct result of the industrialized nations gradually developing alternative sources of energy — mainly coal, natural gas, and nuclear energy — and also promoting more efficient use of oil.

Oil prices subsequently dropped and income was reduced. This process in turn resulted in a slowdown of development in the various countries of the Middle East.

Political History

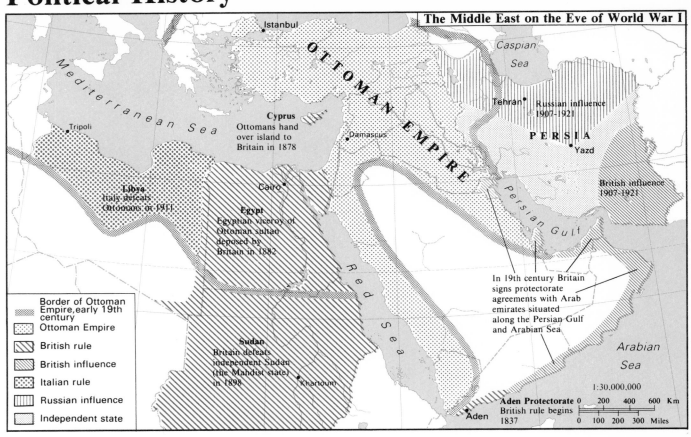

The Middle East on the Eve of World War I

Istanbul

OTTOMAN EMPIRE

Caspian Sea

Mediterranean Sea

Tripoli

Cyprus
Ottomans hand
over island to
Britain in 1878

Damascus

Tehran • Russian influence
1907-1921

P E R S I A
• Yazd

Cairo •

Libya
Italy defeats
Ottomans in 1911

Egypt
Egyptian viceroy of
Ottoman sultan
deposed by
Britain in 1882

Persian Gulf

British influence
1907-1921

Red Sea

In 19th century Britain
signs protectorate
agreements with Arab
emirates situated
along the Persian Gulf
and Arabian Sea

Sudan
Britain defeats
independent Sudan
(the Mahdist state)
in 1898

Khartoum •

Arabian Sea

1:30,000,000

Aden Protectorate 0   200   400   600 Km
British rule begins
1837   0 100 200 300 Miles

• Aden

░	Border of Ottoman Empire, early 19th century
⣿	Ottoman Empire
▨	British rule
▤	British influence
⣿	Italian rule
⦚	Russian influence
⣿	Independent state

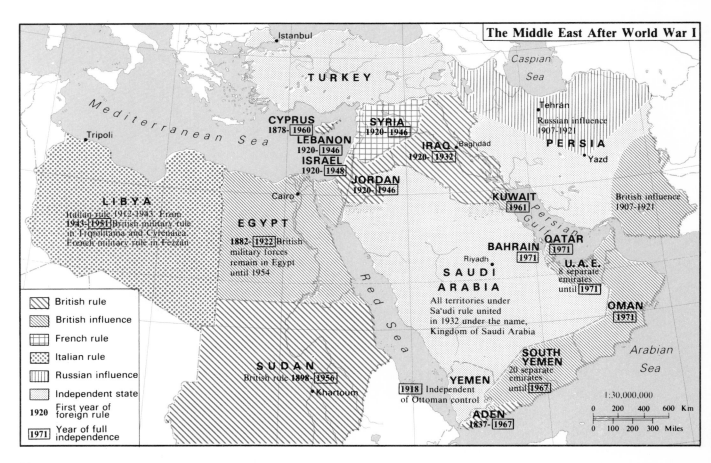

The Middle East After World War I

Istanbul

T U R K E Y

Caspian Sea

Mediterranean Sea

Tripoli

CYPRUS
1878- 1960
LEBANON
1920- 1946
ISRAEL
1920- 1948

SYRIA
1920- 1946

IRAQ • Baghdad
1920- 1932

Tehran •
Russian influence
1907-1921

P E R S I A
• Yazd

JORDAN
1920- 1946

LIBYA
Italian rule 1912-1943. From
1943- 1951 British military rule
in Tripolitania and Cyrenaica.
French military rule in Fezzan.

Cairo •

E G Y P T

1882- 1922 British
military forces
remain in Egypt
until 1954

KUWAIT
1961

Persian Gulf

British influence
1907-1921

QATAR
1971

BAHRAIN
1971

Riyadh •

S A U D I
A R A B I A

All territories under
Sa'udi rule united
in 1932 under the name,
Kingdom of Saudi Arabia

U.A.E.
8 separate
emirates
until 1971

OMAN
1971

Red Sea

Arabian Sea

SUDAN
British rule 1898- 1956

• Khartoum

1918 Independent
of Ottoman control

YEMEN

SOUTH
YEMEN
20 separate
emirates
until 1967

1:30,000,000

0   200   400   600 Km
0 100 200 300 Miles

ADEN
1837- 1967

▨	British rule
▤	British influence
▦	French rule
⣿	Italian rule
⦚	Russian influence
⣿	Independent state
1920	First year of foreign rule
1971	Year of full independence

Political Division of the Middle East Most of the political entities in the area known as the Middle East were carved out of the dismantled Ottoman Empire following World War I. Only Egypt and Persia (today Iran), countries with age-old traditions of their own, had defined boundaries at the beginning of the twentieth century.

The boundaries of the majority of countries were established by agreements between Britain and France, the two dominant powers in the area at that time, and by arrangements Britain made with local rulers and chieftains, mainly in the Arabian Peninsula. These arrangements in many instances ignored the geographical distribution of ethnic and national groups such as, for example, the Kurds in Turkey, Iraq, and Syria. Most boundaries, mainly those in desert areas and sparsely populated regions, were not clearly defined and were never demarcated on the ground.

The arbitrary treatment of most boundaries has been the cause of border disputes between various countries. On the Arabian Peninsula, these disputes became pronounced with the discovery of oilfields.

There have been few changes in these boundaries since they were formed in the early 1920s. The most prominent: in 1938 the Hatay district in northwest Syria was ceded by France to Turkey; in 1965 the Jordanian–Saudi border was redefined by agreement; from 1949 to 1975 border changes occurred between Israel and neighboring countries, and in 1979–1982, between Israel and Egypt.

The border disputes in the Middle East fall into three categories:

1. Active border disputes with frequent border tension and violent incidents. Such disputes exist between Iraq and Iran, the Arab states and Israel, Syria and Turkey, Libya and Chad, the two parts of Cyprus, and between Turkey and Greece on the Aegean Sea.

2. Standing border disputes that rarely result in violence, for example, between Iraq and Kuwait, Egypt and Libya, and Syria and Jordan. Many disputes relating to territorial waters occur between the Persian Gulf states.

3. Dormant claims without hostile actions, but with insistence on rights, such as between Egypt and Sudan, Turkey and the Soviet Union, and Saudi Arabia and Iraq.

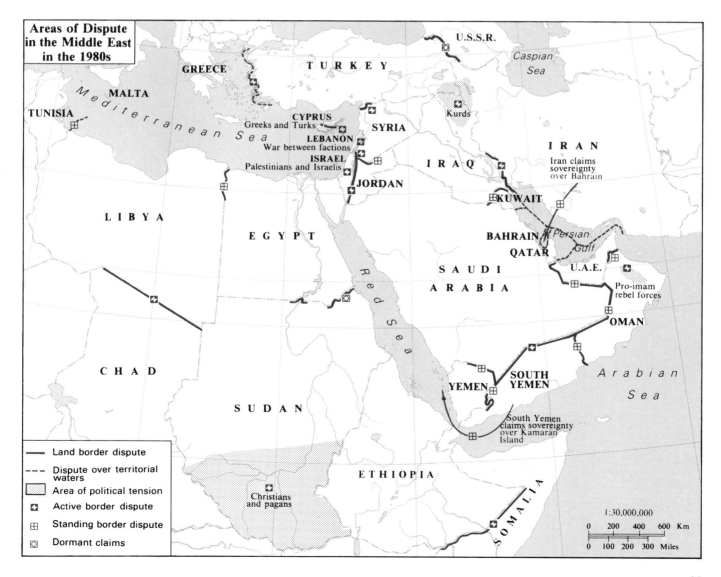

Areas of Dispute in the Middle East in the 1980s

Legend:
- —— Land border dispute
- - - - Dispute over territorial waters
- Area of political tension
- Active border dispute
- Standing border dispute
- Dormant claims

1:30,000,000

0 200 400 600 Km

0 100 200 300 Miles

Military Balance in the Middle East, 1986

	No. of soldiers, in thousands Regular + Reserve		Tanks	Fighter planes	Warships	Rate of defense cost as part of GDP
Libya	76.5	30	2280	550	33	7.5%
Egypt	320	360	2250	587	42	8.2%
Sudan	58.5		235	43	—	5.5%
Yemen	37	40	685	99	2	8.3%
South Yemen	27.5	45	470	62	8	17.6%
Saudi Arabia	73		550	226	20	20.9%
Oman	22		70	37	7	25.5%
United Arab Emirates	40		216	65	6	8.4%
Qatar	6		24	17	3	3.6%
Bahrain	2.8		—	12	4	3.4%
Kuwait	13		260	80	8	7.9%
Iraq	475	480	4500	590	23	65.5%
Iran	654	350	1000	60	16	6.8%
Turkey	650	950	3700	412	34	3.1%
Cyprus	13 + 30 (Greek zone) / 25 (Turkish zone)		8 (Greek zone) / 5 (Turkish zone)	— / —	— / —	Greek zone 3.4% *
Syria	407	270	4000	650	24	18.0%
Lebanon	No figures available					
Israel	140	504	3900	676	28	25.0%
Jordan	70	30	1000	109	6	17.3%

Source: The International Institute for Strategic Studies, The Military Balance, 1987-1988.

* No figures available for Turkish zone

THE
COUNTRIES

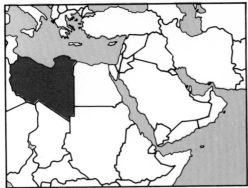

LIBYA

Area **679,358 sq. miles (1,759,540 sq.km)**
Population (1985 estimate) **3,900,000**
Capital city **Tripoli**
Gross domestic product (GDP) per capita (1984) **$7,175**

Population in main cities (1985 estimates)	Tripoli 700,000 Benghazi 300,000 Miṣrātah 100,000	Az-Zawiyah 80,000 Sabhā 50,000

Libya is located at the center of North Africa, and stretches from the Mediterranean Sea in the north down into the heart of the Sahara desert. Libya is bordered by Tunisia and Algeria to the west; Niger, Chad, and Sudan to the south; and Egypt to the east. Nearly all of its land surface is desert.

Topography Libya consists of two principal geographical regions. The western region includes the provinces of Tripolitania and Fezzān, and the eastern region comprises the Cyrenaica province and the Libyan desert. The Gulf of Sirte penetrates the coastline some 125 miles (200 km) between the two regions.

Tripolitania lies in the northwest of Libya. Its coastal plain, from the Tunisian border to the Gulf of Sirte, is 219 miles (350 km) long, and is called the Gefara plain. Much of the coastal plain is covered with sand, although in its eastern section — near the Gulf of Sirte — there are salt marshes. South of the coastal plain is a limestone massif, which reaches a height of approximately 3,250 ft (1,000 meters) and is called Jabal Nafūsah. The eastern extremities of the plateau reach almost to al-Khums on the coast. To the south, the plateau descends in a series of steps, with an area of volcanic rock, called Jabal as-Sawdā' at the plateau's southeastern edge.

The Sirte desert, to the south of the Gulf of Sirte, forms the eastern part of Tripolitania. In the vicinity of the coast there are salt lakes formed by dunes that close up outlets of sporadic streams. South of the coastal region lies a mountainous area called al-Harūj al-Aswad built of volcanic rocks.

The Fezzān region, lying to the south of Tripolitania, includes a series of depressions extending in an east–west direction, most of which are arid and covered by dunes and gravel. Groundwater found in some of these depressions feed the Fezzān oases, namely Sabhā, Murzuq, and Zuwaylah. To the south and southwest of the Fezzān region there are mountainous areas, comprising the edges of the Ajjer and Mangueni Plateaus (most of the former in Algeria, and the latter in Niger).

Cyrenaica, in the east of Libya, covers nearly half of the country's total area. In the north, near the Mediterranean Sea, the highlands of al-Jabal al-Akhḍar rise to a height of about 2,600 ft (800 meters). The northern and western slopes of al-Jabal al-Akhḍar are steep, bordered by a very narrow coastal plain. The eastern and southern slopes descend gently to the Libyan desert.

Nearly all of the area of Cyrenaica south of al-Jabal al-Akhḍar is covered by the Libyan desert. This is a large desert mostly covered by undulating sand dunes that sometimes reach 325 ft (100 meters) in height. A few oases are scattered throughout the desert, the largest being al-Khufrah, Jālū, and al-Jaghbūb.

A massif, known as the Tibesti Mountains, built mostly of granite, rises in the southern part of the desert. The highest peak inside Libya is 7,440 ft (2,268 meters). Most of the massif area, which stands out prominently in the Sahara desert, is in Chad.

Climate Libya's climate is characterized by hot and arid desert conditions. In the north, the Mediterranean Sea has a moderating influence on temperatures and is also responsible for greater rainfall there than in other parts of the country. The average monthly temperature in the hottest month (July) in the coastal region (Tripoli) is 85° F. (29° C.) decreasing to 57° F. (14° C.) in the coldest month (January). Further south, the average maximum temperature in the hottest month (July) reaches 104° F. (40° C.), decreasing to only 72° F. (22° C.) in the coldest month (January). At al-Jabal al-Akhḍar the temperatures are lower throughout the year than in other regions.

Libya's rainfall occurs in winter. The high parts of al-Jabal al-Akhḍar receive the largest average amount of precipitation — about 20 in (500 mm). An average of 12 in (300 mm) falls annually in the coastal regions of al-Jabal al-Akhḍar and Tripolitania and the higher parts of the adjoining plateau. Throughout the rest of Libya, including the coast of the Gulf of Sirte, the average annual precipitation is less than 4 in (100 mm).

Climate

RAINFALL AND TEMPERATURE

Annual temperature

Average monthly rainfall

8.6 in Total annual rainfall

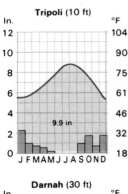

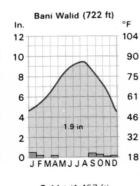

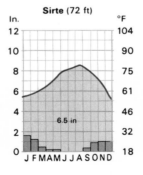

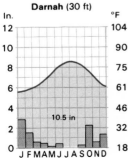

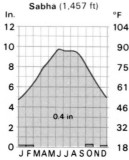

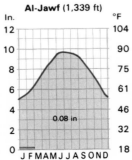

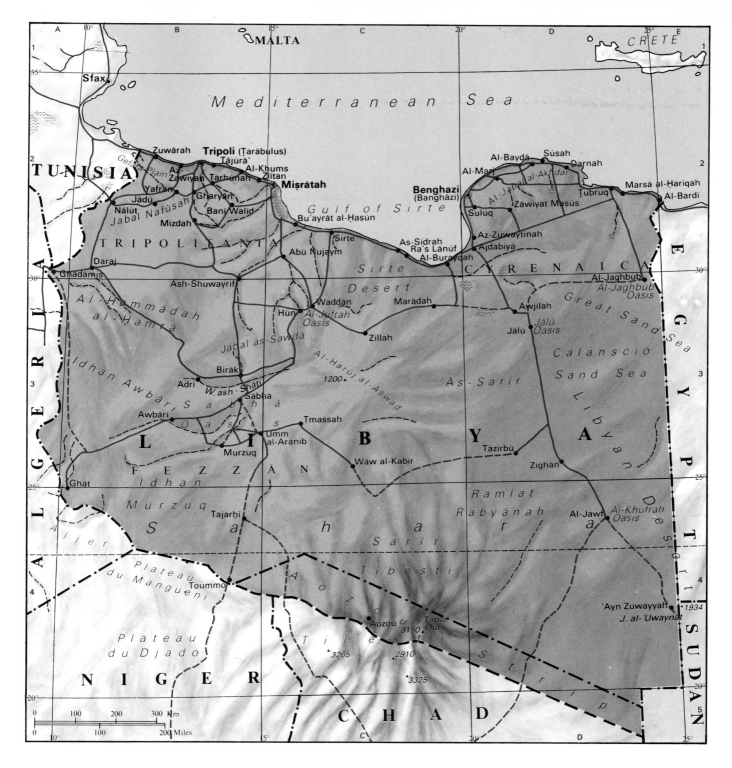

Between April and June, the *ghibli*, a hot, dry, and dust-carrying wind, blows over this region from the south, causing temperatures to rise by 60° to 70° F. (15° to 20° C.) within a matter of hours.

Population Ninety-seven percent of the country's population are Sunni Muslim Arabs. The Arabs first migrated to Libya in the seventh century and eventually became assimilated with the indigenous Berber population. The dominant language is Arabic although some inhabitants still speak a Berber dialect. The Berber culture is maintained to this day in villages of the plateau region and in the mountains in the west (Tripolitania). About 2 percent of the population are Christians, mainly of European origin. The population includes several tens of thousands of blacks (Sunni Muslims by religion), nomads of the Tuareg tribe who live in the Central Sahara, and members of the Tebu tribe, originating in Chad and living in the mountainous regions in the south and southwest of the country. There are also 500,000 foreign residents in Libya; the largest communities are Egyptians — 175,000, Tunisians — 75,000, and Turks — 45,000.

Some 85 percent of the population reside along the Mediterranean coast, the remainder live in

AGRICULTURE

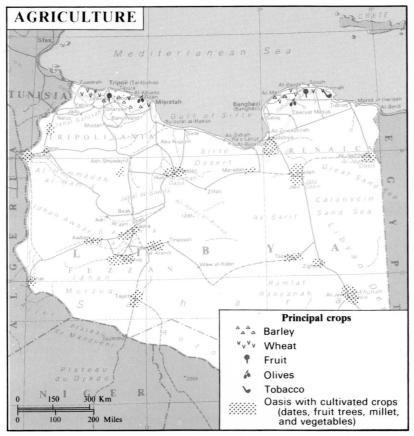

Principal crops
- △ᵃ△ Barley
- ᵛᵛᵛ Wheat
- ♀ Fruit
- ♪ Olives
- ↘ Tobacco
- :::::: Oasis with cultivated crops (dates, fruit trees, millet, and vegetables)

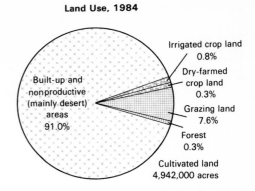

Land Use, 1984

Built-up and nonproductive (mainly desert) areas 91.0%

Irrigated crop land 0.8%
Dry-farmed crop land 0.3%
Grazing land 7.6%
Forest 0.3%
Cultivated land 4,942,000 acres

NATURAL INCREASE
(1980-1984)
3.5%

LIFE EXPECTANCY
(1980-1985)
male - **56.1** years
female - **59.4** years

DOCTORS
(1982)
15.7 per 10,000 inhabitants

HOSPITAL BEDS
(1982)
4.8 per 1,000 inhabitants

INFANT MORTALITY
(1985)
84.0 per 1,000 births

scattered oases in the interior. About 60 percent of the population reside in urban settlements, and 35 percent live in villages; the remaining 5 percent are nomads or seminomads.

Economy In 1957, petroleum was discovered in Libya. Commercial production began in the early 1960s. Until then, Libya's economy had been based on primitive agriculture and pasture. The discovery of oil, and with it the growth of petroleum and natural gas industries, have transformed Libya's economy. Oil revenues became the principal component of national income, enabling development to take place in all economic sectors.

Agriculture The cultivated area in Libya encompasses about 5 million acres — 1.1 percent of the country's land surface — and most of it is under irrigation. In addition, approximately 32 million acres — 7.6 percent of the land area — are used for pasture.

Most of the cultivated area is in the north, close to the sea, on the Gefara plain in the west, on al-Jabal al-Akhḍar in the east, and on the adjacent coastal plain. Some of these areas receive sufficient rain for dry-farming as well as for replenishing the groundwater reserves used for irrigated agriculture. The principal crops are barley, wheat, vegetables, olives, and citrus. In other areas, agriculture is confined to a number of oases in which dates, millet, and some vegetables are grown. Livestock plays an important part in Libyan agriculture, with 130,000 head of cattle, 7 million sheep and goats, over 100,000 camels, and a large poultry branch.

Since the total area under cultivation (dry and irrigated) is relatively small, Libya is obliged to import about 40 percent of its food requirements (especially wheat, barley, oil, vegetables, fruit, and meat).

Agriculture is a prime factor in national economic policy; some 10 percent of the national

budget was invested in it in the 1980s. Despite this, agricultural output has not substantially increased, mainly due to a lack of experienced manpower.

Since 1984, Libya has been running an ambitious project to exploit the enormous groundwater reservoirs in the al-Khufrah and Sarir regions in the east of the country and in the Fezzān region in the west. This project includes about 1,250 miles (2,000 km) of piping that carries water to the coastal region. These "artificial rivers" will expand the irrigated area by about 470,000 acres. A further 25,000 acres will be made fit for cultivation in the oases, particularly at al-Khufrah. The purpose of the project is to enable the country to produce its entire domestic food requirements. However, the "artificial river" project has not progressed as planned — the projected completion date is 1990 — due to a reduction in financial resources and lack of professional manpower.

Minerals Petroleum is Libya's major mineral resource. Most of the oilfields are concentrated southeast of the Gulf of Sirte. Additional fields are located close to the Algerian border. Libya also has an offshore oilfield (the Burī field), 75 miles (120 km) north of Tripoli.

Oil was first discovered in the Fezzān region near the border with Algeria. Production began in 1959 with output continually increasing until 1970, in which year 170 tons of crude oil were produced. After 1970, output was reduced due to the partial nationalization of oilfields operated by foreign oil companies, and the desire on the part of Libya's rulers to conserve oil reserves. In 1985, 52 million tons of crude oil were produced. The proven petroleum reserves in Libya total 3.5 billion tons.

Three refineries operate in Libya — at az-Zawiyah, Ra's Lānūf, and al-Burayqah. A fourth refinery is near completion at Ṭubruq. The annual output of the refineries totals 5.7 million tons. Most of the oil is exported through the seven oil terminals located along the Mediterranean coast, connected by pipelines to the oilfields.

Libya also produces natural gas. The gas reserves stand at 600 billion cubic meters. The output of gas in 1983 was 10.6 billion cubic meters. In addition, Libya has deposits of iron, potassium, magnesium, phosphates, lead and salt. However, these are not exploited due to inaccessibility and high production costs. There are plans to begin iron ore mining at Wādī ash-Shāṭi.

Industry Industry in Libya was relatively undeveloped until the mid-1970s, producing mostly basic foodstuffs, soft drinks, tobacco, and construction materials. Only 26,000 people were employed in industry in 1975 (4.8 percent of the work force). Increased oil revenues between 1975 and

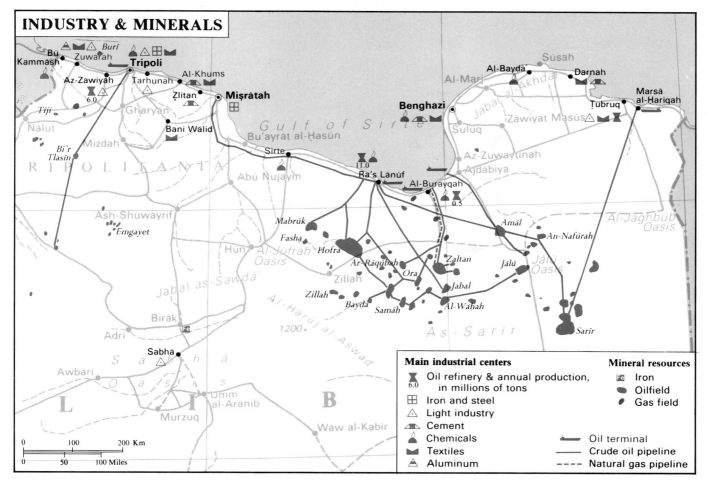

INDUSTRY & MINERALS

Main industrial centers

⚒ Oil refinery & annual production, 6.0 in millions of tons
⊞ Iron and steel
△ Light industry
⛰ Cement
♨ Chemicals
▰ Textiles
△ Aluminum

Mineral resources

Fe Iron
⬮ Oilfield
❟ Gas field

━◣ Oil terminal
——— Crude oil pipeline
- - - - Natural gas pipeline

1980 provided the resources for the development of heavy industry, especially industry based on crude oil resources. At the same time, a wide range of auxiliary industries were developed: an aluminum plant at Zuwārah, iron and steel works at Miṣrātah, and petrochemical works producing disinfectants, pesticides, plastics, and paints at Ra's Lānūf and al-Burayqah. The petrochemical plants supply synthetic materials for textile plants, which have been established near Tripoli, at Banī Walīd, Darnah, and other places. In addition, car, truck, and tractor assembly plants, tire factories, cement works, and plants for food production were set up during this period.

History Until modern times, there had never been a centralized independent authority in Libya. For the most part, power was in the hands of warring tribes or fell under the control of extensive empires of which the territory of Libya was a part. From the middle of the sixteenth century, the coastal region — and later on, areas to the south of the Mediterranean littoral — came under the suzerainty of the Ottoman Empire. Between 1711 and 1835, the inhabitants were granted autonomous rule, but Turkey reimposed its direct control over Libya in 1835 and declared it a Turkish Administrative District (*vilayet*). In September 1911, Italy declared war on Turkey and invaded Tripolitania. In the following year (October 1912), Turkey recognized Italian sovereignty over Libya.

The Italian administration was opposed by the local inhabitants, and Italy managed only to control Cyrenaica and Fezzān in the 1930s, by means of an iron-fist policy against its opponents. During the period of Italian control, tens of thousands

Oil Production and Income

Millions of tons / Billions of dollars

⊸ Income in dollars from oil production
▨ Crude oil

of Italians colonized the country, contributing to Libya's agricultural and commercial development.

During World War II, the Allies conquered Libya, and the country came under British military rule. In 1949, the United Nations decided to grant Libya independence. The country became an independent monarchy on December 24, 1951, and Idris as-Sanussi was crowned king.

Until 1963, Libya was a federal monarchy comprising three autonomous provinces, each with a local government and house of representatives. In 1963, the provinces were united under one central government controlled by King Idris. The monarchical government used a substantial part of

HIGH SCHOOL PUPILS (1982)
340,700

UNIVERSITY STUDENTS (1982)
25,700

LITERACY RATE (1983) 60%

31

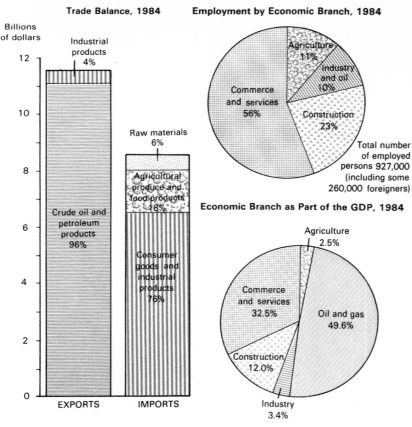

Trade Balance, 1984

Billions of dollars

Industrial products 4%

Crude oil and petroleum products 96%

Raw materials 6%

Agricultural produce and food products 18%

Consumer goods and industrial products 76%

EXPORTS   IMPORTS

Employment by Economic Branch, 1984

Agriculture 11%

Industry and oil 10%

Commerce and services 56%

Construction 23%

Total number of employed persons 927,000 (including some 260,000 foreigners)

Economic Branch as Part of the GDP, 1984

Agriculture 2.5%

Commerce and services 32.5%

Oil and gas 49.6%

Construction 12.0%

Industry 3.4%

the oil revenues to improve living standards and economic development. Agricultural projects were implemented, living conditions were improved, and education and health services were developed. Despite the use of 70 percent of the revenues for these projects, opposition to the government developed among army officers and the educated echelons of the population. These groups held the regime responsible for thwarting more rapid modernization.

In September 1969, a group of army officers led by Mu'ammar al-Qaddafi took over the government without any significant opposition and abolished the monarchy. The new regime reduced the power of the many tribes, particularly those in the Cyrenaica area, from whom much of the support for the monarchy had come.

During the first year of Qaddafi's rule, the British and American army bases were evacuated, the Italian "colony" was expelled and its property confiscated, and the oil companies were forced to increase their payments to the government coffers. During the first decade of Qaddafi's rule, the increased revenue was used to finance programs to improve the standard of living. Qaddafi formulated his own political ideology (contained in the "Green Book"), which he zealously imposed upon the population. His philosophy champions the Islamic religion together with a form of socialism that calls upon the people to rule over themselves. Opposition to his regime has been evidenced by more than thirty attempts to overthrow the government between 1969 and 1985.

Internal unrest has increased since the beginning of the 1980s mainly due to a scarcity of basic foodstuffs, resulting from a decrease in oil revenues. This unrest has generated coup attempts as well as the emigration of tens of thousands of Libyans.

Government and Politics   In theory, since 1977 Libya has enjoyed a popular democracy, through which the masses are involved in the decision-making process. In reality, control is in the hands of one man — Mu'ammar al-Qaddafi. Daily affairs of state are managed by a twenty-member body known as the Revolutionary Command Council. The government's activities are controlled by a secretariat consisting of five representatives who are loyal to Qaddafi's ideology and political methods. Until 1979, Qaddafi served as prime minister. In 1979 he became "leader of the revolution" without any formal position of state.

Throughout the country there are twenty-five "People's Committees," whose members are appointed by the government. These committees implement policy laid down by the central government. Alongside these are "Revolutionary Committees," whose task it is to maintain the principles of the regime and to protect the regime against its opponents, both from inside and from outside the country.

Libya takes an extreme stance on all political and social issues, including the support of terrorist movements throughout the world, whether in the Philippines, Ireland, Germany, or the Middle East, and any organization dedicated to damaging the interests of the United States or Israel. This philosophy is expressed through the financial support given to terrorists, some of whom have training camps and bases within Libya. As a result, Libya maintains close ties with other extremist regimes, such as those of Syria, South Yemen, and Iran, which Libya supports in its war with Iraq. Since the rise of Qaddafi to power, Libya has found itself in a position of diplomatic isolation both in the Arab world and in the West in general.

Economic and strategic interests in neighboring countries have led Libya to undertake subversive policies in Sudan, Egypt, Niger, Algeria, Morocco, and Chad, with which Libya has been engaged in a border war. In 1973, Libyan forces invaded the Aozou Strip of north Chad; most of the area has since remained under Libyan control. Libya's relations with Egypt also worsened following the peace talks between Egypt and Israel, and a number of border incidents took place between the two countries. Libya is also engaged in a dispute with Tunisia over the demarcation of the maritime boundary between the two countries.

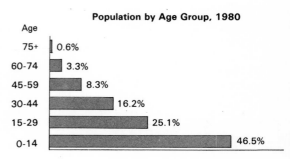

Population by Age Group, 1980

Age

75+ 0.6%

60-74 3.3%

45-59 8.3%

30-44 16.2%

15-29 25.1%

0-14 46.5%

EGYPT

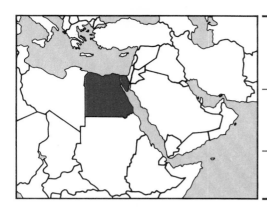

Area **386,659 sq. miles (1,001,449 sq.km)**
Population (1986 estimate) **49,000,000**
Capital city **Cairo**
Gross domestic product (GDP) per capita (1984) **$650**

Population in main cities (1983 estimates)		
Cairo 10,500,000	Suez 500,000	Al-Mahalla al-Kubrä 345,000
Alexandria 3,000,000	Port Said 450,000	
Giza 1,500,000	Isma'iliya 400,000	Asyüṭ 300,000

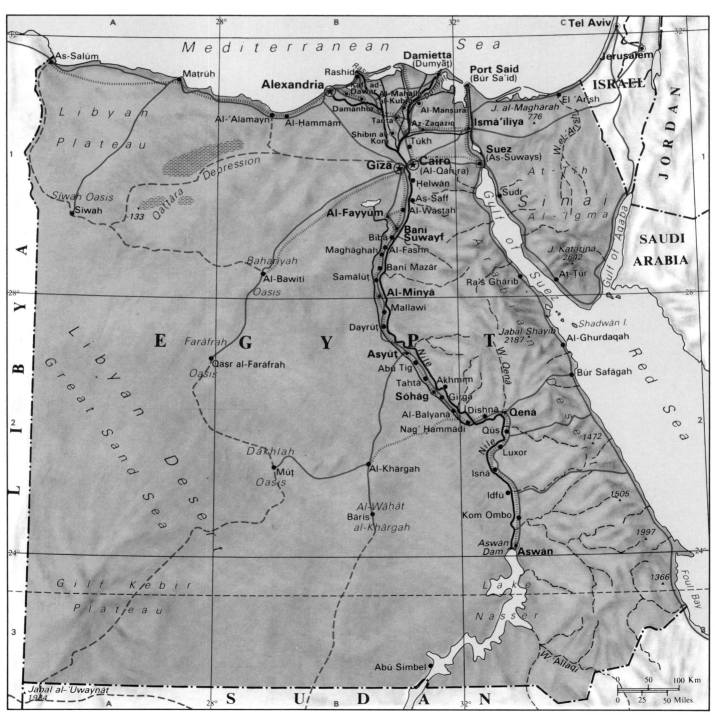

Egypt borders on Libya, Sudan, and Israel, with a coastline along the Mediterranean and. Red Sea.

Topography There are five geographical regions in Egypt: the western desert, the eastern desert, the Nile valley, the Nile delta, and the Sinai Peninsula.

1. The western desert (the Libyan desert) lies to the west of the Nile valley stretching beyond the Libyan border. This region covers approximately two-thirds of the country's total land surface — 270,300 sq. miles (700,000 sq.km). In the southwest of the region, there is a mountain area, Jabal al-'Uwaynāt (6,345 ft [1,934 meters]), built of crystalline rocks. From here, the desert slopes gently to the northeast interrupted by a series of cuestas, their steep side facing the southwest. Pre-Cambrian sandstone beds are exposed near Jabal al-'Uwaynāt. Younger limestone strata underlie the sand dunes that cover much of the desert. In the north, there is a chalk plateau with gravel taking up much of the desert surface. The plateau extends to the Nile valley in the east where a series of terraces rise to heights of 650 ft (200 meters). In the vicinity of the Libyan border, extensive areas are covered by sand dunes. Due to lack of rain the western desert does not have a permanent drainage system. Seasonal streams have formed channels in the north leading into the Mediterranean.

The western desert is crossed by a series of eight depressions, extending for hundreds of miles parallel to the Nile valley. In these depressions, the groundwater is near the surface, enabling the formation of oases with rich natural vegetation. Parts of some depressions are below sea level.

The largest of these is the Qattāra Depression, covering an area of 5,790 sq. miles (15,000 sq.km). Its lowest point is 436 ft (133 meters) below sea level. Most of it is covered by salt pans, which expand in winter and partly dry up in summer. It is possible that the salinity results from the penetration of sea water into the depression. Other important depressions are Sīwah, 80 ft (25 meters) below sea level, and al-Fayyūm, near the Nile valley. Cultivation takes place in most depressions.

2. The eastern desert stretches from the Nile valley in the west to the Gulf of Suez and the Red Sea in the east. It covers an area of approximately 84,900 sq. miles (220,150 sq.km), most of which is mountainous. The mountains form part of the Arabo-Nubian Massif and are mostly built of granite. The peaks reach nearly 6,560 ft (2,000 meters). The eastern desert mountains are extremely dissected, with narrow, steep valleys formed by occasional streams. Transportation through these mountains from the Nile valley to the Red Sea is extremely difficult, with the exception of the route that links Būr Safāgah on the Red Sea coast with Qenā in central Egypt. The northern and western parts of the eastern desert form thick beds of

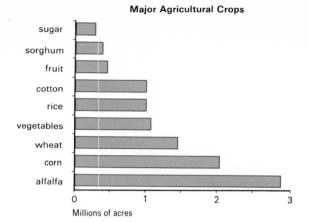

Major Agricultural Crops

Millions of acres

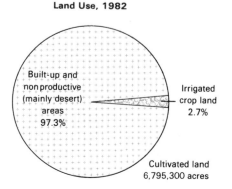

Land Use, 1982

Built-up and non productive (mainly desert) areas 97.3%

Irrigated crop land 2.7%

Cultivated land 6,795,300 acres

limestone. The northern extremity of the eastern desert is Jabal 'Ataqa, west of the city of Suez.

3. The Nile valley crosses Egypt from south to north. From the border with Sudan to the delta, its length is about 750 miles (1,200 km). Since the completion of the Aswān High Dam, the narrow part of the Nile valley in Upper Egypt has been transformed into a large water reservoir. The Aswān dams, new and old, were constructed at locations where the Nile cuts through dikes of granite. North of Aswān, the Nile flows through sandstone beds, the valley narrowing to only 1–3 miles (2–5 km). North of Isnā, limestone beds are exposed and the valley widens to widths of 7–10 miles (12–15 km) near Asyūt. For most of its course, the river flows close to the eastern edge of the valley. Most of the cultivated area is therefore located west of the river. Cairo and its outskirts form the northern end of the Nile valley.

4. The Nile delta is a low-lying plain, about 120 miles (200 km) wide, covering approximately 7,720 sq. miles (20,000 sq.km). The whole area is built of thin sediments, deposited in large quantities over thousands of years by the Nile. North of Cairo, the river forks into two main channels: Rashīd in the west and Dumyāt in the east. In ancient times, the Nile delta had several more branches. A dense network of canals and dikes, serving the needs of irrigation and preventing floods, has been constructed in the delta.

In the delta's northern margins, parallel to the coastline, there is a narrow belt covered by swamps and lagoons. Following the completion of the Aswān High Dam, the river ceased to carry sediments to the delta. The delta's building process came to an end and the sea began to erode the coastline.

5. The Sinai Peninsula stretches from the Suez Canal and the Gulf of Suez to the Gulf of 'Aqaba and the border with Israel. Granite mountains rise in the south of the peninsula, the highest peak, Jabal Katarīnā, reaching 8,668 ft (2,642 meters). These mountains are characterized by very rugged relief, and are dissected by many narrow and steep ravines. To the north of the mountains lies the Tīh Plateau, built of limestone and sandstone beds. This area is also deeply dissected by narrow valleys.

The northern part of the peninsula is an undulating lowland, partly covered by sand dunes and rows of hills. This lowland slopes gently northward toward the Mediterranean coast. Much of the region between the Tīh Plateau and the sea is drained by Wādī el-'Arīsh, flowing into the sea near the town of El 'Arīsh.

The Nile The sources of the Nile are located outside Egypt, mainly in the East African and

Climate

RAINFALL AND TEMPERATURE

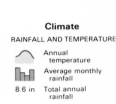

Annual temperature

Average monthly rainfall

8.6 in Total annual rainfall

Matrūh (82 ft)

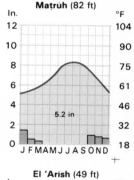

5.2 in

El 'Arīsh (49 ft)

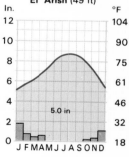

5.0 in

Dākhlah Oasis (360 ft)

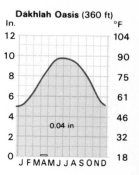

0.04 in

34

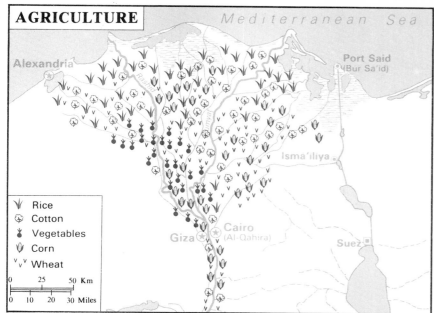

Rice
Cotton
Vegetables
Corn
Wheat

0 25 50 Km
0 10 20 30 Miles

AGRICULTURE

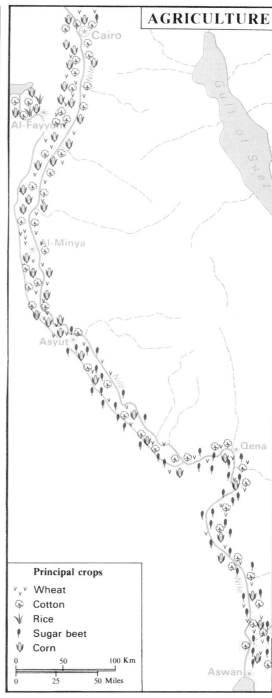

Principal crops

Wheat
Cotton
Rice
Sugar beet
Corn

0 50 100 Km
0 25 50 Miles

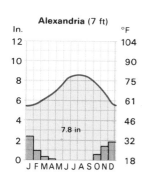

Alexandria (7 ft)

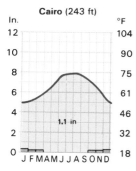

Cairo (243 ft)

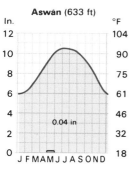

Aswān (633 ft)

Ethiopian Plateaus. The river is characterized by a very low gradient within Egypt, especially beyond Aswān. On entering Egypt, the river bed is 597 ft (182 meters) above sea level, but at Aswān it has descended to 308 ft (94 meters). The distance of the river from Aswān to the sea is 560 miles (900 km). The river brings to Egypt approximately 84 billion cubic meters of water per year. Until the Aswān High Dam began operations in 1971, the river regularly caused floods during four months each year, due to the heavy summer rains in the Ethiopian Plateau. The high floods lasted from mid-June until October. From the end of October until the next high flood, the Nile had a low discharge, resulting in a decreased intensity in the water flow.

The operation of the Aswān Dam and the formation of Lake Nasser (with an area of 1,550 sq. miles [4,000 sq.km] and a maximum storage capacity of 160 billion cubic meters of water) to the south of the dam enabled the water flow to be regulated on an annual basis. A regulated irrigation system was put into operation for most of the arable land.

As a result of the operation of the Aswān High Dam, the cultivated area in the Nile valley and in the delta was expanded by about 1.3 million acres, resulting in an increase in agricultural yields. The previous irrigation system — based on flooding during periods of high flood — was transformed into a regulated system which covers approximately 692,000 acres.

Climate Egypt experiences desert climatic conditions. The summer is hot, while the winter is cool. There is a large diurnal temperature range (52–61° F. [11–16° C.]). In the northern region, along the coast, the sea has a moderating influence on the high temperatures and the diurnal temperature range. During the winter, cold northerly winds cause relatively low temperatures in north and central Egypt. In spring, from mid-March until May, hot, dry southerly winds (*ḥamsin*) cause sandstorms and high temperatures. The average August temperature at the northern coast (Alexandria) is 79° F. (26° C.), decreasing to 55° F. (13° C.) in January. In Upper Egypt (Aswān), the average August temperature is 93° F. (34° C.), decreasing to 61° F. (16° C.) in January.

In most regions, precipitation is low and irregular. In the coastal region, the average annual rainfall amounts to 6–7 in (150–180 mm); in the southern part of the delta region and in the upper parts of the eastern highlands, it is 2–4 in (50–100 mm); while in the rest of the country it does not exceed 2 in (50 mm). Occasionally, large amounts of rain fall in a short period, resulting in flash floods.

Population Approximately 99 percent of the country's inhabitants are Egyptian Arabs. Ninety-three percent of the population are Sunni Muslims and a minority (6 percent of the population) are Copts. Tens of thousands of Nubians live in the south. Arab immigrants from other Middle Eastern countries, including Palestinians, live in the north, particularly in Cairo and north Sinai. Small communities of Greeks (Orthodox Chris-

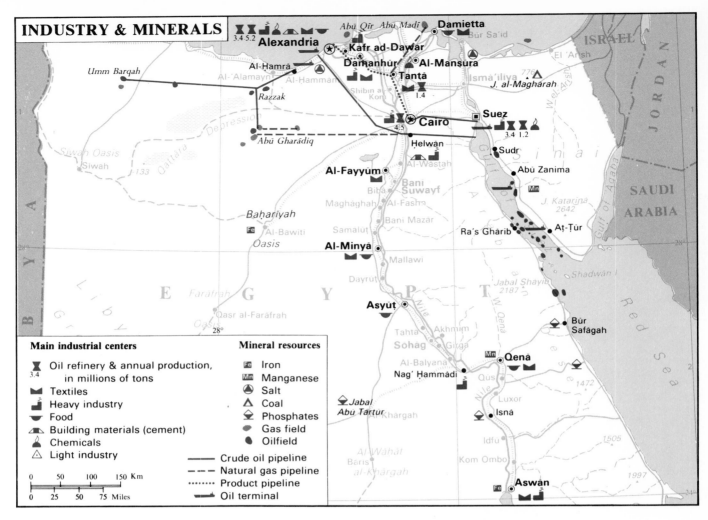

INDUSTRY & MINERALS

Main industrial centers

X Oil refinery & annual production,
3.4   in millions of tons
◣ Textiles
▟ Heavy industry
◣ Food
▃▲ Building materials (cement)
▲ Chemicals
△ Light industry

```
0    50    100   150 Km
0   25    50    75 Miles
```

Mineral resources

Fe Iron
Mn Manganese
◉ Salt
△ Coal
◻ Phosphates
◗ Gas field
● Oilfield

————— Crude oil pipeline
- - - - - - Natural gas pipeline
········· Product pipeline
▃▄◄ Oil terminal

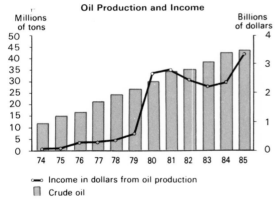

Oil Production and Income

Millions of tons

Billions of dollars

```
50                                    4
45
40                                    3
35
30
25                                    2
20
15
10                                    1
 5
 0                                    0
    74 75 76 77 78 79 80 81 82 83 84 85
```

○— Income in dollars from oil production
▨ Crude oil

tians), Armenians (Armenian Orthodox), Italians (Catholics), and other Europeans (Catholics and Protestants) reside in Cairo and Alexandria. These groups, numbering a few thousand each, are the remainder of what were once large communities, most of whom were forced to leave the country in the 1950s and 1960s following the overthrow of the monarchy. There are also about 300 Jewish inhabitants in Cairo and Alexandria. Tens of thousands of nomads and seminomads live in the eastern desert, and in Sinai.

Nearly 98 percent of Egypt's population is concentrated in 3.5 percent of the country's area, in the delta and along the river Nile. Within this region, the average density (1985) was 3,510 people per sq. mile (1,350 people per sq.km). Only 850,000

people live outside the Nile valley. There has been an average annual natural increase of 1.1 million in the population over the last ten years. Egyptians have traditionally been rural people. However, due to the rapid increase in the rural population — especially during the last fifty years — with no parallel growth in the available agricultural area or other sources of livelihood, there has been a substantial movement of people from the villages to the large cities. As a result, the urban population has increased at a rapid pace.

Because of the severe unemployment, many Egyptians have found their livelihood abroad, particularly in other Middle Eastern and North African countries. It is estimated that some 2.2 million Egyptians are employed in this way (1985).

Economy Egypt's modern economy has its roots in the early nineteenth century, when a subsistence economy was transformed to one based on exports and commerce, especially in agricultural produce. The country's economy developed very slowly in the period between independence (1922) and the early 1950s. Nasser's rise to power (1954) was accompanied by rapid economic development. The banking, transport, commerce, mining, agricultural, and industrial systems all underwent expansion. Most of the initiative for this development came from the government, according to a rigid centralized economic policy.

Following President Sadat's accession to power (1970), economic policy was reoriented. The intention was to encourage local entrepreneurs and foreign investors to participate in the country's economic development. This policy did not bring about widespread development, despite the fact that the 1970s were a period of economic growth, with an average annual increase of 9 percent in the GDP (1974–1981). Economic growth was principally due to oil revenues, income from the Suez Canal, and tourism, as well as money transfers from Egyptian nationals working abroad.

In the early 1980s Egypt began to experience an economic recession. The external debt rose to a total of $40 billion in 1986. Part of the budgetary deficit is covered by loans from the oil-rich Arab states — particularly Saudi Arabia and Kuwait — and assistance from Western nations, most notably the United States.

Agriculture Until the early 1980s agriculture was a major component of the country's economy. In 1982, 36 percent of the work force were employed in agriculture, but this sector contributed only 18.4 percent to the GDP.

Egyptian agriculture is based on intensive cultivation, with many small farm units. Thanks to intensive labor, canal irrigation, and the extensive use of fertilizers, pesticides, and high-quality seeds, the yields are high. The cultivated area in 1982 extended over 6.8 million acres — 2.7 percent of the country's land surface — nearly all of which is located in the Nile valley and delta. Since most of the cultivated area produces more than one annual crop, the area under crops totaled 11.6 million acres. Until the 1970s, agriculture supplied most of the domestic consumption requirements. Beginning in the 1980s, Egypt increased its dependency on imported agricultural produce. In 1983, 5.9 million tons of wheat (72 percent of domestic consumption), corn (28 percent of consumption), oil seeds (70 percent of consumption), sugar (43 percent of consumption), and meat (33 percent of consumption) were imported.

The principal commercial crop in Egypt is cotton. Nearly one-third of the global long-stemmed cotton yield is produced in Egypt. This cotton is of a very high quality. The area devoted to cotton has decreased since the 1950s to 1 million acres in 1983. Despite its commercial importance, only a small area is devoted to sugar cultivation. The area devoted to fruit, vegetables, sugar cane, fodder, and corn has increased.

Extensive efforts have been made to expand the cultivable area and to improve soil quality. Plans for the development of the depressions in the western desert (Faráfrah, Dákhlah, Khárgah, and Bahariyah) were drawn up in the 1950s. This "New Valley" Plan was based on the development of the groundwater reservoirs that had been discovered in the depressions. The plan has not yet been completely implemented due to technical difficulties and because of the unsuitability of the water for irrigation. Other plans to expand the agricultural area were also hindered by difficulties in raising the necessary finances as well as various technical problems. The government is planning to improve a further 1.6 million acres in the Nile delta, south of Port Said and southwest of Alexandria.

Minerals Oil is the principal mineral resource in Egypt. Production began in 1911 at the Ra's Ghárib field on the Red Sea coast. Output finally rose beyond domestic consumption requirements in 1976, following which Egypt began to export petroleum. Oil production increased threefold between 1975 and 1984, from 14.8 million tons to 45.2 million tons per year. Most of the oil comes from seabed fields in the Gulf of Suez. Six refineries operate in Egypt, producing 19.2 million tons per year. Petroleum reserves were estimated

at 640 million tons in 1984.

Since 1974, Egypt has been producing natural gas in the Nile delta. Natural gas production also began in the western desert in 1976 and from seabed fields in the continental shelf near Alexandria and in the Gulf of Suez in 1982. In 1983, natural gas production was 2.2 billion cubic meters, with reserves estimated at 340 billion cubic meters.

Another important mineral is iron. Rich deposits were discovered in the Bahariyah Oasis and in the western desert in the mid-1970s. Following the commencement of mining, output of iron from the Aswán region was reduced due to the medium quality of the ore. Iron ore production was 2 million tons in 1982/83.

Phosphates are mined near Isná on the banks of the Nile and close to Búr Safágah on the Red Sea coast. Other rich deposits have recently been discovered at Jabal Abú Tartúr, west of Dákhlah Oasis in the western desert, but mining has not yet begun. Phosphate production was 630,000 tons in 1982/83.

Small quantities of manganese, gold, zinc, and lead are mined in the eastern desert.

Industry Industry has gradually expanded since the beginning of the twentieth century. Most of the industrial products are destined for domestic consumption, while only a few industrial plants (especially heavy industry) produce goods for export. The principal industrial branches are foodstuffs, metals (aluminum, iron, and steel), textiles, chemicals, and building materials. Since the 1950s development also took place in the chemical and fertilizer industries, the military industry, and car assembly plants. The cement industry, with an output of 4.5 million tons per year, should enable Egypt to reduce its import of some 5.5 million tons per year (1984).

Since the middle of the 1970s, the oil industry has been the major source of national revenue, totaling $3 billion in 1983/84. Nevertheless, pe-

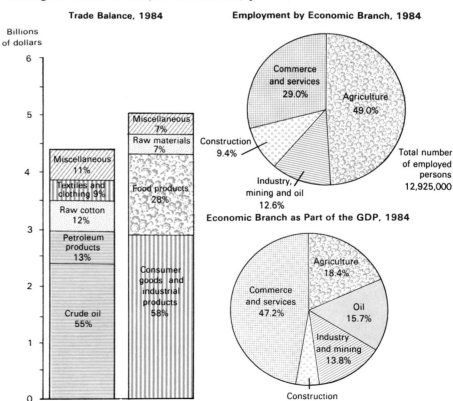

Trade Balance, 1984

Employment by Economic Branch, 1984

Economic Branch as Part of the GDP, 1984

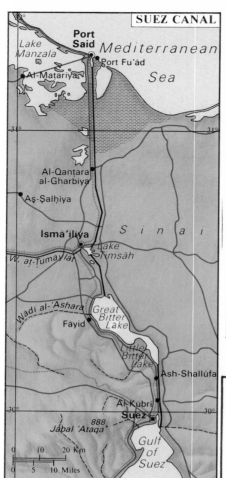

SUEZ CANAL

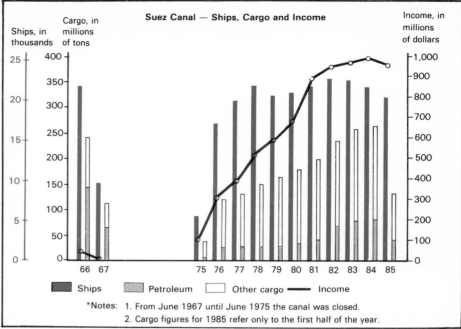

Suez Canal — Ships, Cargo and Income

Ships, in thousands | Cargo, in millions of tons | Income, in millions of dollars

Ships   Petroleum   Other cargo   Income

*Notes: 1. From June 1967 until June 1975 the canal was closed.
2. Cargo figures for 1985 refer only to the first half of the year.

The canal shortens the voyage from the Persian Gulf to Western Europe by about 5,650 miles.

Dimensions of the canal after its extension in 1980

Length from Port Said to Suez: 102.5 miles

Width at water surface level: 1,148 ft

Depth: 64 ft

Passage possible for loaded vessels of 150,000 tons

Passage possible for empty vessels of 370,000 tons

trochemical industries are relatively undeveloped.

Tourism The sites of ancient Egypt, namely the famous pyramids at Gīza and the temples at Abū Simbel and Luxor, attract about 1.3 million tourists each year, with tourism contributing over $1 billion to the national income.

The Suez Canal The first canal in the region was apparently dug around 1800 BCE in Wādī aṭ-Ṭumaylāt. The Ptolemies, and later the Romans, extended the canal, linking the delta lands to the Red Sea. This canal was finally closed in 755 CE for military reasons. In 1799, when Napoleon was in Egypt, his engineers came to the conclusion that there was approximately a 30 ft (10 meter) difference in sea level between the Mediterranean and the Red Sea. Under such conditions, the excavation of a canal would result in the flooding of the Nile delta by water from the Red Sea. Not until 1826 were these conclusions proved to be erroneous.

In 1859, the French obtained a concession from the Egyptian government to dig a new canal. The project took ten years to complete, finally opening to navigation on November 17, 1869. The canal remained open until 1967 (excepting a short period in 1956–1957). As a result of the war between Egypt and Israel, the canal was closed. It did not reopen until June 1975.

The Suez Canal greatly shortens the sea link between Europe and the countries of the Persian Gulf, South and East Asia, East Africa, and Australia. Among other benefits, the canal is an important source of foreign currency for Egypt. Shipping companies pay for the right of navigation through the canal as well as for port services.

History The presence of an agricultural population in the Nile valley dates back to the Early Stone Age. The ancient kingdoms began to develop around 3100 BCE (during which period the pyramids were built). This advanced culture continued to exist until about 500 BCE. In later periods, Egypt formed part of foreign empires, including the Greek, the Roman, and the Byzantine. From the seventh century, Egypt was part of the Islamic caliphates. The Fatimids, the Ayyubids, and the Mamluks ruled in Egypt from the end of the tenth century until the Ottoman conquest in 1517.

Egypt's modern era dates from the beginning of the nineteenth century. Egypt was then part of the Ottoman Empire. From 1805, the governor (*wali*) of Egypt for fifty years was Muhammad 'Ali. He succeeded in transforming Egypt into a virtually independent state, although remaining formally subordinate to the Ottoman Empire. Under his rule, the country underwent an economic and cultural revolution, signs of which remain until the present. In 1842, the Ottoman sultan 'Abd al-Majib recognized the right of Muhammad 'Ali to transfer control to his descendants, and the same family remained in power until 1952.

During the period following Muhammad 'Ali's death, Egypt became burdened with financial debts, resulting in British and French intervention in the country's administration. Britain invaded Egypt in 1882 and took charge of the government, declaring the country a protectorate in 1914. Following this decree, the local population intensified their demands for independence, a struggle led by the Wafd movement. The British acquiesced to these demands in 1922, at the same time retaining the right to maintain and strengthen their military presence in the country.

Following independence, Egypt became a constitutional monarchy. King Fu'ad ruled until 1936, followed by his son Farouk. The extravagance and immoral behavior of the royal household, coupled with Egypt's failure in its war against Israel in 1948/49, were among the factors leading to the military coup in July 1952. Farouk's reign came to an end and the monarchy was abolished. The leaders of the coup, the "free officers," declared the establishment of a republic and appointed General Naguib as president. Early in 1954, Naguib was deposed by Colonel Gamal Abdel Nasser.

Following British and American refusal to finance the construction of the Aswān Dam, Nasser nationalized the Suez Canal Company on July 26, 1956. Nasser saw this move as enabling him to control an additional source of revenue (about $100 million per year) which could be used to finance the Aswān Dam project. In response, the British and French attempted to capture the canal region. Israel also took part in the military operation, its objective being to put an end to terrorist attacks which had been taking place from Egyptian territory. The military expedition ended with Israel capturing the Sinai Peninsula in October 1956. However, due to both American and Soviet pressure, the British and the French abandoned their attempt to capture the Suez Canal while Israel was obliged to retreat from the Sinai Peninsula.

Nasser succeeded in turning the military defeat into a political victory. His prestige rose in the Arab world and this influenced him in his attempt to unite the Arab countries under Egyptian leadership. This found practical expression in the formation with Syria of the United Arab Republic in 1958, dissolved in 1961. Toward the end of 1958, Egypt began to form its first economic and military links with the Soviet Union, resulting in the signing of an agreement between the two countries in December 1958 concerning the joint construction of the Aswān Dam.

Between 1962 and 1967, Egypt became involved in the civil war in Yemen, lending support to the republican cause. War with Israel broke out in 1967, during which Egypt suffered a major military defeat after only six days. The Sinai Peninsula was again conquered by Israel, the Suez Canal was closed, the Egyptian army was largely destroyed, and the national economy was severely damaged. In 1969–1970, Egypt waged a war of attrition against Israel along the Suez Canal. A cease-fire was finally arranged on August 7, 1970. Seven weeks later, President Nasser died from a heart attack.

Nasser's regime was ruthless, but under his rule Egypt underwent important social and economic changes. The most significant changes were the eradication of the Egyptian aristocracy and the confiscation of most of their lands, the development of heavy industry, and the construction of the Aswān Dam. In foreign policy, Nasser succeeded in strengthening Egypt's position in both the Arab and the Western world.

Following Nasser's death, the leadership passed to his deputy, Anwar Sadat. On October 6, 1973, Egypt and Syria coordinated an attack on Israel. Following eighteen days of fierce battles, a cease-fire was arranged. In January 1974, an agreement was signed separating the belligerent forces. Israel retreated, in stages, from the western section of the Sinai Peninsula.

After the war, Sadat instituted a number of changes in the country's economic policy (the "open doors policy") in order to strengthen the national economy. The most prominent change was the promotion of foreign investment, through tax benefits for both local and foreign investors.

In November 1977, Sadat made his historic visit to Jerusalem and recognized the State of Israel. At the end of long negotiations, a peace agreement was signed between Israel and Egypt in March 1979, as a result of which Israel returned the whole of the Sinai Peninsula — in stages — to Egypt.

In October 1981, Sadat was assassinated by a group of revolutionary Muslims. His deputy, Hosni Mubarak, was appointed as president. Mubarak continued Sadat's political and economic policies and even extended the democratization process to internal political and economic affairs.

Government and Politics Egypt is ruled by a president with far-reaching powers who is chosen for a six-year term by a People's Council. This legislative body comprises 458 representatives, whose duty it is to ratify government decisions. Members of government, including the prime minister, are appointed by the president. Appointments to all important administrative and security posts are usually made from among the president's followers. Elections to the People's Council take place every five years. In the elections held in April 1987, carried out according to democratic procedures, the National Democratic party received 346 seats; the Socialist Liberals, Socialist Labor, and Muslim Brotherhood formed a coalition and won 60 seats; and the Wafd party, 35 seats. In addition, seven nonparty representatives were elected, while a further ten representatives were appointed by the president. In the autumn of 1987, Mubarak was elected as president for a second term.

Egypt's borders were demarcated in stages. The border with Libya was fixed in 1925 in an agreement with Italy; the southern border was determined by Britain in 1899; the border with Israel runs along the line of the 1906 border between Egypt (then under British rule) and the Ottoman Empire. This line was fixed as the permanent border in the peace agreement between Egypt and Israel, signed in 1979 and finally implemented in 1982.

The peace agreement with Israel resulted in Egypt's isolation in the Arab world, but only for a short period. Since 1982, Egypt's links with other Arab countries, including Syria who led the opposition to the peace agreement, have gradually been renewed. In the 1980s, partially because of the country's economic difficulties, opposition to the regime intensified among extremist Muslim groups. The tough measures taken by the government have thus far been successful in controlling this subversive activity.

<table>
<tr><td>NATURAL INCREASE (1980-1983)
2.8%</td></tr>
<tr><td>LIFE EXPECTANCY (1980-1985)
male - **55.9** years
female - **58.4** years</td></tr>
<tr><td>DOCTORS (1984-1985)
15.2 per 10,000 inhabitants</td></tr>
<tr><td>HOSPITAL BEDS (1983-1984)
1.8 per 1,000 inhabitants</td></tr>
<tr><td>INFANT MORTALITY (1980-1983)
113.0 per 1,000 births</td></tr>
</table>

<table>
<tr><td>HIGH SCHOOL PUPILS (1982)
1,235,000</td></tr>
<tr><td>UNIVERSITY STUDENTS (1982)
624,000</td></tr>
<tr><td>LITERACY RATE (1984) **40%**</td></tr>
</table>

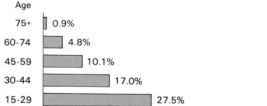

Population by Age Group, 1980

Age

Age	%
75+	0.9%
60-74	4.8%
45-59	10.1%
30-44	17.0%
15-29	27.5%
0-14	39.7%

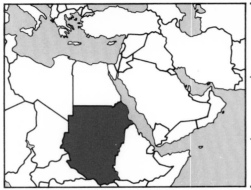

SUDAN

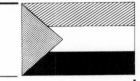

Area **967,494 sq. miles (2,505,813 sq.km)**
Population (1985 estimate) **23,000,000**
Capital city **Khartoum**
Gross domestic product (GDP) per capita (1982) **$440**

Population in main cities (1983 estimates)	Omdurman 530,000	Port Sudan 207,000	'Atbarah 73,000
	Khartoum 500,000	Al-Ubayyiḍ 140,000	
	Khartoum North 350,000	Kassalā 99,000	

Sudan covers a large part of northeast Africa. It borders on Egypt, Libya, Chad, Zaïre, Uganda, Kenya, Ethiopia, and the Red Sea.

Topography   Sudan consists of large undulating plains and plateaus, surrounded by a rim of mountainous areas. Much of these plains is underlain by a basement of very old formations of hard crystalline rocks (mainly granite and gneiss).

The Nile and its tributaries cross Sudan from south to north, draining nearly the entire country. The three large tributaries of the White Nile, the Baḥr al-Ghazāl, Baḥr al-Jābal, and the Baḥr al-'Arab, whose sources lie outside Sudan in the Central African Plateau, flow through the southwest of the country. These rivers carry large quantities of water over a very gentle gradient, resulting in the formation of large swamps (the Sudd Swamps). During the rainy season, approximately 115,000 sq. miles (300,000 sq.km) are covered by swamps. About half of the river flow is lost in these swamps. The White Nile is formed by the convergence of these tributaries, which are joined near the township of Malakāl by another tributary, the Sobat, coming from the southern part of the Ethiopian Plateau.

The White Nile flows north for a distance of 435 miles (700 km) until it meets the Blue Nile at Khartoum. The sources of the latter are in the Ethiopian Plateau. The area in Sudan between the White Nile and the Blue Nile is known as al-Jazīrah (the island). It is covered by a thick mantle of alluvial material, most of which has been deposited by the Blue Nile. During the rainy season (June to September), the Blue Nile is in flood, its level rising by 15–20 ft (5–6 meters) near Khartoum.

North of Khartoum, the Nile flows through the Nubian Desert. South of the confluence with the river 'Atbarah, the Nile cuts through hard granite rocks, forming rapids which cause an obstacle to navigation. 'Atbarah is the last of the perennial tributaries of the Nile.

The extensive plains are surrounded on three sides by mountainous areas. In the northeast the mountains reach elevations of 7,220 ft (2,200 meters), making access from the Red Sea coast to the Nile valley extremely difficult. The Red Sea coastal strip is narrow and arid. Only where the river Baraka reaches the sea does the coast broaden to a width of 30 miles (50 km).

The margins of the Ethiopian and East African plateaus extend, respectively, into the eastern and southern Sudan. The highest mountain in Sudan is Mount Kinyeti (10,456 ft [3,187 meters]) near the border with Uganda.

Jabal Marrah (10,075 ft [3,071 meters]), is a volcanic mountain complex in west Sudan. The extensive area between Jabal Marrah and the Nile valley (approximately 135,000 sq. miles [350,000 sq.km]) is mostly covered by sand dunes.

Climate   Sudan lies between 22 and 4 degrees latitude. As a result, the country's northern regions experience desert conditions, becoming tropical toward the south. Precipitation also increases as one goes south. In the vicinity of the Egyptian border, the average annual precipitation is less than .5 in (10 mm) per year, rising to over 40.0 in (1,000 mm) in the south in the frontier areas with Uganda and Zaïre.

Sudan has three principal climatic regions. North of the sixteenth latitude hot and dry conditions prevail. At 'Atbarah, the average temperature in the hottest month (June) is 97° F. (36° C.), with an average maximum temperature of 110° F. (43° C.). The winter is temperate, with an average January temperature of 72° F. (22° C.). This region receives most of its limited rainfall in the summer, rarely exceeding 1.2 in (30 mm) per year. In Wādī Halfā', near the Egyptian border, the average precipitation is only .2 in (4 mm) per year.

Central Sudan experiences savannah conditions. The average June temperature at Khartoum is 93° F. (34° C.), decreasing to 75° F. (24° C.) in

NATURAL INCREASE (1980-1984) **2.9%**

LIFE EXPECTANCY (1980-1985) male - **48.0** years female - **50.0** years

DOCTORS (1981-1982) **1.1** per 10,000 inhabitants

HOSPITAL BEDS (1982) **0.9** per 1,000 inhabitants

INFANT MORTALITY (1980-1985) **118.0** per 1,000 births

HIGH SCHOOL PUPILS (1984) 460,000

UNIVERSITY STUDENTS (1984) 18,000

LITERACY RATE (1982) **20%**

Land Use, 1982

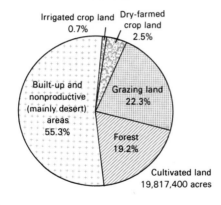

Irrigated crop land 0.7%
Dry-farmed crop land 2.5%
Built-up and nonproductive (mainly desert) areas 55.3%
Grazing land 22.3%
Forest 19.2%
Cultivated land 19,817,400 acres

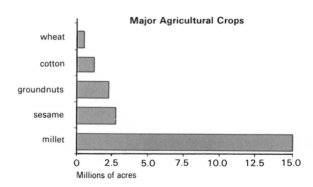

Major Agricultural Crops

wheat
cotton
groundnuts
sesame
millet

0   2.5   5.0   7.5   10.0   12.5   15.0
Millions of acres

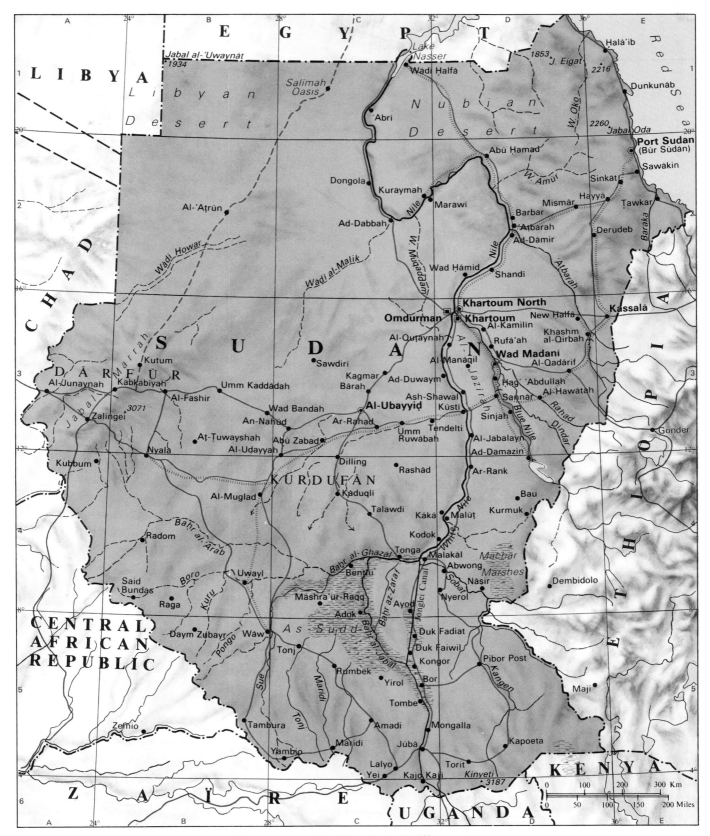

January. The rainy season is longer as one advances south. In the north of the region at Khartoum, the annual rainfall is 8.0 in (200 mm), falling between June and September. In the south at Malakāl, the average annual rainfall is 3.0 in (750 mm), falling mostly between May and October.

An equatorial climate prevails in the extreme south, with only small differences between summer and winter temperatures. At Jūbā, the highest average monthly temperature is 84° F. (29° C.) in March, while the lowest average temperature is 81° F. (27° C.) in October. Rains fall throughout most of the year, especially in the summer, totaling approximately 40.0 in (1,000 mm).

Population Sudan's population is composed of two major racial groups — the Hamites and the Negroids. Each group comprises numerous tribes and subtribes. The Hamites form approximately 40 percent of the population and are concentrated in the northern and central part of the country. The blacks reside in the southern and western regions. Between the tenth and twelfth latitudes, much of the population is made up of a mixture of both groups.

Nubians (comprising 3 percent of the total population) reside mainly in the Nile valley. The Beja tribes (comprising 7 percent of the population) are the main inhabitants of the northeast. In the southwest the population is made up of Sudanese tribes, and in the southeast, of Nilotic tribes. The largest of these are the Dinka (10 percent of the population), and the Nuba in the Kurdufān province (approximately 5 percent of the population). Black Sudanese tribes, who migrated to Sudan from Central Africa, inhabit the western frontier regions of the country.

Most of Sudan's inhabitants (approximately 60 percent of the population) are Sunni Muslims. They are concentrated in the north and center of the country. Most of the inhabitants in the south (32 percent of the total population) are idol worshipers. The remainder (8 percent) are Christians: mostly Catholic (concentrated in the pagan south), with small Coptic and Protestant minorities.

Approximately half of Sudan's inhabitants are concentrated in 15 percent of the area, most of them in the Jazīrah region around Khartoum and along the Nile, north of Khartoum. More than 70 percent of the population live in villages, 18 percent in towns, while 10 percent are nomads. In recent years, the famine conditions in neighboring countries (Ethiopia, Uganda, and Chad) have caused hundreds of thousands of refugees to migrate to southern Sudan in search of food.

Economy Sudan's economy is based on agriculture and cattle breeding. Approximately 70 percent of the labor force is employed in these two sectors, accounting for 40 percent of the GDP (1983). Agriculture accounts for nearly all the country's exports. Despite the improvements in both agriculture and industry since the 1960s, Sudan's economy remains backward. The per capita GDP is only $440 (1982).

The principal factors explaining Sudan's economic difficulties are: internal political instability (the civil war in the south of the country has continued sporadically almost since Sudan gained its independence); lack of professional and skilled manpower; lack of local and foreign finance; scarcity of domestic raw materials. Another factor is the poor state of the highways which is responsible for the delays in exploiting the country's mineral

resources. Since the early 1980s, Sudan has experienced a severe economic recession, resulting from drought in some parts of the south.

Agriculture The cultivable area in Sudan totals 195 million acres, of which some 10 percent is actually cultivated. Much of the area is devoted to dry-farming and is concentrated in the southern and central parts of the country. The yields are low and are dependent on the variable annual precipitation.

The area under irrigation was expanded during the 1970s, covering approximately 4.25 million acres, 22 percent of the cultivated area. About half of the irrigated area lies in the Jazīrah region, the remainder along the rivers (especially in the north of the country), and at the foot of Jabal Marrah in the west.

The most widespread crop is millet, the principal food of the inhabitants, covering 60 percent of the cultivated area. The most important commercial

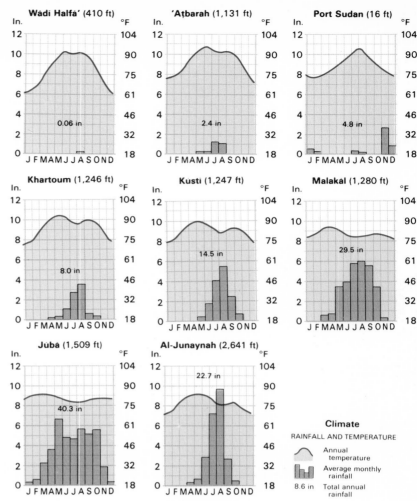

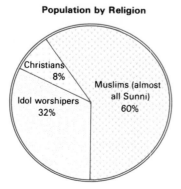

Population by Religion

Christians 8%
Idol worshipers 32%
Muslims (almost all Sunni) 60%

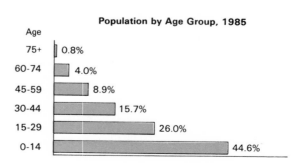

Population by Age Group, 1985

Age	
75+	0.8%
60-74	4.0%
45-59	8.9%
30-44	15.7%
15-29	26.0%
0-14	44.6%

AGRICULTURE

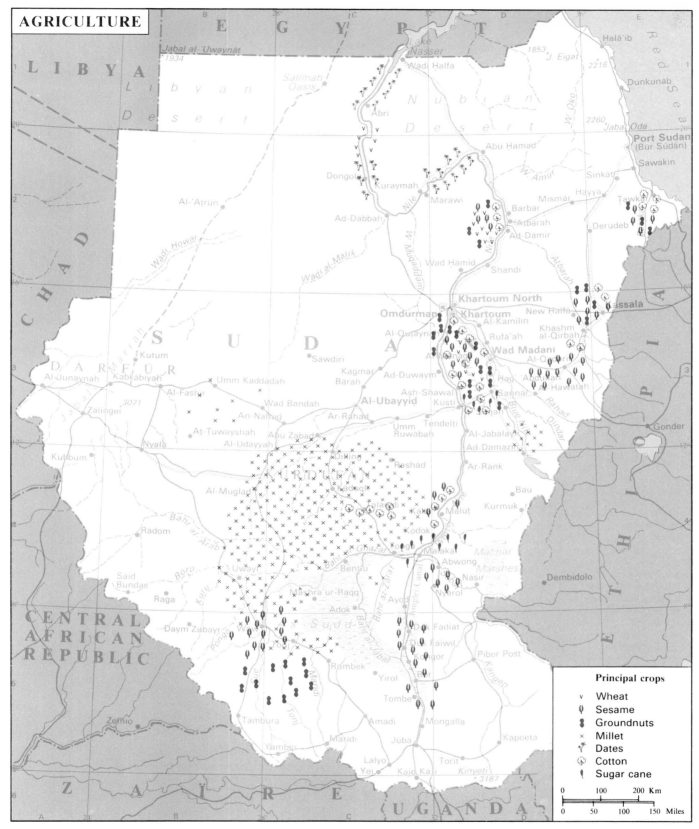

Principal crops

v	Wheat
ⵋ	Sesame
ⵎ	Groundnuts
×	Millet
ⵟ	Dates
⊕	Cotton
ⵏ	Sugar cane

0   100   200 Km

0   50   100   150 Miles

crop is cotton, accounting for 60 percent of the value of exports. Sudan also exports groundnuts, sesame seeds, and gum arabic (produced from the resin of acacia trees which grow in central and west Sudan).

Sudan has extensive pasture (about 140 million acres), with widespread livestock breeding (19.5 million head of cattle, 33 million sheep, and 2.5 million camels). This sector contributes 10 percent to the GDP and approximately 15 percent to export revenues.

Minerals Sudan has a number of commercially important minerals — iron, chromium, manganese, sulfur, copper, zinc, and gold. Most of the deposits

INDUSTRY & MINERALS

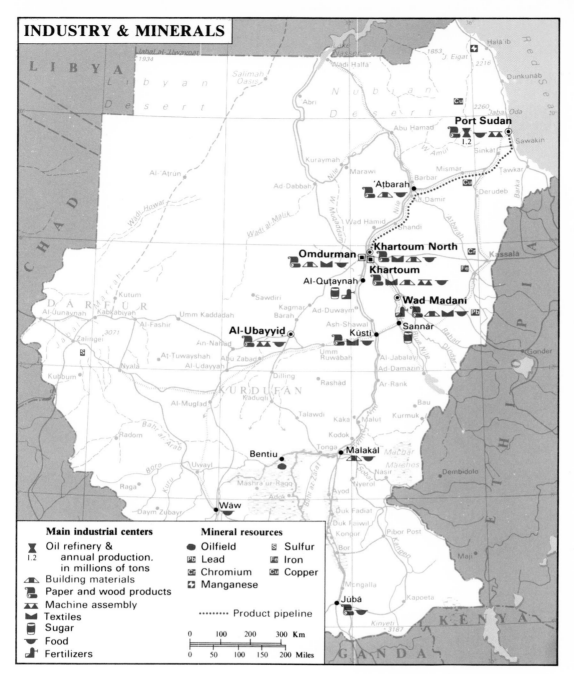

Main industrial centers

- ⊠ Oil refinery &
  1.2   annual production.
      in millions of tons
- ⛰ Building materials
- 📖 Paper and wood products
- ⛰ Machine assembly
- ◪ Textiles
- 🥫 Sugar
- ▽ Food
- 🛠 Fertilizers

Mineral resources

- ● Oilfield
- Pb Lead
- Cr Chromium
- ◪ Manganese
- S Sulfur
- Fe Iron
- Cu Copper

········· Product pipeline

| 0 | 100 | 200 | 300 Km |
| 0 | 50 | 100 | 150 | 200 Miles |

are located in areas to which access is very difficult, especially in the mountains neighboring the Red Sea. The mining of these minerals is therefore very limited. In 1982, 10,000 tons of chromium, and small amounts of gold, copper, and manganese were produced.

In 1979 petroleum was discovered in the Bentiu region in the south of the country. The proven reserves in this field total 35 million tons. But oil production is irregular and is often disrupted by the rebel activity in this region. The country's only oil refinery is at Port Sudan, mostly treating imported crude oil, with an annual production capacity of 1.2 million tons.

Industry Sudan's industry began to develop in the early 1960s. Until then, there were only a few small factories, mostly specializing in processing agricultural products. As a result of government initiatives during the 1960s and 1970s, many additional factories were established, engaging in the manufacture of sugar, preserved foodstuffs, textiles, clothing, leather goods, cement, and fertilizers. Industry's contribution to the national economy nevertheless remains small, contributing only 6 percent to the GDP and employing only 6 percent of the labor force.

Since the early 1980s industrial development has slowed down. Both local and foreign entrepreneurs have reduced their investments in industry, mainly because of the increasing political instability and the growth in revolutionary activities in the south. The oil-rich Arab countries have also reduced the amount of aid given to Sudan. The scarcity of raw materials and the lack of replacement parts, as well as the irregular electricity supply, have been responsible for a reduction in output in most factories.

History The modern history of Sudan began in the early 1820s when it was conquered by Muhammad 'Ali of Egypt. Until then, Sudan had been split by intertribal warfare. Muhammad 'Ali took advantage of this situation to extend his control over Sudan with the dual objective of obtaining slaves and exploiting the country's natural resources. There was much opposition to the corrupt Egyptian administration among the local population. The dissent culminated in the revolution of 1881, headed by the religious leader Muhammad Ahmad Ibn 'Abdullah, who called himself the *mahdi* (teacher of the true way). The British, who took control of Egypt in 1882, did not want to become embroiled in Sudan and therefore refrained from suppressing the rebellion. The *mahdi*'s forces succeeded in conquering nearly all of Sudan's present territory by 1885, thus transforming it into an independent state.

This independence lasted for only thirteen years. In 1898, the British decided to conquer Sudan as part of the power struggle for control in Africa. The British ruled Sudan until 1956, making an important contribution to the country's economic development. Their administration was based on maintaining good relations with both the tribal chieftains — who were given legislative and administrative powers — and the religious leaders, including the *mahdi*'s son. Nevertheless, the educated sectors of the population demanded independence for Sudan, while others aspired to union with Egypt. Following the officers revolution in Egypt (1952), both Britain and Egypt recognized Sudan's right to independence. It was left to the Sudanese to decide between an independent state or union with Egypt. In elections held in 1954, the proponents of union with Egypt emerged victorious. But they subsequently changed their minds and decided to establish an independent state. Sudan declared its independence on January 1, 1956.

Independent Sudan experienced severe problems. In the south, where most of the Christian and pagan tribes reside, a rebellion broke out in 1955 over claims for regional autonomy. This state of affairs has continued to the present. The economic situation was also difficult. The regime was unable to solve these problems, resulting — in 1958 — in a military coup headed by General Ibrahim 'Abbud. 'Abbud's regime was also unsuccessful in finding a solution to the country's problems and in 1964 'Abbud agreed to return parliamentary rule to Sudan.

In May 1969, Colonel Jafar Numeiri took control of Sudan in a military coup. Numeiri instituted a one-party regime in the country. He ruled Sudan for sixteen years, possessing absolute power. During his rule, he nationalized some of the means of production and proposed plans for economic development — of which only a few were implemented — based on socialist principles.

The rebellion in the south continued sporadically until 1972. Hundreds of thousands of people were killed in the violence and thousands of refugees were forced to migrate to neighboring countries. In 1972, Numeiri succeeded in reaching an agreement with the rebels. The agreement granted regional autonomy to residents of the southern regions. But this undertaking was not put into effect and the violent struggle against the central government erupted again.

In 1983, the internal situation worsened following Numeiri's proposal to adopt Islamic law (*Shariah*) as the basis for the country's legal system. He also proposed that he be nominated as president for life. These proposals were bitterly opposed by the non-Muslim residents of the south. This discontent, together with the worsening economic

situation resulting from continuing droughts, resulted in the overthrow of Numeiri by General Siwar-al-Dhahab in April 1985.

The military regime remained in power for a year. In April 1986, general elections were held in which Sadeq al-Mahdi of the National (*Umma*) party emerged victorious. He formed a coalition government, the first democratic regime after seventeen years of dictatorship.

Government and Politics Since May 1986, Sudan has been governed by a democratic regime. The legislative assembly is made up of 301 representatives, elected in regional elections. In the elections of 1986, only 260 representatives were elected since the representatives from the south did not recognize the legitimacy of the elections. The National party headed by Sadeq al-Mahdi was victorious, gaining 99 seats in the legislature. They formed a coalition government with the Democratic Unionist party, which had won 63 seats and several southern groups.

The civil war continued after the elections, despite the fact that the present government is sympathetic to the claims for regional autonomy. By the beginning of 1988, the government still had not succeeded in reaching an agreement with the rebels in the south.

In its foreign policy, the present government takes a neutral stance. It maintains foreign relations with both Eastern and Western countries. This policy is also expressed in regional relations with Iran, Iraq, and the Persian Gulf states, the latter being a major source of financial assistance for Sudan.

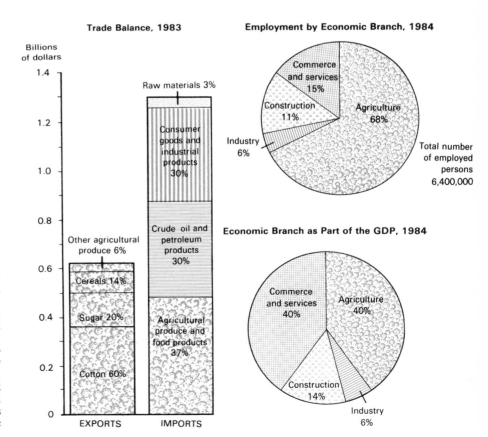

Trade Balance, 1983

Billions of dollars

Raw materials 3%
Consumer goods and industrial products 30%
Crude oil and petroleum products 30%
Agricultural produce and food products 37%

Other agricultural produce 6%
Cereals 14%
Sugar 20%
Cotton 60%

EXPORTS   IMPORTS

Employment by Economic Branch, 1984

Commerce and services 15%
Construction 11%
Industry 6%
Agriculture 68%

Total number of employed persons 6,400,000

Economic Branch as Part of the GDP, 1984

Commerce and services 40%
Agriculture 40%
Construction 14%
Industry 6%

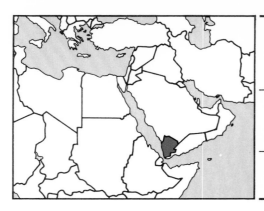

YEMEN

Area **72,290 sq. miles (195,000 sq.km)**
Population (1986 estimate) **9,270,000**
Capital city **San'ā'**
Gross domestic product (GDP) per capita (1982) **$511**

Population in main cities	San'ā' 280,000
(1981 estimates)	Hodeida 130,000
	Ta'izz 120,000

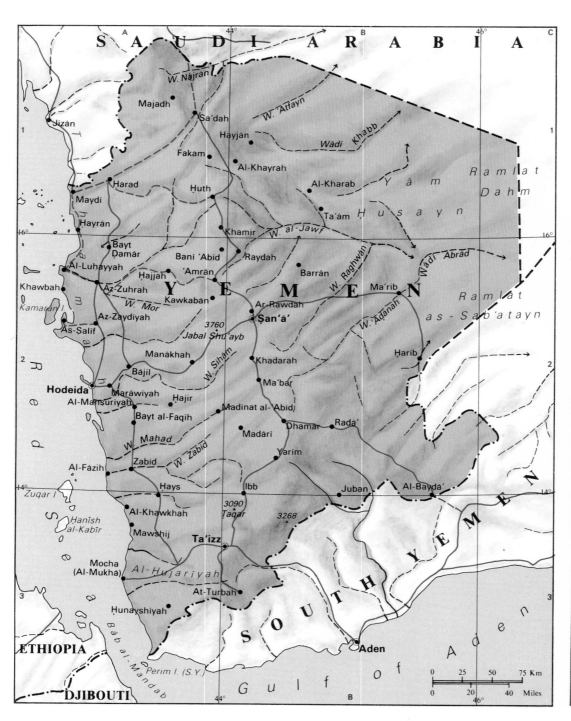

NATURAL INCREASE (1980-1983)
2.7%

LIFE EXPECTANCY (1980-1985)
male - **42.7** years
female - **44.8** years

DOCTORS (1981)
1.2 per 10,000 inhabitants

HOSPITAL BEDS (1982)
0.5 per 1,000 inhabitants

INFANT MORTALITY (1983-1984)
154.0 per 1,000 births

HIGH SCHOOL PUPILS (1981)
35,000

UNIVERSITY STUDENTS (1981)
6,700

LITERACY RATE (1981) **20%**

The Yemen Arab Republic lies at the southern tip of the Arabian Peninsula. It is bordered by Saudi Arabia in the north and the east, South Yemen in the south, and the Red Sea in the west. The center of Yemen is occupied by a 94 mile (150 km) wide basalt plateau, which reaches heights of 6,500–9,100 ft (2,000–2,800 meters).

Topography The coastal plain of the Arabian Peninsula along the Red Sea, in the west of Yemen, is known as the Tihāmah. This plain is up to 31 miles (50 km) wide and is covered by dunes and gravel. Exploitable groundwater is found in the alluvial fans formed by riverbeds.

Yemen's principal region of cultivation and habitation is the plateau that rises steeply above the Tihāmah Plain. The western slopes are dissected by deep riverbeds which descend to the Red Sea. Most of these are seasonal river valleys, and only a few carry water all the time. Even when floods occur, the water is often absorbed into the ground before it reaches the sea. Most of the plateau is covered by basalt supporting fertile soil. The plateau is cut by deep valleys, above which rise extinct volcanic cones, including the highest mountain in the Arabian Peninsula — Jabal Shu'ayb (12,220 ft; 3,760 meters). The eastern slopes of the plateau have a gentle gradient. This is the desert region, built mainly of limestone, with large stretches covered by dunes.

Climate Three climatic regions may be discerned. Hot and humid conditions prevail in the Tihāmah Plain, with summer temperatures reaching 105° F. (40° C.) and humidity rising beyond 70 percent. On the plateau and on its western slopes, the temperatures are comfortable throughout most of the year, with a summer average of 77–81° F. (25–27° C.), decreasing to 52° F. (11° C.) in the coldest month. The eastern slopes of the plateau have a desert climate, with a hot summer and cool winter.

Yemen's rain falls in summer, between March and September. Precipitation totals vary according to the altitude, exposure, and distance from the sea. In the Tihāmah region, precipitation equals approximately 4 in (100 mm) per year. On the western slopes of the plateau, annual rainfall reaches 36–40 in (900–1,000 mm), the largest amount anywhere in the Arabian Peninsula. On the plateau — at heights of 8,125 ft (2,500 meters) — annual precipitation equals 24 in (600 mm). Rainfall decreases eastward, amounting to only 6 in (150 mm) per year near Yemen's eastern border.

Population Most of Yemen's population are Yemeni Arabs, speaking a distinctive dialect of Arabic. Blacks, originating from tribes in East Africa, live along the Tihāmah coast. Almost the entire population is Muslim — about 60 percent

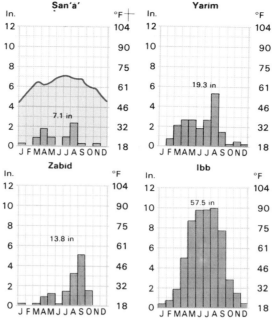

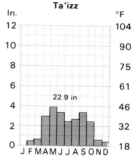

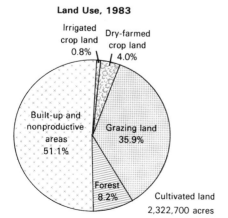

Land Use, 1983

Shiite and 40 percent Sunni. Most of the Shiites belong to two tribal groups, the Bakil and the Hashed. They live in a semi-autonomous tribal framework in the Yemeni mountains. The Sunnis live mainly on the coastal plain and in the north and east of the country. A small Jewish community of about 2,000 people remains in Yemen. Most of the Jews — some 56,000 — emigrated to Israel in 1949.

During the 1970s and 1980s, over one million Yemeni inhabitants emigrated to the oil-rich Arab states of the Persian Gulf, particularly to Saudi Arabia. Only about 10 percent of the country's population reside in urban settlements. Most of the villages are located on the western parts of the highlands. A small number of villages are scattered along the coastal plain and on the eastern slopes of the plateau.

Economy Until the early 1970s, the country's economy was based on subsistence agriculture. After the civil war in 1970, Yemen began to develop a modern economy, which reached its peak at the end of the 1970s. Yemen's modernization was aided by foreign financing, especially from Saudi Arabia and Kuwait, as well as through money transferred home by the Yemeni citizens working in the rich Gulf states and in Saudi Arabia. Development included vast improvements in transport, electricity and water services, and the establishment of banks and a modern public administration system.

Agriculture Intense economic development resulted in a substantial reduction in the contribution of agriculture to the GDP, accompanied by a fall in the number of workers employed in this sector. Nevertheless, agriculture is still the major branch of the economy, contributing 50 percent to the GDP in 1984 (it was 85 percent at the beginning of the 1960s), and employing 65 percent of the total work force (90 percent at the beginning of the 1960s). Some 3.75 million acres of land — 7.6 percent of the country's land surface — is cultivable. In 1984, approximately 2.35 million acres were under cultivation (5 percent of the country's area), 85 percent of which was dry-farmed. As a result crop yields fluctuate annually and in dry years cannot meet local demands. Yemen imports a substantial amount of food pro-

AGRICULTURE

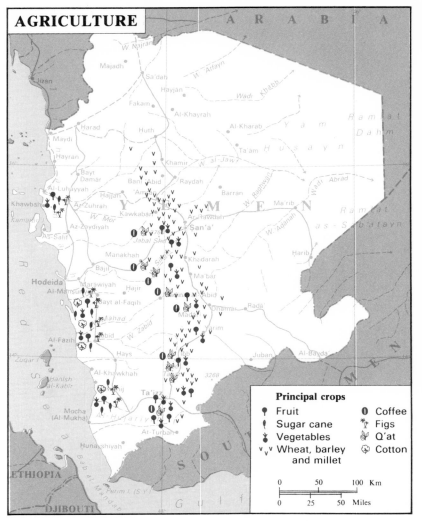

Principal crops

- Fruit
- Sugar cane
- Vegetables
- Wheat, barley and millet
- Coffee
- Figs
- Q'at
- Cotton

ducts, especially wheat (350,000 tons).

The cultivated area lies mainly on the basalt plateau. The principal crops are grains: millet and corn (1.7 million acres), and wheat and barley (275,000 acres). Terraced agriculture is well developed on the western slopes of the plateau, which benefit from summer rains. Cultivation consists mainly of market gardening. Until the beginning of the 1980s, coffee was the most profitable commercial crop. It is grown mainly on the upper parts of the western slopes. Coffee plantations have been reduced in recent years as farmers have discovered that it is more profitable to grow *q'at* (an evergreen shrub with leaves that are used as a narcotic). In 1984, over 125,000 acres were planted with *q'at*. Agriculture along the coastal plain is irrigated, using water from the *wādīs* and groundwater. The principal crops here are fruit (especially apricots and peaches), vegetables, garlic, tobacco, cotton, and sugar cane. With the exception of the Tihāmah region, farms throughout the country are small, and almost no use is made of modern agricultural technology.

Minerals Yemen is poor in mineral resources and deposits are too small to be mined. There are a number of quarries of excellent granite and marble. At aṣ-Ṣalif, on the Red Sea coast, 60,000 tons of salt are produced annually. The salt deposits in this region are estimated at 25 million tons.

In 1984, oil was found in Wādī al-Jawf in the Ma'rib basin 125 miles (200 km) east of Ṣan'ā'. The petroleum reserves here are estimated at 45 million tons. Commercial production began in 1985, while the planning of a pipeline to connect the oil deposits in the Ma'rib basin with an oil terminal to be constructed near aṣ-Ṣalif was begun in 1986. Nickel, zinc, and copper deposits are also found in small quantities but have not yet been exploited.

Industry During the 1980s, the industrial sector expanded, but it remains relatively small. Consisting mostly of light industry, it includes textiles, leather, jewelry, glass, foodstuffs, and building materials for the construction industry, all based on local raw materials. Most of the industrial production is destined for domestic consumption.

The lack of natural resources and the small-scale nature of industry explain the enormous gap between exports and imports. In 1982, Yemen imported goods to the value of $1.9 billion, while revenue from exports totaled only $43 million. Economic assistance from Gulf states and countries in the communist bloc, as well as transfer of salaries of Yemeni residents working abroad, have resulted in increased consumption of imported goods, which adds to the growing foreign trade deficit.

History Yemen is located on an important international trade route. Throughout the centuries, goods have been transported along this route from East Asia to Europe. At different times, this traffic brought great wealth to the region. Despite the contact with foreign traders, Yemen remained isolated from the world at large. The mountainous terrain afforded local inhabitants immunity from foreign invaders. Relatively high rainfall has earned Yemen the name of "Fortunate Arabia" (Arabia Felix) and has enabled its inhabitants to become sedentary farmers.

From the end of the sixteenth century until the eighteenth century the region was, in theory, under Ottoman control. In reality, the Zeidi imams ruled for most of this period. In 1918, at the end of World War I, Imam Yahya declared Yemen independent.

Under his rule, Yemen followed a policy of self-imposed isolation, refraining from establishing links with other countries. Violent border disputes took place with Saudi Arabia and Britain, the latter ruling in neighboring South Yemen. The conservative regime based its policies on the principles of the Koran and eschewed modernization and development. In 1948, the imam was murdered by a group of dissidents whose aim was modernization. However, the attempted coup was brutally suppressed by the imam's son Ahmad. He continued to govern the country along the lines of his father's policy, at the same time permitting outside assistance to strengthen the country's economy. In 1956, strong links were established between Yemen and the Soviet Union, while military aid agreements were signed with Egypt, Saudi Arabia, and Syria. In 1958, Yemen joined Egypt and Syria

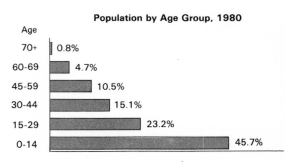

Population by Age Group, 1980

Age	
70+	0.8%
60-69	4.7%
45-59	10.5%
30-44	15.1%
15-29	23.2%
0-14	45.7%

INDUSTRY & MINERALS

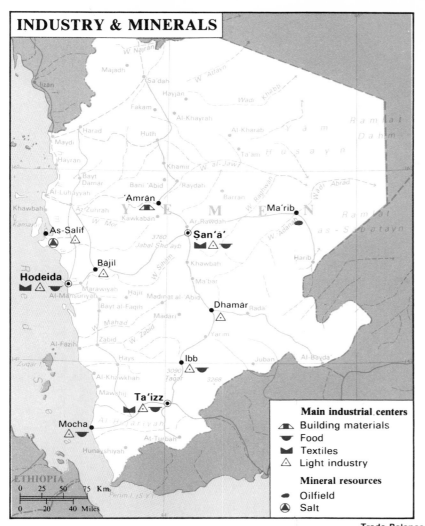

Main industrial centers
- Building materials
- Food
- Textiles
- Light industry

Mineral resources
- Oilfield
- Salt

to assassinate him and overthrow the regime. They were assisted by armed forces from South Yemen, who crossed the border and engaged the Yemen army in battle. At the beginning of 1979, representatives of the Arab League succeeded in mediating between the combatants and brought about the withdrawal of the South Yemen army. Negotiations aimed at the eventual political unification of South Yemen with Yemen began in the same year.

The royalist struggle against the military regime continued sporadically after 1979. In 1982, a further coup attempt was suppressed and the rebel forces fled to South Yemen.

Government and Politics Government is in the hands of an army faction, which elects a president for a five-year term. In reality, the country is headed by a military council comprised of four members. Government affairs are managed by ministers, who are appointed by the military council and are responsible to the president. In 1983 Colonel 'Ali 'Abdullah Salih was elected for a second term as president. In 1979, a Popular Assembly was established consisting of 159 representatives. Fifteen of its members serve as an advisory council to the president. In 1982, a Popular Congress was established, comprising 1,000 representatives — 700 of whom are elected and 300 appointed — who meet once every two years. The representatives are elected every four years.

There are seven administrative districts in Yemen, each controlled by a military governor. The internal political situation in the country is affected by the power struggles between the various groups in Yemeni society. Tension exists between the royalists (who support the imams) and the republicans (who support the existing regime); between Shiites (Zeidis) and Sunnis (Shafe'is); and between immigrants from South Yemen (who mostly reside in the Ta'izz district) and the local residents. There are also occasional intertribal disputes.

in the United Arab Republic (UAR).

Following Imam Ahmad's death in 1962, the leadership passed to his son, al-Badr. A week later, in a military coup, General 'Abdullah Sallal declared Yemen a republic. 'Abdullah Sallal attempted to modernize Yemen with the assistance of foreign aid and by strengthening the country's international ties. There were many opponents to this scheme among the royalists, particularly the deposed imam, al-Badr. A civil war broke out in which the royalists were assisted by Saudi Arabia and the republicans were aided by Egypt, which dispatched military units to Yemen. The war lasted until 1970. During the final years of the war, the republicans held a clear advantage, controlling most of the country. In the treaty that was finally signed between the republicans and the royalists, the latter were promised a share in the country's leadership.

After the civil war, 'Abdullah Sallal was deposed by another military coup. A presidential council with three representatives was established, headed by 'Abdul Rahman al-Iryani. In 1971, a constitution was drawn up and an advisory council to the president was elected. But the struggle for power continued, both within the army and against its royalist opponents. Al-Iryani was deposed in 1974, and his successor, Muhammad al-Hamadi, was assassinated a year later.

In 1978 the army faction appointed Colonel 'Ali 'Abdullah Salih as president of the republic. Soon after his rise to power, royalist rebels attempted

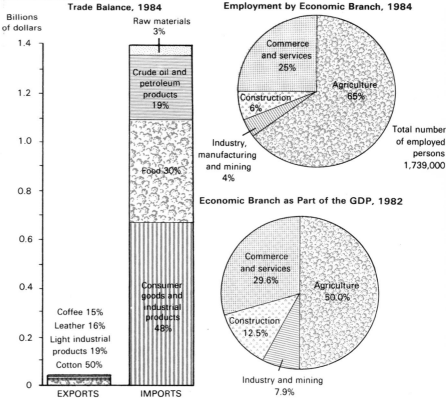

Trade Balance, 1984

Billions of dollars

EXPORTS:
- Coffee 15%
- Leather 16%
- Light industrial products 19%
- Cotton 50%

IMPORTS:
- Raw materials 3%
- Crude oil and petroleum products 19%
- Food 30%
- Consumer goods and industrial products 48%

Employment by Economic Branch, 1984

- Commerce and services 25%
- Agriculture 65%
- Construction 6%
- Industry, manufacturing and mining 4%

Total number of employed persons 1,739,000

Economic Branch as Part of the GDP, 1982

- Commerce and services 29.6%
- Agriculture 50.0%
- Construction 12.5%
- Industry and mining 7.9%

49

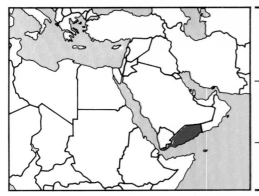

SOUTH YEMEN

Area **129,876 sq. miles (336,380 sq.km)**
Population (1985 estimate) **2,250,000**
Capital city **Aden**
Gross domestic product (GDP) per capita (1983) **$510**

Population in main cities (1984 estimates)	Aden 450,000	Madinat ash-Sha'b 25,000
	Al-Mukallā 60,000	
	Say'ūn 30,000	

South Yemen borders on Yemen to the west, Saudi Arabia to the north, and Oman to the east. The country also includes the island of Socotra in the Arabian Sea (1,200 sq. miles; 3,100 sq.km) and the island of Perim (5 sq. miles; 13 sq.km) in the Bāb al-Mandab Strait.

Topography South Yemen has a long, narrow coastal strip of 744 miles (1,190 km) along the Gulf of Aden. Part of the strip is rocky, and the remainder is covered by dunes. Remains of volcanic activity are in evidence along sections of the coast.

Most of the country's land surface consists of a desert plateau, rising steeply from the coastal plain and eventually descending in a gentle gradient to the Rub' al-Khālī, the large sand desert of the Arabian Peninsula. The average height of the plateau is about 3,280 ft (1,000 meters), above which rise a number of mountain massifs, the highest of which is Jabal Thāmār (8,241 ft [2,512 meters]). The plateau is made up of limestone layers over bedrock.

The plateau is incised by numerous *wādīs* (seasonal riverbeds), which descend steeply to the Gulf of Aden. The longest and most important is Wādī Hadramawt (its lower section is called Wādī Masīlah) with a length of 250 miles (400 km) and a maximum width of 12.5 miles (20 km). A large amount of the summer rains drain into this *wādī*. Numerous springs are to be found in the upper part of the plateau where the groundwater lies close to the surface. For part of its length Wādī Hadramawt is perennial and some of its waters are used for irrigation.

Climate South Yemen has a tropical climate, with high temperatures throughout the year and only small amounts of precipitation.

The coastal region is extremely hot and humid. The average temperature in the hottest month (June) is 94° F. (34° C.) and in the coldest month (January) it is 77° F. (25° C). The climate is more moderate in the interior plateau, with an average June temperature of 90° F. (32° C.), falling to 83° F. (28° C.) in January. There is a large diurnal temperature range in the plateau.

The plateau and the mountains inland receive rainfall in the summer months, particularly April and May. Annual precipitation in these regions is 8 in (200 mm), although in wet years, precipitation in the mountains can reach 16 in (400 mm). The average annual precipitation in the northern reaches of the plateau is only 0.2 in (5 mm). Along the coast, the annual precipitation is 1.2 in (30 mm), mostly falling between December and April. South Yemen experiences severe sand storms during April and May, which often cause considerable damage.

Population Approximately 93 percent of the population are Yemeni Arabs, the majority of whom are Sunni Muslims with a minority of Shiite Muslims. About 2.5 percent of the population are Hindus from India and Pakistan, while 2.2 percent are Africans (Muslims) of Somali origin. The remaining 2.3 percent are Chinese, Iranians, and Europeans (especially British and French).

A large proportion of the country's inhabitants belong to tribal groups, which fall into two major divisions: the Qu'ayti in the south and the west, and the Kathīrī in the north and east. Fifty-two percent of the country's population live in villages around desert oases or in fishing villages along the coast; 38 percent of the population reside in urban settlements, the majority in the port city of Aden. The principal towns inland, Saywun, Tarīm, and Shibām, function as market towns and administrative centers for the tribes in the region. Some 10 percent of South Yemen's inhabitants are nomads or seminomads, principally engaged in raising livestock and in subsistence agriculture.

On the island of Socotra, where there is a naval base for the Soviet fleet and a Palestine Liberation Organization (PLO) training camp, there are some 20,000 inhabitants, nearly all of whom are foreigners.

Economy South Yemen is one of the most underdeveloped countries in the world. The per capita GDP was only $510 in 1983. This is due to a scarcity of natural resources, a lack of sufficient water, and climatic conditions that make agriculture extremely limited.

Until South Yemen became independent in 1967, its economy was largely dependent on revenue accruing from the port at Aden. Its importance derives from its location on the navigation route between Europe and South and East Asia. This free-trade port served as a center of international trade. Approximately 6,000 ships called annually at Aden, making use of its storage and resupply facilities. Part of the crude oil in transit from the Persian Gulf countries to Europe was refined in the

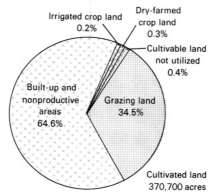

Land Use, 1984

Irrigated crop land 0.2%
Dry-farmed crop land 0.3%
Cultivable land not utilized 0.4%
Built-up and nonproductive areas 64.6%
Grazing land 34.5%
Cultivated land 370,700 acres

NATURAL INCREASE (1980-1983) **3.1%**

LIFE EXPECTANCY (1980-1985) male - **45.3** years female - **47.7** years

DOCTORS (1982) **1.3** per 10,000 inhabitants

HOSPITAL BEDS (1985) **1.7** per 1,000 inhabitants

INFANT MORTALITY (1983-1984) **138.4** per 1,000 births

HIGH SCHOOL PUPILS (1982) 28,600

UNIVERSITY STUDENTS (1981) 400

LITERACY RATE (1984) **40%**

50

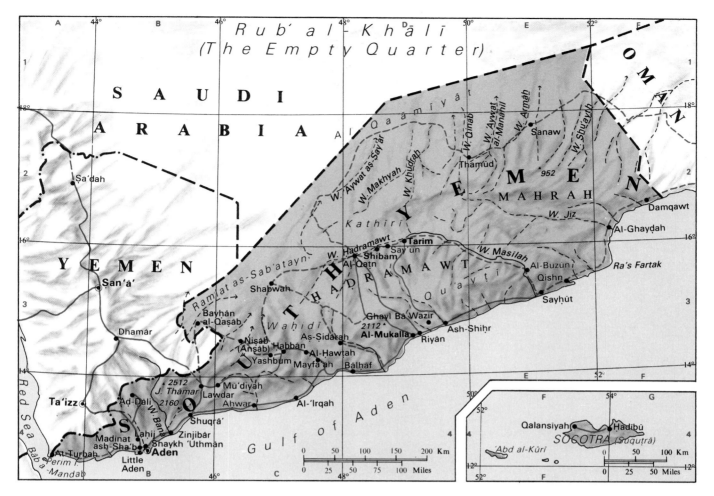

Map labels:

*Rub' al-Khālī
(The Empty Quarter)*

OMAN

SAUDI ARABIA

Sa'dah

W. Aywat as-Say'ar *W. Makhyah* *W. Khudrah* *Al Qaāmiyaât* *W. Qinab* *W. Aywat al-Manāhil* *W. Armāh* *W. Shu'ayb*

Sanaw

Thāmud

• 952

YEMEN

MAHRAH

Kathirī *W. Jiz* Damqawt

Al-Ghaydah

YEMEN

San'a'

W. Hadramawt Tarim Shibam Say'un *W. Masilah* Al-Qatn Al-Buzun Qishn Ra's Fartak

Ramlat as-Sab'atayn UTH HADRAMAWT *Qu'aytī* Sayhūt

Dhamār Shapwah *Wahidī* Ghayl Ba Wazir 2112 Ash-Shihr

Bayhān al-Qasāb As-Sidārah Al-Mukallā Riyān

Nisāb (Ansāb) Habbān Al-Hawtah

Yashbum Mayfa'ah Balhāf

2512 Mū'diyah

J. Thamar 2160 Lawdar

Ta'izz Ad-Dāli Ahwar Al-'Irqah

W. Bana Shuqrā'

Gulf of Aden

SOUTH

Lahij Zinjibār

Madinat ash-Sha'b Shaykh 'Uthmān

Al-Turbah Aden

Perim I. Little

Bab al- Aden

Mandab

Red Sea

0 50 100 150 200 Km
0 25 50 75 100 Miles

SOCOTRA (Suqutrā)

Qalansiyah Hadībū

'Abd al-Kūrī

0 50 100 Km
0 25 50 Miles

large refinery at Aden. In addition, the presence of British military garrisons in the town provided employment and income for local residents.

Following independence in 1967, the British evacuated Aden and ceased granting financial aid to South Yemen. In the same year, the Suez Canal was closed to navigation, causing a substantial decrease in the number of ships passing through Aden. Following a change in government at the end of 1970, the port of Aden no longer functioned as a free-trade area. As a result South Yemen fell into an economic recession. The reopening of the Suez Canal in 1976 did nothing to improve the situation, because by then cargo vessels had increased their capacity and only a small number of ships needed to take advantage of the facilities offered by the port at Aden. In 1984, only 2,088 ships called at the port.

In recent years, the country's revenue has come mainly from oil refining, foreign currency sent home by Yemenis employed in the oil-rich states of the Persian Gulf, and fishing. Since the cost of imports far exceeds the national income, the country's economy is largely dependent on financial aid from the Soviet Union, China, East Germany, and North Korea.

Agriculture Agriculture constitutes the principal source of employment. As in most socialist–Marxist regimes, agricultural land is largely allocated either as state ranches or as cooperative farms. There are also a small number of private farms. Out of 700,000 acres fit for agriculture, only 370,700 acres are actually cultivated. The major obstacle standing in the way of further development is the lack of water. Existing agriculture already uses most of the small amounts of precipitation and groundwater. Most of the agricultural area is to be found in the Hadramawt valley, where millet (125,000 acres), cotton, wheat, q'at (an evergreen shrub with leaves that are used as a narcotic), fruit (melons, bananas, and dates) and vegetables (tomatoes, cucumbers, carrots, beans, potatoes, and eggplant) are grown. Tobacco is grown in small quantities along the coast. The livestock economy in South Yemen consists mostly of sheep and goats. Rich fishing grounds are found close to the country's shores, the annual catch totaling some 75,000 tons.

Minerals Relatively few economically viable minerals have been discovered in South Yemen. Silica, used in the glass industry, is mined near the town of Habbān, while high-quality marble is quarried near Mū'diyah. Salt was produced for hundreds of years, mainly along the coast and near the ancient city of Shabwah (Sheba), close to the border with Yemen. However, the extent of salt

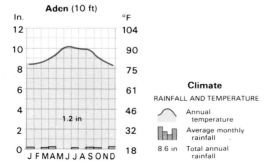

Aden (10 ft)

In. °F
12 104
10 90
8 75
6 61
4 46
2 32
0 18
J F M A M J J A S O N D

1.2 in

Climate

RAINFALL AND TEMPERATURE

Annual temperature

Average monthly rainfall

8.6 in Total annual rainfall

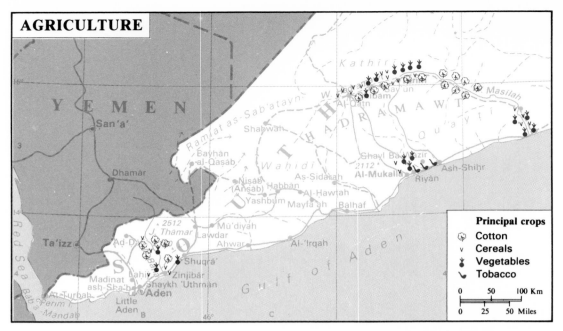

AGRICULTURE

Principal crops
- Cotton
- Cereals
- Vegetables
- Tobacco

```
0        50      100 Km
0    25      50 Miles
```

mining has substantially declined. Copper, iron ore, and titanium are found in small, noncommercial quantities, while oil has yet to be found.

Industry Despite the developments in this sector since the 1970s, industry remains limited in scope. In 1983, 23,000 people — 5 percent of the total work force — were employed in industry. Factories are mostly government-owned and mainly process agricultural produce. Only a few produce consumer goods for the local market such as plastics, paper, clothing, footwear, wood, aluminum, iron, and chemical goods. The largest plant in the country is the oil refinery near Aden, employing 2,300 workers, with an annual production capacity of 8.8 million tons. However, only 3.6 million tons of refined oil were produced in 1984. The raw material for the refinery comes mainly from Saudi Arabia.

History Until 1839, the southern part of the Arabian Peninsula was a remote and insignificant area of the Ottoman Empire. Ottoman control was somewhat fictitious, with real power lying in the hands of local rulers.

The operation of a regular steamship route from India to Europe via Egypt began in 1837 (goods were transferred overland through Egypt). The use of this route gave South Yemen, and in particular Aden, a new importance, thanks to its natural harbor and convenient anchorage. Because of its strategic advantages the British seized Aden in 1839 and established a port. The opening of the Suez Canal in 1869 gave additional impetus to Aden's development. In order to strengthen its hold on the region, Britain signed protection and friendship treaties with the sultanates and emirates in the interior of the country. Relations improved after World War I, during which the Turks finally left the region. In the treaties of friendship, the British promised to provide protection against external threats, in return for a monopoly over all foreign trade. In effect, the treaties gave rise to British protectorates. These were administratively divided into an eastern protectorate containing three sultanates, and a western protectorate with seventeen emirates and sheikdoms. In 1937, the city of Aden became a crown colony.

The emirates of the protectorate were each too small to maintain independent status. In addition, there was much internal conflict among the emirates which made it difficult for them to face the annexationist claims of Yemen. As a result, in the 1950s the British proposed the formation of a federation. Six emirates in the Western Aden Protectorate agreed to the proposal and the Federation of Southern Arab Emirates was established in 1959. This nucleus was later joined by other emirates.

In 1962, the name of the federation was changed to the Federation of South Arabia. As a result of British pressure, Aden — which had autonomous rule — joined the federation in 1963. This act provoked violent reaction on the part of nationalists in Aden, who opposed joining a federation that they regarded as a failure. At the same time subversive activity escalated throughout South Yemen, with demands for the complete evacuation of the British and the deposition of the rulers of the emirates. In 1966, the British announced that they would grant independence to the Federation of South Arabia within two years. The underground organizations refused to recognize the federation and its emirates. In 1967 the federal army rose up against its rulers. Most of the sultans and emirs fled and the federation was dissolved.

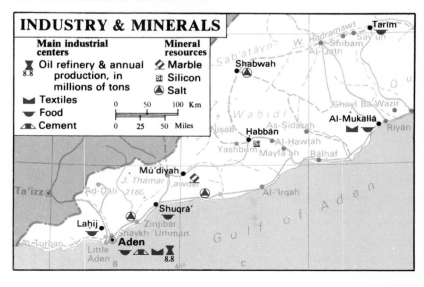

INDUSTRY & MINERALS

Main industrial centers
- Oil refinery & annual production, in millions of tons
- Textiles
- Food
- Cement

Mineral resources
- Marble
- Silicon
- Salt

```
0        50      100 Km
0    25      50 Miles
```

The British were forced to recognize the left-wing National Liberation Front as the official representative for the transfer of power. In a violent struggle, this organization defeated its rival, the Front for the Liberation of Occupied South Yemen which was supported by Egypt.

On November 30, 1967, power was transferred to Qahtan ash-Sha'bi, the leader of the National Liberation Front. He became both president and prime minister of the country. His government was composed of members of his organization, which became the country's sole political party. During Sha'bi's rule, there was a continuous internal struggle, both within the party itself and between the tribes, which resulted in civil war. In June 1969, Sha'bi's government was overthrown by an extreme leftist group. Salem Rubai' 'Ali became president of the country, a new constitution was drawn up, and the name of the country was changed to the People's Democratic Republic of Yemen. All important foreign assets were nationalized and South Yemen began to receive financial aid from China, the Soviet Union, and other Eastern European countries.

During the 1970s, there was a constant struggle for leadership of the party and of the country by the different factions of the ruling party. In June 1978, street battles broke out in Aden, during which President Salem Rubai' 'Ali was executed. The government was seized by 'Ali Nasser Muhammad, supported by the extremist factions in his party.

In January 1986, an attempt to overthrow the government took place, during which 10,000 people were killed in street fighting. The leader of the attempted coup was 'Abd al-Fattah Isma'il, who had served as chairman of the National Council and leader of the party during the 1970s. In 1980, he had been exiled to Sofia and Moscow. The attempted coup occurred following his return to South Yemen, at the invitation of the president. Muhammad fled the country and his deputy was murdered. The coup finally ended in failure and 'Abd al-Fattah Isma'il was killed. In February 1986, Heidar al-Attas was appointed president of the country.

Government and Politics The organization of government in South Yemen is similar to that of communist countries. The president — the country's leader — is also secretary general of the Yemen Socialist party. In theory, there is an Upper Popular Council (Parliament), whose purpose is to function as an advisory body to the president and the government ministers. In practice, council members do not possess any real powers. With the sole exception of the party in power, all political organizations are banned.

The country is divided into six administrative districts. Five of them comprise the twenty emirates that existed during the period of British rule, while the sixth is the Greater Aden region. Each district

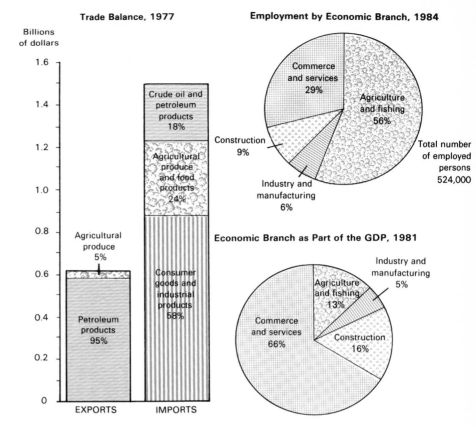

Trade Balance, 1977

Employment by Economic Branch, 1984

Economic Branch as Part of the GDP, 1981

has an appointed governor who is responsible for internal affairs.

The country's boundaries with Yemen, Saudi Arabia, and Oman are in dispute, resulting in sporadic border incidents. Since 1972, there have been frequent border clashes with Yemen, which lays claim to a large area in the west of South Yemen. During 1983–1984, there was fighting with Saudi Arabia over border disputes. Despite the tension between South Yemen and Yemen, the two countries are in the process of negotiating a union. The discovery of oil in Yemen strengthened the desire for union on the part of South Yemen. However, the January 1986 attempt to overthrow the government led to a postponement of the talks.

Since 1968, South Yemen has maintained strong links with the Soviet Union and with other countries in the communist bloc. The Soviet Union is the major source of financial and military aid to South Yemen in return for which it has strategic use of the port of Aden, the island of Socotra, and the country's airfields.

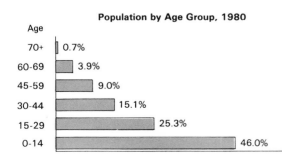

Population by Age Group, 1980

Age	
70+	0.7%
60-69	3.9%
45-59	9.0%
30-44	15.1%
15-29	25.3%
0-14	46.0%

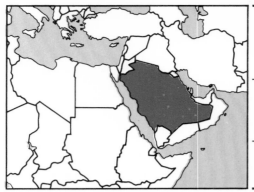

SAUDI ARABIA

Area **830,115 sq. miles (2.150,000 sq.km)**
Population (1985 estimate) **10,500,000**
Capital city **Riyadh**
Gross domestic product (GDP) per capita (1985) **$8,000**

Population in main cities (1984 estimates)		
Riyadh 1,200,000	Ad-Dammām 400,000	Al-Hufūf 100,000
Jiddah 1,000,000	Medina 350,000	
Mecca 600,000	At-Ṭā'if 350,000	

Saudi Arabia is a desert kingdom, occupying most of the Arabian Peninsula. The country borders on Kuwait, Iraq, Jordan, Yemen, South Yemen, Oman, the United Arab Emirates (UAE), and Qatar. Islam's most holy city, Mecca, is located in Saudi Arabia.

Topography The Arabian Peninsula includes a large section of the Arabo-Nubian Massif. This massif is built of igneous rocks, partly overlaid by younger limestone outcrops and volcanic outpours. The Syrian-African Rift valley cuts the massif into two at the Red Sea. Thus the eastern part of ths section of the rift valley is located in the Arabian Peninsula.

Saudi Arabia consists of a number of distinct geographical units. In the west, along the Red Sea, is a narrow coastal plain called the Tihāmah, east of which rises a mountainous belt. This belt is actually the western margin of a plateau mainly built of ancient crystalline rocks that are part of the Arabo-Nubian Massif (the Hejaz and the Asir mountains). The plateau slopes gently eastward toward the Persian Gulf, and much of it is desert — an-Nafūd, ad-Dahnā', and Rub' al-Khālī. The al-Ḥasa Plain is in the Persian Gulf region.

The Tihāmah Plain, mostly covered by sand and gravel, lies parallel to the length of the Red Sea. In some sections, the mountains reach the coastline while in other parts the coastal strip is several miles wide. In a number of locations, the *wādīs* (riverbeds) empty into the sea forming a fan-shaped alluvial plain, in part of which is fresh groundwater. Corals are to be found along the coast.

The Hejaz and the Asir mountains are built mainly of granite. Their average height ranges from 4,900 to 6,600 ft (1,500 to 2,000 meters) with peaks reaching 9,800 ft (3,000 meters). Steep slopes descend to the Red Sea and are deeply incised by narrow, deep ravines. Most of the rivers are short, with only Wādī al-Ḥamḍ completely crossing the highlands, providing convenient access from the Red Sea to the center of the country. In the Hejaz mountains, there are basins containing large oases, in which the cities of Mecca, Medina, and Taymā' have developed.

The Najd Plateau, northeast of the Hejaz and Asir mountains, is built of limestone formations interspersed with beds of sandstone. They are bound in the southwest by precipitous slopes, with gentle slopes northeast. This region receives relatively large amounts of rain, between 6–10 in (150–250 mm) per year. The rainwater seeps into the permeable limestone, forming groundwater sources at the foot of the strata. These sources provide the desert oases with their water supply.

Northeast of the Najd Plateau are large sand deserts. The Nafūd is in the north of the country, cov-

ering an area of 27,000 sq. miles (70,000 sq.km) with an average elevation of 2,000–2,300 ft (600–700 meters) above sea level. Virtually all of the Nafūd is covered by mobile sand dunes, rising to heights of 430 ft (130 meters) above their base. The dunes have been formed as a result of the erosion of the crystalline rocks of the Arabo-Nubian Massif. In the northern margins of the Nafūd are two large oases: the Jawf and the Sākākah. The Dahnā' desert stretches to the east of the Nafūd, 620 miles (1,000 km) long and approximately 50 miles (80 km) wide.

The Rub' al-Khālī (the empty quarter) is the largest sand desert in the world, covering approximately 232,000 sq. miles (600,000 sq.km). It occupies most of the southeastern part of the Arabian Peninsula. Extensive areas of the Rub' al-Khālī are completely desolate, often with little if any rain for several years in a row. In the east of the region, the dunes reach heights of 650 ft (200 meters) above the surrounding area. The dunes have largely been formed from limestone erosion.

The al-Ḥasa region stretches east of the Dahnā' desert to the Persian Gulf and comprises a 185 mile (300 km) wide plain, covered by sand and gravel. The rock beds found in the interior of this region are similar in structure to that of the Najd Plateau.

Climate Saudi Arabia has a desert climate. In most regions, temperatures are high in summer and relatively moderate in winter. In the interior of the country, the average temperature for the hottest month (July) is 95° F. (35° C.) with maximum temperatures occasionally reaching 122° F. (50° C.). The average temperature in the coldest month (January) is 59° F. (15° C.), although in some places, the minimum temperature can fall below 32° F. (0° C.). In the Asir mountains in the southwest, summer temperatures are moderate. At aṭ-Ṭā'if (4,840 ft [1,475 meters]) the average temperature for the hottest month (June) is 84° F. (29° C.), descending to 61° F. (16° C.) in the coldest month (January).

Along the Red Sea and Persian Gulf coasts, the sea has a moderating influence on the range of temperatures. At Jiddah, on the Red Sea coast, the average temperature for the hottest month (August) is 90° F. (32° C.), descending to 75° F. (24° C.) in the coldest month (January). High humidity (80–100%) prevails throughout most of the year.

Throughout most of Saudi Arabia, annual precipitation is less than 4 in (100 mm). Rains fall over most of the country between November and March. In summer (June to September), rainfall occurs in the Asir mountains and some areas in the southwest, with annual precipitation reaching 12.6 in (320 mm) in the uplands.

NATURAL INCREASE (1980-1985) **3.3%**

LIFE EXPECTANCY (1980-1985) male - **54.5** years female - **57.6** years

DOCTORS (1985) **13.6** per 10,000 inhabitants

HOSPITAL BEDS (1985) **2.9** per 1,000 inhabitants

INFANT MORTALITY (1983) **103.0** per 1,000 births

HIGH SCHOOL PUPILS (1985) **530,540**

UNIVERSITY STUDENTS (1984-1985) **93,000**

LITERACY RATE (1984) **52%**

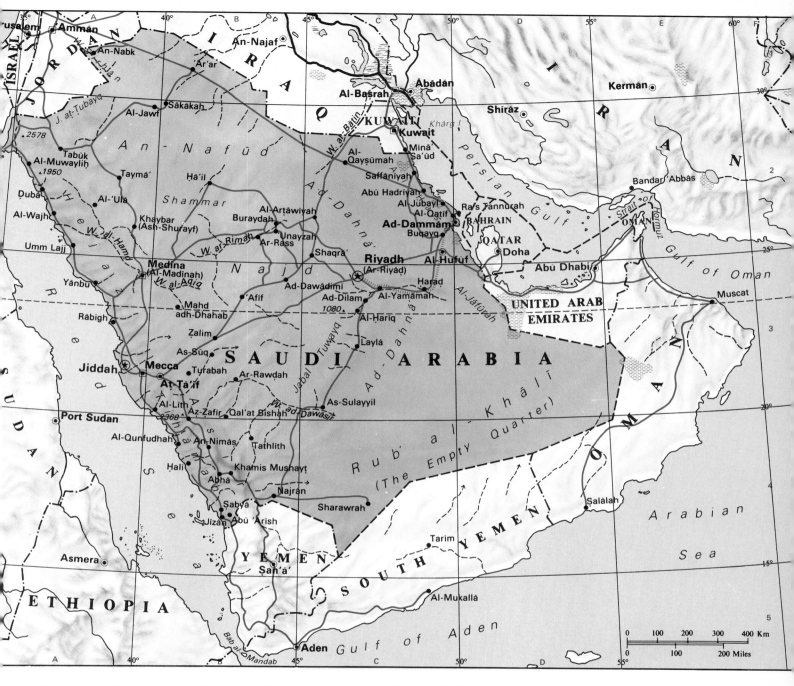

Population There are approximately 8 million citizens in Saudi Arabia (1985). Roughly 93 percent of the inhabitants are Arabs, the remainder blacks who are descendants of the slaves brought to Arabia from East Africa. Ninety-two percent of the country's inhabitants are Sunni Muslims; 6 percent are Shiite Muslims who live mostly in the al-Hasa region. The remainder of the population is made up of Zeidi Muslims, a Shiite faction originating in Yemen, living in the Asir mountains.

There are many foreign residents in Saudi Arabia, all of whom are employed in industry and services. They include 1.2 million Yemenis (most of whom are Zeidis), 400,000 Egyptians, 300,000 Pakistanis, and approximately 300,000 Palestinians, mostly Jordanian citizens. The rest of the foreign workers are from around the world.

Since the 1950s, there has been much internal migration of villagers and nomads to the urban settlements. In the early 1960s, approximately 25 percent of the population lived in urban areas; this figure had risen to 70 percent by the mid-1980s. At the same time, the percentage of nomads decreased from 50 to 5 percent. The process of sedentation is continuing to this day. Approximately 25 percent of the population live in villages.

Economy Until the early 1970s, Saudi Arabia's economy was based on subsistence agriculture and animal husbandry. Another major source of income was the annual Muslim pilgrimage to the holy cities of Mecca and Medina. Despite the fact that oil production and marketing began in the 1940s, the initial revenues were small and did not enable widespread economic development. The national economy finally began to benefit in the late 1960s due to the large and rapid increase in oil revenues. In 1970, oil revenues reached $1.1 billion, rising to $29 billion by 1975. This enabled widespread economic development in all sectors.

During the first phase of development, in the early 1970s, most of the resources were channeled into the development of a transportation network and welfare services for the country's citizens. During the second phase, industrial development commenced, accompanied by the expansion of the cultivated area. In the third phase, most of the resources were channeled into the development of heavy industry, using oil and natural gas as raw materials and sources of energy.

Since the early 1980s, there have been delays in meeting the planned targets. These difficulties are due mainly to the decline in oil revenues as a result of the fall in production and lower prices in the world market.

Agriculture The desert conditions preclude agriculture in most of the regions. In 1985, the cultivated area covered only 1.5 million acres, or 0.3 percent of the country's total area. Most of the cultivated area is located in the Asir and Hejaz regions, with additional areas in desert oases and valleys of seasonal streams that drain the mountain regions (especially in the Hejaz region in the northwest of the country). Most of the cultivation consists of dry-farming of barley, corn, and wheat. Irrigated agriculture, accounting for approximately 250,000 acres, includes vegetables, wheat, and fodder crops, while 350,000 acres are devoted to fruit trees and other perennial crops.

Since the early 1970s, substantial resources have been channeled into the development of water resources to expand the irrigated area. For this purpose, dams are being constructed for the storage of flood waters, enabling a regulated flow of water to the fields. By 1980, 41 dams had been constructed. In addition, several wells exploiting the groundwater are dug each year, while a number of desalination plants have also been constructed.

In its attempt to increase the agricultural output, the government has provided generous financial assistance in promoting mechanization, the use of fertilizers, and modern cultivation techniques. These efforts have resulted in increased wheat, vegetable, and fodder yields. Nevertheless, a high proportion of its domestic food requirements has to be imported.

Climate
RAINFALL AND TEMPERATURE

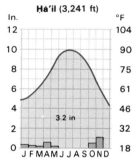

Annual temperature

Average monthly rainfall

8.6 in   Total annual rainfall

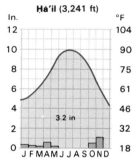

Ḥā'il (3,241 ft)

3.2 in

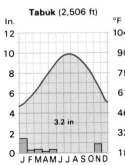

Tabūk (2,506 ft)

3.2 in

Riyadh (1,994 ft)

4.0 in

Medina (2,073 ft)

1.4 in

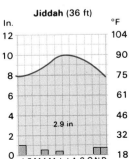

Jiddah (36 ft)

2.9 in

Aṭ-Ṭā'if (4,780 ft)

7.6 in

Jizān (10 ft)

1.4 in

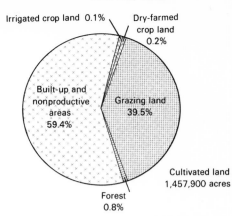

Land Use, 1985

Irrigated crop land 0.1%

Dry-farmed crop land 0.2%

Built-up and nonproductive areas 59.4%

Grazing land 39.5%

Cultivated land 1,457,900 acres

Forest 0.8%

The livestock economy, especially the domestic poultry industry, has been developing since the 1970s. This sector now supplies most of the domestic demand for poultry and eggs. A select breed of cattle, imported from Europe toward the end of the 1970s, and sheep imported from Australia have formed the base for a diversified livestock economy. Nevertheless, the contribution to domestic consumption requirements remains small.

In 1985, approximately 600,000 people (14 percent of the work force) were employed in agriculture, contributing only 2.1 percent to the GDP.

Minerals Petroleum is the principal natural resource. In 1985, the known oil reserves of Saudi Arabia totaled 23.5 billion tons, equaling one-third of the known oil reserves in the Western world.

Most of the oilfields are concentrated in the east of the country, in the al-Hasa region, and offshore. Among these is the world's richest and largest oilfield — the Ghawar field — with proven reserves of 11 billion tons. The Saffāniyah and Manifa fields (proven reserves of 4 billion tons) are jointly owned with Kuwait, while the Abū Sa' Fah field is jointly owned with Bahrain. The fields are connected by pipelines to six refineries with an annual production capacity of 67 million tons (1985).

In addition to the large amounts of gas that are produced along with the petroleum, Saudi Arabia also holds large natural gas fields. The proven reserves of these fields total 3,500 billion cubic meters. In 1985, 7.1 billion cubic meters of natural gas were produced, all of which was used domestically.

Other minerals include iron, nickel, copper, zinc, manganese, coal, lead, and phosphates. However, these are not exploited commercially. In 1987, a gold mine at Mahd adh-Dhahab in the west of the country began to operate, with an expected output of over 2,200 lbs (1,000 kg) per year.

Industry The industrial sector began to develop in the 1970s. Until then, there had been only three refineries (at Riyadh, Ra's Tannūrah, and Jiddah) and a small number of factories, concentrated in the major towns and specializing in construction materials, cement, basic foodstuffs, leather goods, and simple metal products. The large increase in oil revenues brought about rapid industrial development. The main plants use petroleum and natural gas as their raw materials. Most of the factories are concentrated in two locations — at al-Jubayl in the east of the country and at Yanbu' in the west. The plants include refineries (one at al-Jubayl and two at Yanbu'), fertilizer plants, factories for the production of liquid gas, iron and steel plants,

AGRICULTURE

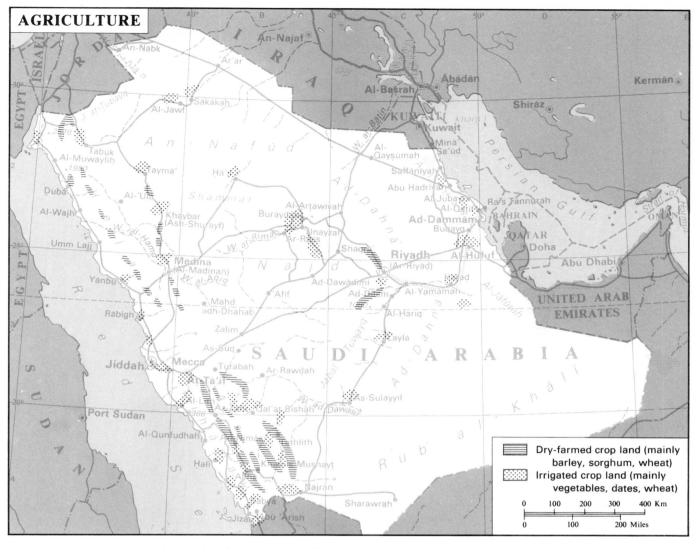

Dry-farmed crop land (mainly barley, sorghum, wheat)

Irrigated crop land (mainly vegetables, dates, wheat)

and petrochemical industries. The petrochemical products became the second most important source of export revenue after the crude oil itself. In recent years, there has been a significant increase in the revenues from petrochemical exports. In 1985, revenues from the export of crude oil equaled $28 billion, while revenues from petrochemical exports reached only $2 billion.

In addition to the heavy industries, other industries have developed in Saudi Arabia's major cities, specializing in the manufacture of agricultural equipment, paper, textiles, foodstuffs, construction materials, cement, and consumer goods.

History The major event in Arabia's history was the formation of the Islamic religion by Muhammad in the middle of the seventh century. In less than a hundred years, Muhammad and his successors controlled an area stretching from Persia to Spain, within which Islam was the main religion of most inhabitants. The location of the Arabian Peninsula was not suitable as a center for an empire. As a result, the Arab rulers moved their capital to other sites. The peninsula returned to its former isolated and politically unimportant status.

The beginnings of the modern Saudi monarchy date back to the early eighteenth century. Muhammad Ibn Sa'ud, the ruler of a small emirate in the Najd region, accepted the Wahhabi doctrine stressing the need to revive the Muslim traditions

as originally taught by Muhammad. Ibn Sa'ud and his successors conquered the whole of the Arabian Peninsula, disseminating the Wahhabi doctrine by means of force. When they also began to threaten Iraq and Syria, the Ottomans reacted by delegating Muhammad 'Ali, the Egyptian ruler, to defeat the Wahhabis. Following seven years of warfare (1811–1818), the Saudi state was destroyed.

In 1824, the Sa'ud family managed to renew their rule in the Riyadh area. During the nineteenth century, there was a continuous struggle between the Saudis and the Rashidis, the latter controlling the Mount Shammar area and professing loyalty to the Ottomans. The Saudis were defeated and were obliged to exile themselves to Kuwait (1891).

It was apparent that the House of Sa'ud had lost its status in Arabia. However, in 1902, 'Abd-ul-'Az-

Population by Age Group, 1980

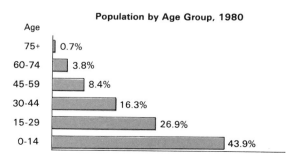

Age	
75+	0.7%
60-74	3.8%
45-59	8.4%
30-44	16.3%
15-29	26.9%
0-14	43.9%

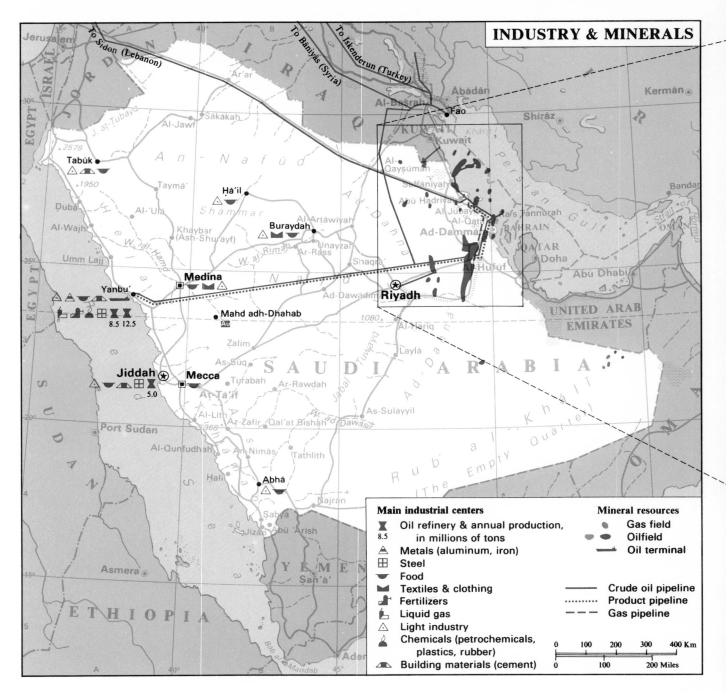

Main industrial centers

⊠	Oil refinery & annual production,
8.5	in millions of tons
△	Metals (aluminum, iron)
⊞	Steel
▽	Food
⋈	Textiles & clothing
⚒	Fertilizers
⬒	Liquid gas
△	Light industry
◊	Chemicals (petrochemicals, plastics, rubber)
⬠	Building materials (cement)

Mineral resources

▮	Gas field
◖◗	Oilfield
⊢	Oil terminal

——	Crude oil pipeline
······	Product pipeline
– – –	Gas pipeline

iz Ibn Sa'ud managed to reaffirm his control over Riyadh. He signed a treaty with Britain and recommenced the dissemination of the Wahhabi doctrine among the local tribes. In 1913, he captured the al-Hasa region from the Ottomans. Following the termination of World War I and the Turkish defeat, 'Abd-ul-'Aziz overcame the Rashīdīs and captured Shammar (1919–1921). In 1924–1925, he also captured the Hejaz from Hussein Ibn 'Ali (the Hashemite Sharif of Mecca). The conquered territories were united in 1932 under the name of the Kingdom of Saudi Arabia.

Until his death in 1953, Ibn Sa'ud preserved the existing social and tribal structure of his kingdom. He did not intervene in the internal affairs of the tribes. The administration of the kingdom was based on the personal relationships between the king and the various sheiks. The royal family established marital links with the families of the

sheiks, while the national revenue was distributed to the tribal leaders on a personal basis. This system created internal political stability. The discovery of petroleum toward the end of the 1930s brought in large revenues for the royal household, part of which was used in the development of the country and its economy.

Following Ibn Sa'ud's death, his son Sa'ud Ibn 'Abd-ul-'Aziz became the country's ruler. His squandering resulted in a budgetary deficit, despite the large oil revenues. In its foreign policy, Saudi Arabia became embroiled in disputes with both Britain and Egypt. Sa'ud was forced to transfer the administration of the country's internal and foreign affairs to his brother, Feisal, who served as prime minister from 1958. In 1964, Sa'ud was deposed and was replaced on the throne by Feisal.

During the eleven years of his rule, Feisal endeavored to develop the country's economy. The

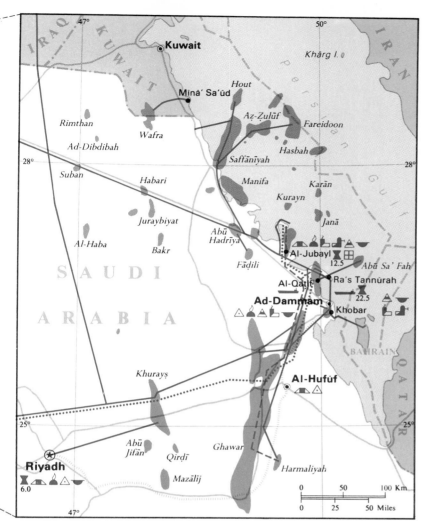

dependent on Saudi Arabia's financial assistance, to mediate in inter-Arab conflicts. In 1976, the negotiations aimed at bringing about an end to the civil war in Lebanon took place in Riyadh, as did the appeasement talks between Egypt and Syria. Saudi Arabia adopted a policy of moderation concerning oil prices and opposed any exaggerated price increase, fearing that such an action would damage the world economy.

Until the late 1970s, Saudi Arabia enjoyed internal political stability, with widespread support for the royal family and the government institutions. In 1979, the political framework was shaken when a group of fundamentalist Mahdi Sunnis, who accept the basic religious doctrines in their simplest form, took control of the Ka'ba Mosque in Mecca for a period of two weeks. Shortly afterward, there were outbreaks of violence by the Shiites in the al-Ḥasa region in the east of the country. When these disturbances began to spread to other parts of the country in February 1980, they were mercilessly repressed. Subsequently, the government began development in the al-Ḥasa region, especially in the cities of al-Hufūf and al-Qaṭif, in order to appease the local Shiite inhabitants. The region's transportation, electricity, water, education, and health networks were all expanded.

Khaled died in 1982 and was replaced by his half-brother Fahd. The main thrust of his policies has been aimed at the strengthening of the country's military status and the diversification of the country's economy to include industries not dependent solely on oil. The strengthening of the army is of particular importance because of the Iranian threat to Saudi Arabia which has increased as a result of the assistance given by Saudi Arabia to Iraq. Approximately one-third of the national budget is used for military expenditure and the development of defense networks.

Government and Politics Saudi Arabia is ruled by a king who is both prime minister and national

administrative network was extended, the education system was developed (education became mandatory), and the communications and transport networks were expanded.

In foreign policy, Feisal followed a pro-Western line. This policy brought about a worsening of relations between Saudi Arabia and Egypt during the 1960s, due to Egypt's dominance in the pro-Soviet Arab states. The two sides found themselves in direct military conflict in the civil war in Yemen. Saudi Arabia supported the royalists, while Egypt assisted the republican cause. During Feisal's reign, agreements concerning oil concessions and rights in the Persian Gulf were signed with Iran, while the boundary line between Saudi Arabia and Jordan was demarcated (1965). In 1973, Saudi Arabia was one of the initiators of the oil embargo on the Western countries. However, in the following year, Feisal initiated the termination of the embargo because he feared that Saudi Arabia's economy, as well as that of other oil-producing countries, would be severely damaged.

In March 1975, Feisal was assassinated by a mentally unstable member of his family. In his place, Feisal's half-brother Khaled was crowned as king. Khaled continued his predecessor's policy of development but at a slower pace than before. His most notable contribution was the development of the agricultural sector, which until then had been of negligible importance. In his foreign policy, Khaled took advantage of the country's wealth, and the fact that so many Arab countries were

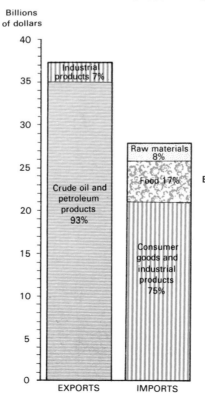

Trade Balance, 1984

Billions of dollars

EXPORTS: Industrial products 7%; Crude oil and petroleum products 93%

IMPORTS: Raw materials 8%; Food 17%; Consumer goods and industrial products 75%

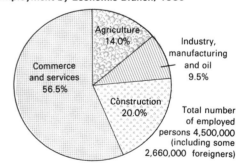

Employment by Economic Branch, 1985

Agriculture 14.0%
Industry, manufacturing and oil 9.5%
Construction 20.0%
Commerce and services 56.5%

Total number of employed persons 4,500,000 (including some 2,660,000 foreigners)

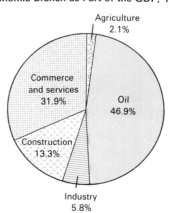

Economic Branch as Part of the GDP, 1983

Agriculture 2.1%
Oil 46.9%
Industry 5.8%
Construction 13.3%
Commerce and services 31.9%

Oil Production and Income

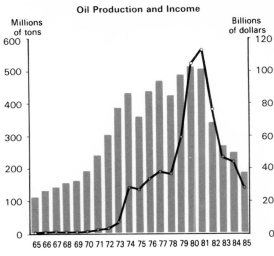

Millions of tons / Billions of dollars

○—○ Income in dollars from oil production
▪ Crude oil

important social significance. The tribal leaders function as mediators between the population and the government institutions. The country's law is based on the Islamic religion (the *Shariah*), with the addition of decrees relating to modern social and economic issues.

The ethnic homogeneity — nearly all of the population are Sunni Muslims — and the high economic level of welfare, maintain internal political stability. The principal group to oppose the regime is the Shiite Muslims in the al-Hasa region, where the large oilfields are located. The rise of Ayatollah Khomeini to power in Iran has led to much unrest among this minority. But apart from the disturbances that broke out in 1979, their antigovernment activities have remained limited.

The precise demarcation of Saudi Arabia's boundaries with South Yemen, Oman, Qatar, and the United Arab Emirates (UAE) remains under dispute. However, skirmishes only occur with South Yemen, on whose border Saudi Arabia retains an active military force.

Saudi Arabia's economic strength has transformed it into an important political power not only in the Middle East but in the world as a whole. Saudi Arabia provides economic and military support for many of its neighbors, especially Iraq, which receives much financial assistance in its war against Iran. In addition, Saudi Arabia stands at the head of the group of countries in conflict with Israel. Its relatively moderate foreign policy enables Saudi Arabia to act as a mediator in a number of conflicts within the Middle East, such as between different PLO factions and in attempts to reach a cease-fire between Iran and Iraq. Saudi Arabia has close relations with the United States and with European countries, all of which provide it with much military equipment.

religious leader. The king is chosen from among the senior and most influential members of the royal family. The choice is also dependent on the agreement of the important religious leaders (the *'Ulama*) and the heads of the most powerful tribes. The mandate given to the king is subject to continual supervision by the senior members of the royal family who, in certain circumstances, can depose him. The government comprises 25 ministers who are all appointed by the king. Ministerial responsibility is only to the king, and he is empowered to veto and change any of their decisions. All forms of political organization are forbidden in the kingdom. However, there is a great deal of tribal affiliation and loyalty, and this has

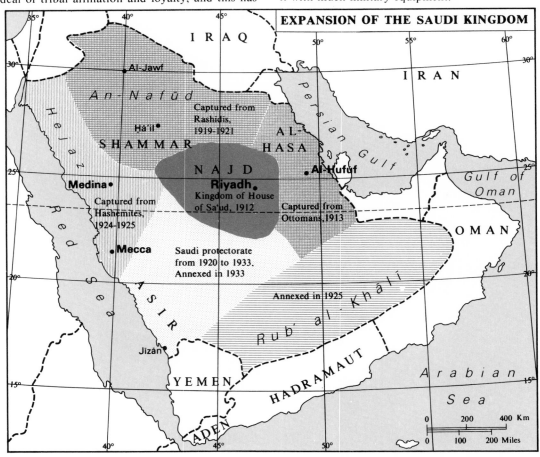

EXPANSION OF THE SAUDI KINGDOM

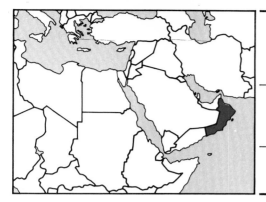

OMAN

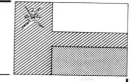

Area **104,247 sq. miles (270,000 sq.km)**
Population (1985 estimate) **1,000,000**
Capital city **Muscat**
Gross domestic product (GDP) per capita (1984) **$7,816**

Population in main cities (1983 estimates)	Muscat 50,000 Sib 25,000 Ṣuḥār 25,000	Nizwā 25,000 Ṣalālah 15,000

Oman lies at the eastern edge of the Arabian Peninsula, bordering on the United Arab Emirates, Saudi Arabia, and South Yemen. It also includes the Musandam Peninsula, physically separated from Oman by the United Arab Emirates; the island of Maṣīrah near Oman's southeast coast; and the islands of Kūriā Mūriā close to the southwest coast.

Topography Oman comprises two mountainous regions: the Oman mountains in the north (including the western and eastern Ḥajar mountains and al-Jabal al-Akhḍar) and Jabal al-Qarā in the south. Between the two mountain ranges is a low-lying area forming a continuation of the Rub' al-Khālī desert.

The Oman mountains consist of ranges mainly built of limestone beds. They are approximately 60 miles (100 km) wide, stretching parallel to the Gulf of Oman, with steep northeastern slopes. Their highest peak is 9,900 ft (3,018 meters) at al-Jabal al-Akhḍar. A narrow, flat coastal strip, known as the Bāṭinah, stretches from the border with the United Arab Emirates to the town of Muscat. The coastal strip has an average width of up to 9 miles (15 km) and is covered by alluvial material, sand, and gravel. To the southeast of Muscat, the width of the coastal strip decreases to a few hundred feet, while in some places the mountains actually reach the seashore. To the southwest, these mountains slope gently toward the Rub' al-Khālī desert. Since the rain-bearing clouds reach Oman from the west, the western slopes receive relatively large amounts of precipitation, resulting in forest and bush vegetation.

To the south of the Oman mountains, the land has a gentle southerly slope, descending from an altitude of 1,640 ft (500 meters) at the foot of the Oman mountains to 660 ft (200 meters) near the coast of the Gulf of Maṣīrah, and then rising toward Jabal al-Qarā in the south. The flat areas opposite the Gulf of Maṣīrah are covered by sand dunes. This region is an extension of the Rub' al-Khālī desert sands.

Jabal al-Qarā lies parallel to the southern coastline. These mountains slope gently in a northern direction, while the southern slopes descend steeply to a narrow coastal strip. This coastal strip receives more rain than other parts of the southern coast and is covered by fertile soils suitable for cultivation.

Oman's coastline extends for over 1,050 miles (1,700 km), with long stretches lined by coral reefs.

The Musandam Peninsula, covering an area of approximately 770 sq. miles (2,000 sq.km), is mostly mountainous. Steep mountain slopes descend to the sea in the west and east, leaving an extremely narrow coastal strip. There are many inlets along the peninsula's coastline, some of which penetrate as far as 9 miles (15 km) inland.

Climate Most of Oman is characterized by desert conditions. The summer is extremely hot while the winter is temperate and dry. Winds from the Arabian Sea have a moderating influence on the eastern coast.

The climate is hot and humid in the coastal regions. The average temperature in the hottest month (May) in Muscat is 93° F. (34° C.), decreasing to 72° F. (22° C.) in the coldest month (January). Maximum temperatures often reach 110° F. (43° C.) in the summer with humidity as high as 90 percent. In Ṣalālah, in the Dhufār region, the average temperature in the hottest month (May) is 82° F. (28° C.), descending to 70° F. (21° C.) in January. In the al-Jabal al-Akhḍar highlands, the temperatures are more moderate. The inland desert regions are hot and dry, with an average high temperature of 106° F. (41° C.) in July, and 77° F. (25° C.) in January.

Throughout most of Oman, rain falls between November and April. In the mountainous north of the country and in the Dhufār region in the south there are summer rains. In the northern coastal region (around Muscat) and in the coastal region of Dhufār, annual rainfall is approximately 4 in (100 mm). Precipitation is greater in the al-Jabal al-Akhḍar highlands and in the western Ḥajar mountains. At some of the higher altitudes, average annual rainfall totals 20 in (500 mm). In the desert regions to the west and the south of the country, precipitation is less than 1.2 in (30 mm) per year.

Population No population census has, as yet, been carried out in Oman. The following figures are, therefore, based on estimates.

Over 90 percent of Omani citizens are Arabs, some 60 percent of whom belong to the Ibadiyya sect (a special Muslim sect). The largest ethnic minority are the Baluchis, with other minorities including Pakistanis, Indians, Iranians, and blacks. An unknown number of foreign workers from Southeast Asia, the Middle East, and Europe also

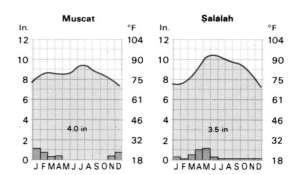

Climate

RAINFALL AND TEMPERATURE

⌒ Annual temperature

▥ Average monthly rainfall

8.6 in Total annual rainfall

61

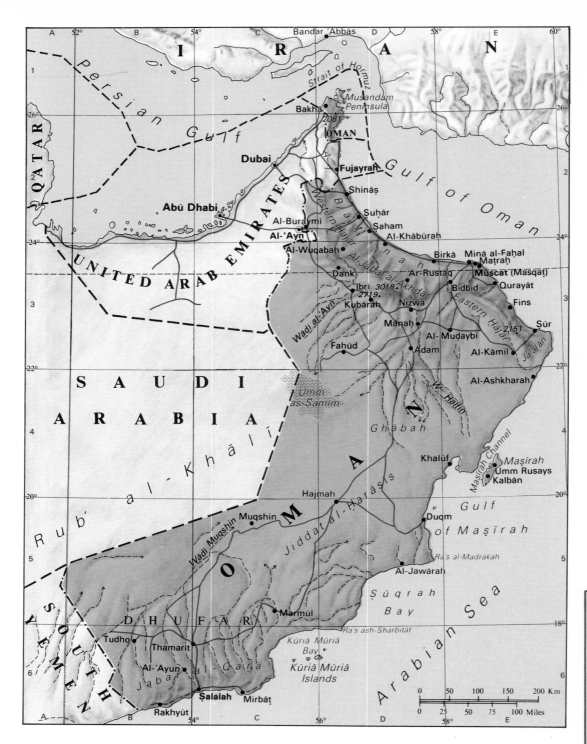

NATURAL
INCREASE
(1980-1983)
3.1%

LIFE
EXPECTANCY
(1980-1985)
male - **48.7** years
female - **50.9** years

DOCTORS
(1982)
7.5 per 10,000
inhabitants

HOSPITAL BEDS
(1982)
2.2 per 1,000
inhabitants

INFANT
MORTALITY
(1983)
122.0 per 1,000 births

reside in Oman. These workers came into the country after the discovery of oil in the 1960s. Oman also has tens of thousands of nomads.

Approximately 30 percent of the country's inhabitants are concentrated in the Bāṭinah coastal plain, 50 percent in the mountains to the east of the coastal plain, with the remainder in the Dhufār region. The Musandam Peninsula has approximately 13,000 inhabitants. The majority of the country's inhabitants live in villages, urban settlements accounting for only 15 percent of the population.

Economy Until the discovery of oil during the early 1960s, most of Oman's population was part of a subsistence economy based on agriculture, fishing, and the raising of sheep and camels. Industry was backward, mostly consisting of the manufacture of basic consumer goods in small workshops. Throughout the country, the level of services and infrastructure was low. There was a lack of essential services, such as electricity, water, roads, health, welfare, and education.

Toward the end of the 1960s, there was a turnaround in Oman's economy. Oil revenues (\$.92 billion in 1969, \$2.4 billion in 1979) assisted the rapid development of industry, agriculture, services, and infrastructure. As a result, there was a marked improvement in the standard of living of Oman's inhabitants.

Despite the broadening base and diversification

Land Use, 1985

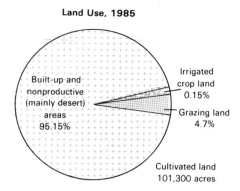

Built-up and nonproductive (mainly desert) areas 95.15%

Irrigated crop land 0.15%

Grazing land 4.7%

Cultivated land 101,300 acres

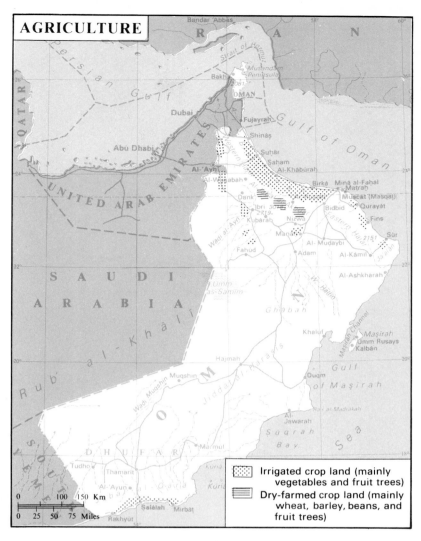

AGRICULTURE

Irrigated crop land (mainly vegetables and fruit trees)

Dry-farmed crop land (mainly wheat, barley, beans, and fruit trees)

of the industrial infrastructure, the petroleum industry became the backbone of the country's economy. Oil makes up 48 percent of the GDP and 88 percent of the country's export revenues (1984) despite employing only 4,000 workers. Oil exports have resulted in a surplus trade balance in recent years. In 1984, export revenues were $1.2 billion larger than imports.

Agriculture Sixty-five percent of the country's inhabitants are engaged in agriculture (1984). However, this sector contributes only 3 percent to the GDP.

In 1985, the cultivated land extended over 101,000 acres. The agricultural lands are in the Baṭinah Plain, the coastal strip to the south of the Dhufār region, and in the Oman mountains. Irrigation, exploiting local springs and groundwater, is widespread in the Baṭinah Plain. It is mostly carried out by means of *qanats* (underground channels that bring groundwater to the surface). Crops include fruit, dates, bananas, citrus, mangos, vegetables, and fodder. In the Oman mountains, especially at altitudes above 4,500 ft (1,400 meters) there is sufficient precipitation for dry-farming. The principal crops here are wheat, barley, millet, beans, and market gardening. In the coastal strip to the south of the Dhufār region, fruit trees and vegetables are cultivated, mostly by means of irrigation.

Since the agricultural area is limited and the crop yields are small, Oman is obliged to import a substantial portion of fruit and vegetables. This makes up 13 percent of the country's total import bill.

Oman's livestock economy is sufficient to meet most of the local demand. Oman possesses good grazing lands in the coastal plain and in the mountains above altitudes of 3,280 ft (1,000 meters). There is poultry farming in the Dhufār region. Approximately 10 percent of the country's population is employed in fishing, the catch mainly going to the local market.

To relieve the scarcity of water in Oman, the government has invested in the construction of dams to store flood water. The largest dam was constructed to the south of Muscat, storing 100 million cubic meters of water.

Minerals Petroleum is the country's most important mineral resource. The proven oil reserves stood at 550 million tons in 1984. Oil was first discovered in 1964 at Fahūd, 150 miles (250 km) southwest of Muscat. Production from this field began in August 1967. Additional oilfields were discovered during the 1970s south of Fahūd and in the Dhufār region. When commercial production began, these fields were linked to the oil terminal at Minā al-Fahal. Oman also produces gas, mostly as

a by-product of the oilfields. Natural gas fields were discovered in 1984 in the Dhufār region. Oman produced 1.36 billion cubic meters of natural gas in 1985, and proven natural gas reserves stood at 76 billion cubic meters.

The second most important mineral is copper. Deposits are concentrated to the west of Ṣuhār. Copper production began in 1983. The copper deposits in this area are of medium quality. Approximately 3,500 tons of pure copper were produced in Oman in 1985, and it is estimated that 13 million tons of copper deposits remain to be exploited in this region. Small chromium deposits were found in the same region but these are not exploited. Other minerals in Oman include coal, iron, lead, manganese, and nickel, also not mined.

Industry Industry developed rapidly during the 1970s and early 1980s. The most important single project was the construction of the oil refinery at Minā al-Fahal with an annual capacity of 2.5 million tons. Its completion in 1982 enabled the establishment of a variety of petrochemical industries. At the same time, other industries, such as fertilizers and liquid gas, were developed and expanded. Following the discovery of the copper deposits in the early 1970s, a plant for copper refining and the manufacture of copper products was established. Light industry was also developed during this period, including foodstuffs, beverages, construction materials, and cement.

In spite of the rapid development of industries

HIGH SCHOOL PUPILS (1982) **26,000**

LITERACY RATE (1983) **25%**

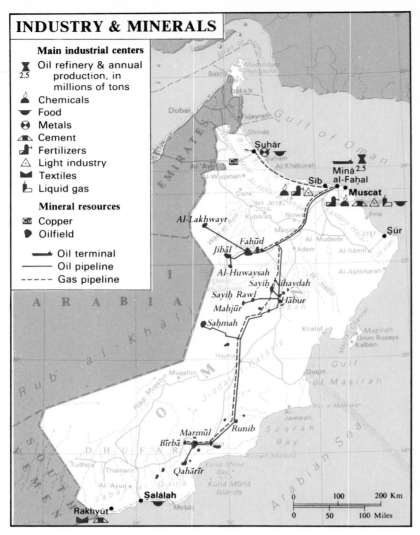

INDUSTRY & MINERALS

Main industrial centers

- ⚒ (2.5) Oil refinery & annual production, in millions of tons
- ♨ Chemicals
- ◥ Food
- ⊖ Metals
- ⛰ Cement
- ⚒ Fertilizers
- △ Light industry
- ⋈ Textiles
- ⚓ Liquid gas

Mineral resources

- Cu Copper
- ● Oilfield

- ▬► Oil terminal
- ─── Oil pipeline
- ----- Gas pipeline

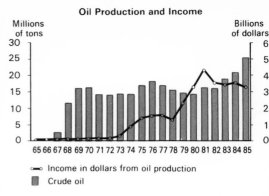

Oil Production and Income

Millions of tons / Billions of dollars

65 66 67 68 69 70 71 72 73 74 75 76 77 78 79 80 81 82 83 84 85

- ○— Income in dollars from oil production
- ▮ Crude oil

forces from West Arabia into territories that had been under the sultan's control resulted in a weakening of the status and authority of the sultanate. Following the death of Sultan Sa'id in 1856, a war of succession broke out. This led to the division of the country into an Asian sultanate with its capital at Muscat, and an African sultanate controlled from Zanzibar.

In the second half of the nineteenth century, there was a struggle between the local tribes of the Asian sultanate over their respective spheres of control. There were also occasional violent struggles between the sultan's forces and the tribes further inland. The tribes wanted to reduce their dependency on the sultan and to increase their own independence. In 1913, the tribes in al-Jabal al-Akhdar chose their own imam to serve as their religious and political leader. This led to a significant reduction in the power and influence of the sultan in the country's interior, especially in the mountain regions. A new imam, Muhammad al-Halili, took over the leadership in 1920. He signed an agreement (the Sib Treaty) with Sultan Sa'id ibn Taimur, in which a cease-fire was declared and autonomous status was granted to the imam in the mountain regions.

The conditions laid down in the Sib Treaty were adhered to until the appointment of Ghaleb ibn 'Ali as imam in 1954. Under his leadership, the mountain tribes revolted against the sultan. They demanded full independence according to the provisions of the treaty. The violent struggle continued until 1959, when the British intervened in the conflict. The followers of the imam continued to demand independence for the areas under their influence.

In 1970 Sultan Sa'id ibn Taimur, who had ruled Oman since 1932, was deposed by his son Qabus, aided by the British. Qabus brought about an end to the imam's revolt and extended his absolute authority throughout the country. The title of imam as a religious and political leader in the mountain region was officially abolished.

When Qabus came to power, Oman was a back-

not dependent on the oil industry, their economic importance remains minor. They engage only 1.5 percent of the labor force and contribute only 4 percent to the GDP (1984). Industrial exports comprise 12 percent of the value of total exports.

History Oman's inhabitants accepted the Islamic faith in the seventh century. The Ibadiyya sect struck roots in this region. In 1508, the Portuguese gained control of parts of the coast of Oman, which they held until they were finally driven out by Oman's inhabitants in 1650. Since then, Oman has enjoyed an independent status, the longest period of uninterrupted independence enjoyed by any Arab nation in recent history. The Omani inhabitants were not satisfied with the expulsion of the Portuguese. They established a strong naval force, which between 1650 and 1730 succeeded in capturing the Portuguese strongholds in Eastern Africa (Mogadishu, Mombasa, the Mafia Islands, and Zanzibar). This navy served as the foundation for Oman's increasing skill in maritime commerce, as well as the slave trade and ocean piracy.

Toward the end of the eighteenth century, Britain began developing its links with Oman, resulting in the signing of a protectorate treaty in 1898. Britain gradually extended its influence and presence in the sultanate. The British tried to abolish the slave trade, which until the nineteenth century had constituted one of the major elements of Oman's economy. The strengthening of Britain's position in the region and the invasions of Wahabbi

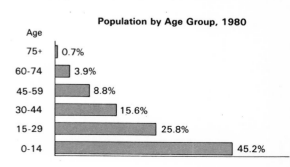

Population by Age Group, 1980

Age

- 75+ : 0.7%
- 60-74 : 3.9%
- 45-59 : 8.8%
- 30-44 : 15.6%
- 15-29 : 25.8%
- 0-14 : 45.2%

Trade Balance, 1984

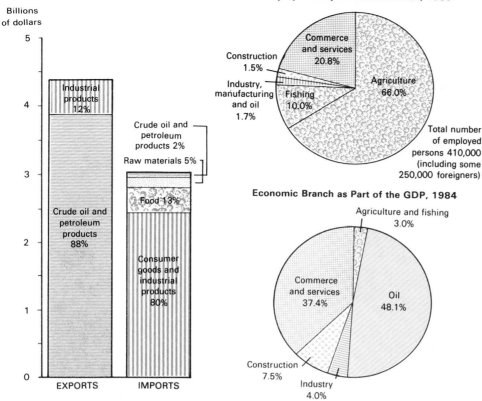

Billions of dollars

EXPORTS
- Industrial products 12%
- Crude oil and petroleum products 88%

IMPORTS
- Crude oil and petroleum products 2%
- Raw materials 5%
- Food 13%
- Consumer goods and industrial products 80%

Employment by Economic Branch, 1983

- Commerce and services 20.8%
- Construction 1.5%
- Industry, manufacturing and oil 1.7%
- Fishing 10.0%
- Agriculture 66.0%

Total number of employed persons 410,000 (including some 250,000 foreigners)

Economic Branch as Part of the GDP, 1984

- Agriculture and fishing 3.0%
- Commerce and services 37.4%
- Oil 48.1%
- Construction 7.5%
- Industry 4.0%

ward and extremely isolated country. Sultan Sa'id ibn Taimur had done little to develop his country. Qabus — who has continued to rule Oman since 1970 — introduced substantial changes in internal and foreign policy. In his efforts to overcome the backwardness of the sultanate, Qabus permitted the entry of Western influences into the country, particularly through the expansion of economic links with Western countries.

Within the country, Qabus has been making continuous efforts to modernize the whole economy. He completely crushed his opponents at home. He also tried to reduce the level of hostility between the tribes making up the sultanate's population.

Government and Politics Oman is governed by a sultan, who has absolute legislative, judiciary, and executive powers. The sultan appoints the government, whose task is to assist him in the administration of the country's affairs. The sultan himself serves as defense minister, the army and the internal security forces being directly responsible to him. Most of the other key government appointments are controlled by members of the sultan's family. Oman does not have a written constitution or a legislative assembly. The source of the country's law stems from the religious Islamic law (*Shariah*), which is interpreted by *qadis* (religious leaders) who are appointed by the government. In the interior of the country, the law is often made up of local customs.

A number of militant groups are opposed to the absolute rule of the Abu Sa'id family. In 1971 and 1972, following Qabus's rise to power, the opponents widened the scope of their activities, leading to violent conflict with the army. Following the receipt of military aid from Saudi Arabia, Jordan, Iran, and Pakistan, Qabus gradually succeeded in defeating his opponents. Most of the militant groups were expelled from Oman in 1975. Since then they have undertaken sporadic operations from bases in South Yemen.

Oman's geographical location close to the Strait of Hormuz bestows considerable strategic importance on the country. This importance has increased following the outbreak of the Iran–Iraq war, especially since Oman possesses an oil terminal outside the Persian Gulf area. As a result of Oman's strategic importance, the United States, with Oman's full agreement, has positioned military forces on the island of Maṣīrah.

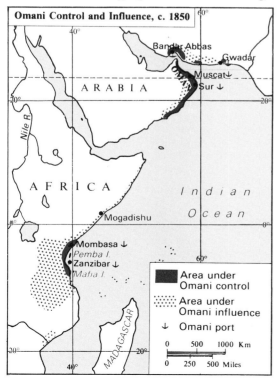

Omani Control and Influence, c. 1850

ARABIA
- Bandar Abbas
- Gwadar
- Muscat ↓
- Sur ↓

Nile R.

AFRICA

Indian Ocean

- Mogadishu
- Mombasa ↓
- Pemba I.
- Zanzibar ↓
- Mafia I.

MADAGASCAR

- ■ Area under Omani control
- ⋯ Area under Omani influence
- ↓ Omani port

0   500   1000 Km
0   250   500 Miles

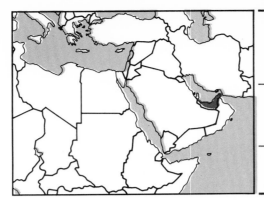

UNITED ARAB EMIRATES

Area **32,278 sq. miles (83,600 sq.km)**
Population (1985 census) **1,622,462**
Capital city **Abū Dhabi**
Gross domestic product (GDP) per capita (1984) **$21,800**

Population in main cities **(1983 estimates)**	Dubai 280,000 Abū Dhabi 252,000 Sharjah 137,000	Al-'Ayn 115,000

The United Arab Emirates is a union of seven emirates: Abū Dhabi (26,000 sq. miles; 67,350 sq.km), Dubai (1,470 sq. miles; 3,880 sq.km), Sharjah (1,000 sq. miles; 2,590 sq.km), Ra's al-Khaymah (656 sq. miles; 1,700 sq.km), Umm al-Qaywayn (290 sq. miles; 750 sq.km), Fujayrah (444 sq. miles; 1,150 sq.km), and 'Ajmān (100 sq. miles; 260 sq.km). The country is located along the Persian Gulf coast and is bordered by Qatar, Saudi Arabia, and Oman.

Topography Most of the United Arab Emirates' land surface is a continuation of the Rub' al-Khālī desert in the south of the Arabian Peninsula. The area is covered with gravel, rocky slopes, and dunes. Near the coast is a strip of salt flats, some several miles in width. The coastline is highly indented, while the continental shelf is shallow with many coral reefs and shoals.

In the south of the country, in a depression, is a group of about thirty oases known as al-Līwā'. This group of oases is fed by springs and by groundwater resources lying close to the surface. The western slopes of the Western Ḥajar mountains, which are in neighboring Oman, are in the east of the country. This region consists of hills and low mountains which in some places extend to the coastline.

Climate Desert conditions prevail in the Emirates with high temperatures throughout most of the year and little precipitation. Due to the proximity of the sea, high humidity prevails on the coastal plain — 85 percent in summer months and 75 percent in winter. The average temperatures for the summer months (July–September) is 90° F. (32° C.). The temperature occasionally reaches 119° F. (48° C.). The average winter temperature (November–April) is 65° F. (18° C.). The diurnal temperature range increases as one moves away from the coast.

The rainy season is between November and April, with an average annual precipitation of 3–4 in (80–100 mm). The northeastern mountain region — Ra's al-Khaymah — receives 4.5 in (115 mm) of rain annually.

Population In 1985, the population of the Emirates totaled 1,622,462 inhabitants, of whom only 30 percent (467,000) were citizens of the Union. The remainder were foreign residents seeking employment in the Emirates.

Most of the citizens are Muslim. Seventy-five percent are Sunni Muslim Arabs, 20 percent are Shiite Muslims, 3.8 percent are Christian Arabs, 0.5 percent are black Muslims (descendants of the slaves who were brought to the region up until the nineteenth century), and the remainder are Hindu.

The number of foreign residents in the country is not constant. In recent years, there has been a growing tendency to reduce the size of the foreign work force due to the decreasing oil revenues and the reduction in economic activity that accompanied it. Approximately 35 percent of the foreign residents are Indian, 20 percent Pakistani, 20 percent Bengali, and 5 percent European. The remainder are Omani, Palestinians, Jordanians, Egyptians, and Yemeni.

Approximately 75 percent of the Union's inhabitants live in urban settlements, half of them in Abū Dhabi, Dubai, and Sharjah. The remainder live in villages. Nomads, totaling 10 percent of the population, are to be found in Abū Dhabi, Sharjah, Fujayrah and Ra's al-Khaymah.

Economy Until the discovery of oil and its commercial production in 1963, most of the inhabitants were nomads or seminomads. They existed on livestock raising, subsistence agriculture, fishing, pearl-diving, or trading. Until the middle of the nineteenth century, some of the inhabitants were sea pirates.

The revenues from oil production and royalties completely changed the region's economy, transforming the Union into one of the world's richest countries. The growth in oil revenues during the 1970s (from $.55 billion in 1972 to $19.5 billion in 1980) has enabled the establishment of a broad spectrum of industry in addition to the development of high-quality services. The major advances

Population of the U.A.E., according to 1985 Census

Abū Dhabi	670,125
Dubai	419,104
Sharjah	268,723
Ra's al-Khaymah	116,470
'Ajmān	64,318
Al-Fujayrah	54,425
Umm al-Qaywayn	29,299

NATURAL INCREASE (1980-1984) **2.3%**

LIFE EXPECTANCY (1980-1985) male - **61.6** years female - **65.6** years

DOCTORS (1984) **12.2** per 10,000 inhabitants

HOSPITAL BEDS (1984) **3.2** per 1,000 inhabitants

INFANT MORTALITY (1983) **45.2** per 1,000 births

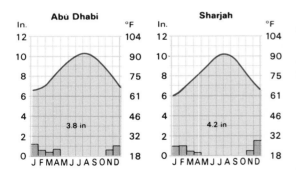

Abū Dhabi — 3.8 in
Sharjah — 4.2 in

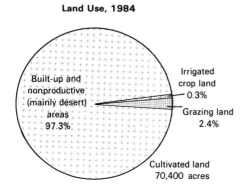

Land Use, 1984

Built-up and nonproductive (mainly desert) areas 97.3%

Irrigated crop land 0.3%

Grazing land 2.4%

Cultivated land 70,400 acres

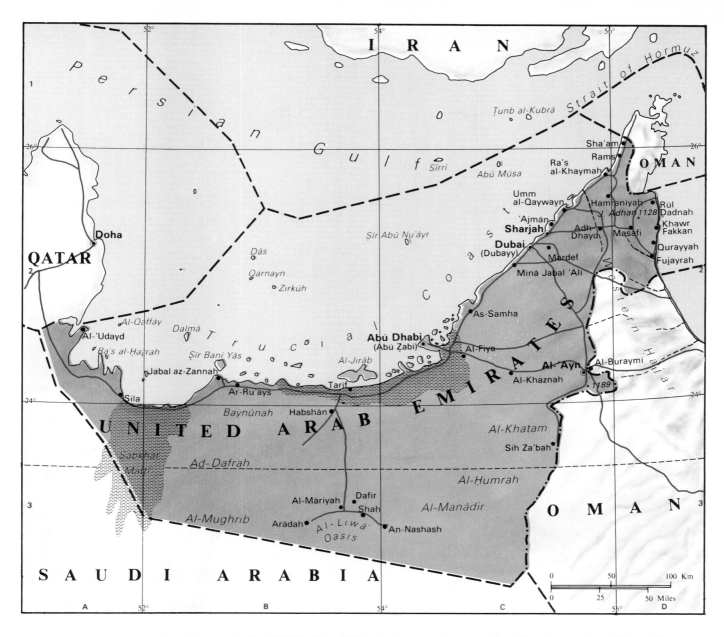

have been made in Abū Dhabi and Dubai, where most of the petroleum and gas reserves are concentrated. These two emirates annually give part of their revenues to the other members of the Union, enabling the latter also to benefit from a high level of development.

Agriculture The agricultural sector is only of minor importance to the country's economy. There is a scarcity of water throughout the Emirates. Annual water consumption totals 565 million cubic meters. Less than half the required amount is supplied by groundwater, the remainder coming from the desalination of sea water. In recent years, dams have been constructed in the *wādis* (riverbeds) descending from the mountains, in order to store flood waters.

Because of the shortage of water, the harsh climate, and the unsuitability of the soil for cultivation, dry-farming and even irrigated agriculture is limited. As a result, the Union is forced to import a large amount of its food. During the past decade, intensive efforts have been made to expand the area under irrigation through the use of modern cultivation techniques such as green-houses, drip irrigation, and sprinklers. The area under irrigation totaled 71,000 acres in 1984, three times that in 1973. Most of the agricultural area is concentrated in Ra's al-Khaymah and at the al-'Ayn oasis. The principal crops are vegetables, fruit, and fodder for the small livestock economy (dairy cattle and poultry).

Minerals The only natural resources to be exploited in the country are petroleum and gas. The large and rich oilfields are located in Abū Dhabi

HIGH SCHOOL
PUPILS
(1984-1985)
21,000

UNIVERSITY
STUDENTS
(1984-1985)
5,700

LITERACY RATE
(1985) **69%**

Population by Age Group, 1980

Age	
70+	0.7%
60-69	2.8%
45-59	9.0%
30-44	28.3%
15-29	28.9%
0-14	30.3%

67

and Dubai, while smaller oilfields are found in Sharjah, Ra's al-Khaymah, 'Ajman, and on the adjoining continental shelf. Oil is also found in Umm al-Qaywayn and Fujayrah, but the fields are not exploited because of the limited quantity of oil. The proven oil reserves of the Emirates totaled 4.38 billion tons in 1985.

Annual oil production in 1985 stood at 41.5 million tons in Abū Dhabi, 18.9 million tons in Dubai, 3.2 million tons in Sharjah, 450,000 tons in Ra's al-Khaymah, and 300,000 tons in 'Ajmān.

Rich natural gas fields are also found in the Emirates. The proven gas reserves total some 2.5 trillion cubic meters (about 0.7% of the proven world reserves). Annual gas output totaled 9.5 billion cubic meters in 1984, which makes it the third largest producer in the Middle East after Saudi Arabia and Iran.

Industry Industry in the Union is varied, and includes many factories: oil refineries, liquid gas plants, petrochemical plants, cement works, metal-works, textile factories, and shipyards.

Most of the factories are concentrated in the four centers of ar-Ru'ays, Mīnā Jabal 'Alī, Abū Dhabi, and Dubai. Ar-Ru'ays was constructed in recent years as a center for petrochemical industries. The refineries here produce 1.9 million tons of refined oil per year, while liquid gas plants annually produce 2.1 million tons (1984). There are also fertilizer and steel factories. Mīnā Jabal 'Alī is another new industrial centre. Abū Dhabi has a deep water port and functions as a trade depot for goods in transit. There are small industrial centers in 'Ajmān, Sharjah, Ra's al-Khaymah, and Fujayrah.

History Two Bedouin tribes, the Quwaysin and the Banī Yās, lived in this area in the past. They existed on piracy and the slave trade. Constant struggles took place between the two tribes over control of land and sea. At the beginning of the nineteenth century, the British, in their efforts to ensure the freedom of navigation to India and the Far East, dispatched military forces and later signed treaties with the local sheiks to ensure the eradication of sea piracy and the termination of the slave trade. In the first treaty, signed in 1820,

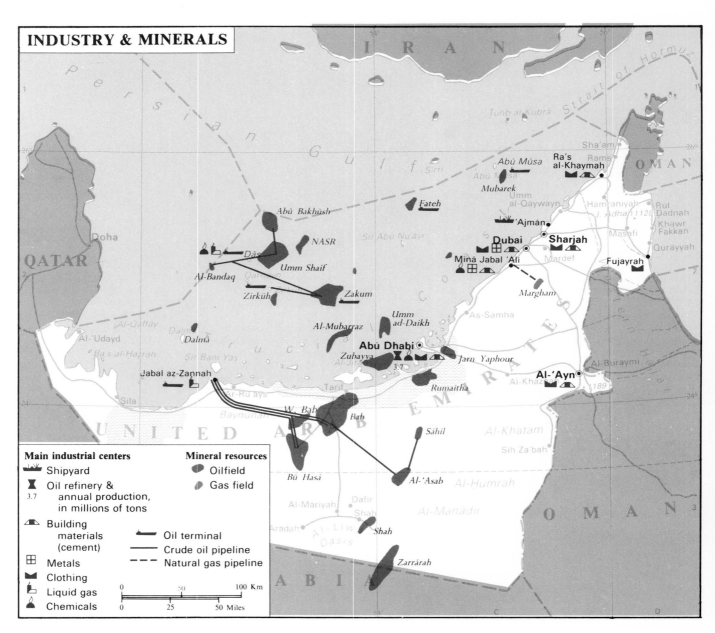

INDUSTRY & MINERALS

Main industrial centers
- Shipyard
- Oil refinery & annual production, in millions of tons — 3.7
- Building materials (cement)
- Metals
- Clothing
- Liquid gas
- Chemicals

Mineral resources
- Oilfield
- Gas field

— Oil terminal
— Crude oil pipeline
--- Natural gas pipeline

0   50   100 Km
0   25   50 Miles

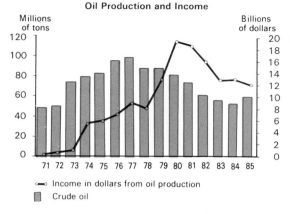

Oil Production and Income

- ○—○ Income in dollars from oil production
- ▨ Crude oil

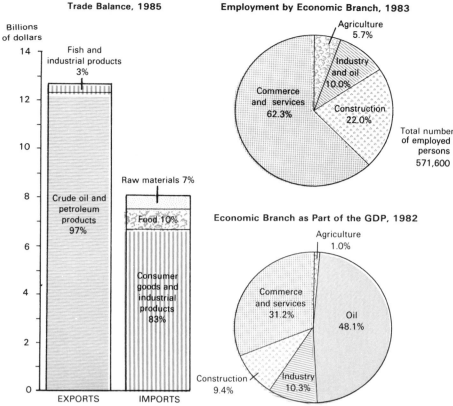

Trade Balance, 1985

Billions of dollars

EXPORTS
- Fish and industrial products 3%
- Crude oil and petroleum products 97%

IMPORTS
- Raw materials 7%
- Food 10%
- Consumer goods and industrial products 83%

Employment by Economic Branch, 1983

- Agriculture 5.7%
- Industry and oil 10.0%
- Construction 22.0%
- Commerce and services 62.3%

Total number of employed persons 571,600

Economic Branch as Part of the GDP, 1982

- Agriculture 1.0%
- Oil 48.1%
- Industry 10.3%
- Construction 9.4%
- Commerce and services 31.2%

Britain took on the responsibility of maintaining security in the coastal region. Britain's position in the region was strengthened through the signing of additional treaties in 1835, 1853, and 1892, which transformed the area into a British protectorate known as the Trucial Coast.

The areas to be controlled by the different sheiks were not defined under these arrangements. The focus of power lay in the hands of the Qassimi family, to whom the 'Ajmān, Umm al-Qaywayn, Sharjah, Fujayrah and Ra's al-Khaymah sheiks were subservient. In order to maintain stability in the region, the British established a Trucial Council in 1952, providing an orderly forum for discussions between the Emirate sheiks. The relative power status of the Emirates changed as a result of the discovery of oil in Abū Dhabi in 1958 and in Dubai in 1966. In 1968, these two Emirates became linked by a covenant, which was later signed by the other Emirates, with the exception of Ra's al-Khaymah. In December 1971, the British annulled their protectorate treaties with the Emirates. The member nations of the covenant declared the establishment of a Union to be known as the United Arab Emirates. Ra's al-Khaymah joined in 1972.

The process of state formation continues despite many difficulties, arising mainly out of historical rivalries between tribes and differences in economic levels of development. Despite this, the various Emirates are careful not to be drawn into violent conflict. Where differences of opinion occur, they are usually discussed in the joint government institutions.

Government and Politics The supreme federal institution is the Council of Rulers comprised of the rulers of the Emirates. The council is chaired by a president and vice president. The president appoints the prime minister and the council of ministers, who are responsible for the administration of the federation's daily affairs. There is a legislative authority (Advisory Council) of forty representatives: 8 from Abū Dhabi, 8 from Dubai, 6 from Sharjah, 6 from Ra's al-Khaymah, 4 from Fujayrah, 4 from 'Ajmān, and 4 from Umm al-Qaywayn. These representatives serve for a two-year term. The function of the Advisory Council is to ratify government decisions, but it lacks any real power to modify such decisions.

Each of the Emirates is an absolute monarchy, possessing total autonomy in its internal affairs (taxes, internal security, and legal system). No political parties are allowed.

The borders of the Union are not precise. A dispute with Saudi Arabia and Oman over the control of the al-Buraymī desert oasis (on the border between Abū Dhabi and Oman) was resolved in 1974 by the division of the area. There remains a dormant dispute with Iran concerning control over the Ṭunb Islands, which were invaded by Iran in 1971.

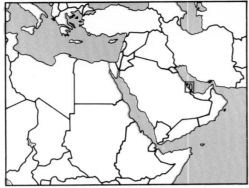

QATAR

Area **4,416 sq. miles (11,437 sq.km)**
Population (1985 estimate) **275,000**
Capital city **Doha**
Gross domestic product (GDP) per capita (1984) **$22,100**

Population in main cities (1984 estimates)	Doha 190,000 Umm Said 30,000

Qatar extends over a peninsula, 35–45 miles (60–80 km) wide and 100 miles (165 km) long, on the northeastern coast of the Arabian Peninsula. Qatar borders on the United Arab Emirates and Saudi Arabia.

Topography Most of Qatar's territory consists of a low-lying desert plateau, built of limestone formations with a gentle west–east slope. To the west and in the interior of the peninsula are mobile dunes, separated by areas of gravel. There are groundwater sources in the north. Along the coast are bays and lagoons, interspersed with salt pans.

Climate Qatar's climate is characterized by desert conditions. Along the coast, humidity is extremely high throughout the year, reaching 90 percent in summer. The average temperature in the hottest month (August) is 99° F. (37° C.), with temperatures reaching 113° F. (45° C.). Conditions are more moderate in winter, with an average January temperature of 79° F. (26° C.).

Annual precipitation averages 3 in (80 mm). Most of the rain falls during January and February.

Population Qatar's population totaled 275,000 in 1985, half of whom were citizens and half foreign workers on temporary contracts. Due to the slowing down of economic activity in recent years, thousands of the foreign work force have left the country.

The country's citizens are Muslim Arabs, approximately 75 percent of whom are Sunni and most of the remainder Shiite. The largest foreign communities are Iranians (60,000), Pakistanis (40,000), Indians (25,000), and Palestinians (15,000).

Approximately 85 percent of Qatar's inhabitants live in urban settlements. The largest city, Doha, had 190,000 inhabitants in 1985.

Economy Until the discovery of oil in the late 1930s, Qatar's economy was dependent on pearl diving and trading, fishing, and the breeding of animals. The discovery of petroleum and its commercial marketing from 1949 onward, transformed the country's economy. The oil industry gradually

became the economy's most important constituent. Oil revenues were used to develop the country's agriculture (which did not exist until the 1950s) and the heavy industrial sector, which uses oil and gas as its raw materials.

The global decline in demand for oil in recent years has resulted in a reduction in national revenue and a subsequent slowing down of the economy. In an effort to strengthen its economy and to diversify its sources of revenue, Qatar has expanded the export side of its heavy industry. This has been achieved with assistance from Saudi Arabia,

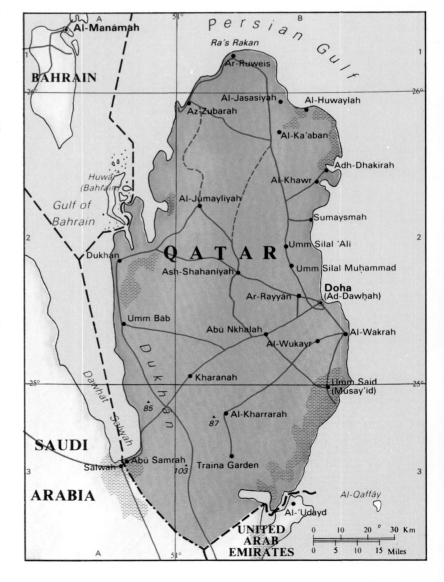

Land Use, 1984

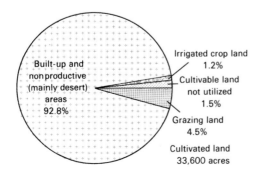

Built-up and nonproductive (mainly desert) areas 92.8%

Irrigated crop land 1.2%

Cultivable land not utilized 1.5%

Grazing land 4.5%

Cultivated land 33,600 acres

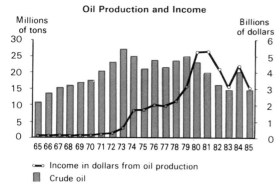

Oil Production and Income

Legend for chart:
- Income in dollars from oil production
- Crude oil

Japan, and France. Oil and related products continue to contribute 86 percent of export revenues (1986).

Agriculture The scarcity of precipitation and of groundwater (part of Qatar's water comes from the desalination of sea water), and the poor quality of the soil combine to prevent widespread cultivation. Approximately 82,000 acres — 2.7 percent of the total area — are cultivable. Of this, 33,600 acres were actually cultivated in 1984, all of it by irrigation. Despite Qatar's intensive efforts to develop the agricultural sector, the country is obliged to import a substantial portion of its food.

Most of the agricultural area is concentrated in the north of the country. In this region there are groundwater sources near the surface. Small cultivated areas are also found in the interior of the peninsula. The principal agricultural crops are vegetables (10,000 acres), fruit, and fodder.

Minerals The country's principal mineral resources are oil and natural gas. The large oilfields are located in the west of the peninsula, in the vicinity of Dukhān and on the seabed to the east of the peninsula. Since 1977, all of the oil concessions have been owned by Qatar itself.

As a result of the decline in world demand for oil and Qatar's desire to preserve its oil reserves (450 million tons in 1985), output was reduced in 1984, amounting to 14.5 million tons in 1985. Two refineries are in operation at Umm Said, their production capacity totaling 3.15 million tons per year.

Qatar produces natural gas from fields adjacent to the Dukhān oilfield and from fields in the continental shelf west of the peninsula. In 1972, a gas field was discovered on the seabed north of Qatar, one of the largest such fields in the world. The proven reserves at this field total 2,000 billion cubic meters. As of 1987, commercial production had not yet begun at this location. The country's total gas reserves from all of its fields amount to 4,200 billion cubic meters.

In addition to oil and gas, gypsum, salt, nitrate, and magnesium have also been discovered in Qatar. Of these, only the gypsum is mined, being used as raw material in the production of cement.

Industry Qatar's economy is dependent on the oil industry, based on the production and export of refined oil.

In the second half of the 1970s, the gas industry was developed, particularly the production of liquid gas. Once production gets underway at the Northwest Dome sea field (planned for 1988), it is expected that this sector will become the major industrial branch. At present, there are two plants for the production of liquid gas and two plants for the manufacture of gas-related products. The gas is mainly used in the fertilizer and petrochemical industries.

INDUSTRY & MINERALS

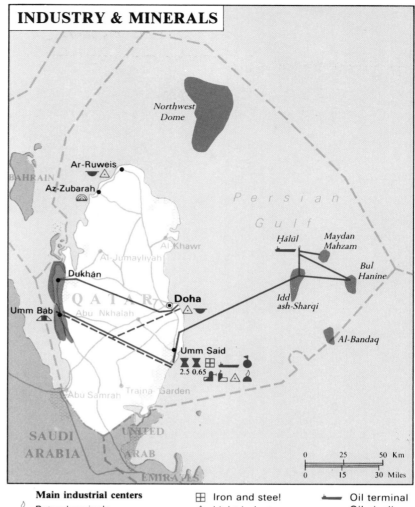

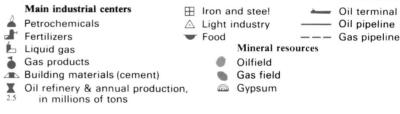

Main industrial centers
- Petrochemicals
- Fertilizers
- Liquid gas
- Gas products
- Building materials (cement)
- Oil refinery & annual production, in millions of tons — 2.5
- Iron and steel
- Light industry
- Food

Mineral resources
- Oilfield
- Gas field
- Gypsum

- Oil terminal
- Oil pipeline
- --- Gas pipeline

Qatar also has plants for the manufacture of iron, steel, and cement. Many of the heavy industrial plants were established in cooperation with multinational companies, due to the lack of professional manpower in Qatar and because of the recent decline in oil revenues, which have resulted in difficulties in financing new investments.

Qatar's light industry includes textile, foodstuffs, and furniture factories.

History During the 1760s, a number of families of the al-Khalifa tribe (then resident in Kuwait) settled along Qatar's northwest coast. They established the settlement of az-Zubarah, which became a center for pearl diving and trading. Qatar remained under the influence of the al-Khalifa tribe — with their base in Bahrain — until the middle of the nineteenth century.

During the 1860s, the al-Thani tribe threatened the status of the al-Khalifa. In 1872, Qatar came under Ottoman control, which was supported by local groups headed by the al-Thani leader Qassem ibn Muhammad, who was subsequently appointed as Qatar's governor.

The Ottomans were not visibly present in Qatar, and their control was limited to a tax on pearl

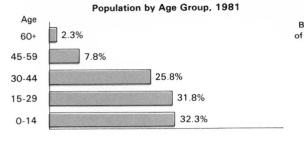

Population by Age Group, 1981

Age	
60+	2.3%
45-59	7.8%
30-44	25.8%
15-29	31.8%
0-14	32.3%

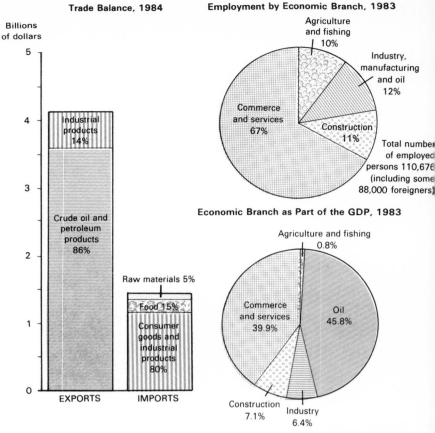

Trade Balance, 1984

Billions of dollars

EXPORTS
- Industrial products 14%
- Crude oil and petroleum products 86%

IMPORTS
- Raw materials 5%
- Food 15%
- Consumer goods and industrial products 80%

Employment by Economic Branch, 1983

- Agriculture and fishing 10%
- Industry, manufacturing and oil 12%
- Construction 11%
- Commerce and services 67%

Total number of employed persons 110,676 (including some 88,000 foreigners)

Economic Branch as Part of the GDP, 1983

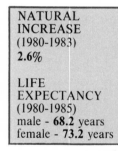

- Agriculture and fishing 0.8%
- Oil 45.8%
- Commerce and services 39.9%
- Construction 7.1%
- Industry 6.4%

diving and trading. In 1915, during World War I, the Ottomans withdrew from Qatar. The leaders of the al-Thani tribe signed a treaty with Britain, according to which Britain promised to supply Qatar with military aid and assistance in the development of its foreign relations.

In effect, Qatar was under British control until 1970. Nevertheless, its internal affairs were administered by the al-Thani dynasty. Qatar became an independent state in 1971 following the British withdrawal from the Persian Gulf region. The country's ruler was Emir Ahmad ibn 'Ali.

In February 1972, in a nonviolent coup, the crown prince and prime minister, Khalifa ibn Hamad al-Thani, deposed the emir. Khalifa made efforts to develop the country's economy. As part of this process, he gradually nationalized sections of the oil industry that were owned by foreign companies, taking control of all the oil concessions. At the same time, he limited the extent of powers held by his family. His economic policy and his efforts to develop the standard of services throughout the country resulted in a significant improvement in the quality of life.

Government and Politics The country is ruled by an emir — a member of the al-Thani family — who possesses absolute power. The emir also stands at the head of the government and appoints all of its ministers (most of whom are members of his family). There is no elected assembly and political parties are forbidden.

Qatar has a territorial dispute with Bahrain concerning sovereignty over a number of islands in the Gulf of Bahrain. The dispute centers around the control of the island of Huwār, at present controlled by Bahrain. Qatar enjoys close relations with Saudi Arabia, which is closely involved in the country's economic activities and also provides military assistance to Qatar — especially since the beginning of the Iraq–Iran war in 1980.

NATURAL INCREASE (1980-1983) **2.6%** LIFE EXPECTANCY (1980-1985) male - **68.2** years female - **73.2** years	DOCTORS (1983) **7.5** per 10,000 inhabitants HOSPITAL BEDS (1985) **3.2** per 1,000 inhabitants INFANT MORTALITY (1984) **45.0** per 1,000 births	HIGH SCHOOL PUPILS (1984-1985) **6,186** UNIVERSITY STUDENTS (1985-1986) **5,057** LITERACY RATE (1984) **25%**

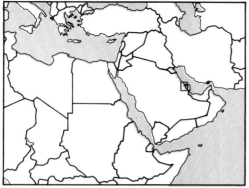

BAHRAIN

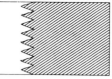

Area **258 sq. miles (669 sq.km)**
Population (1985 estimate) **400,000**
Capital city **Al-Manāmah**
Gross domestic product (GDP) per capita (1985) **$12,600**

Population in main cities	Al-Manāmah 121,000
(1981 census)	Al-Muharraq 62,000

Bahrain comprises thirty-three small islands in the Persian Gulf, northwest of the Qatar peninsula. Of these islands, the most populated are Bahrain and Muharraq. The main island, Bahrain — 30 miles (50 km) long and 9 miles (15 km) wide — comprises 85 percent of the country's total land area. The island is connected to Saudi Arabia by means of a 15 mile (25 km) causeway passing through Umm Na'sān island, which is the private property of the emirate's ruler. The islands of Sitrah and Muharraq are connected to the nearby island of Bahrain by means of bridges.

Topography The island of Bahrain is an undulating plain with low hills, mostly built of limestone beds covered by sand and gravel. The island has a good supply of groundwater and springs, formed by rain that falls over a wide area and accumulates in aquifers underlying the limestone beds. The highest point in the island is 440 ft (135 meters).

Climate Bahrain is characterized by an arid climate, with high humidity and high temperatures throughout most of the year. The average temperature of the hottest month (July) is 97° F. (36° C.). In the coldest month (January) the average temperature is 62° F. (17° C.). Precipitation is low, with only an average of 3 in (80 mm) of rain per year, all of which falls in the winter.

Population According to the 1981 census, there were 359,000 people in Bahrain. Of these, 244,000 were local citizens, while 115,000 were foreigners, mostly Pakistanis, Indians, and Iranians. There were also about 10,000 Europeans and Americans.

Approximately 89 percent of Bahrain's inhabitants are Arabs; 3 percent are Iranian, 2.8 percent are Pakistani, 1.8 percent are Indian, and the remainder is European.

In terms of religious affiliation, 48 percent of the population are Shiite Muslims, 44 percent are Sunni Muslims, 6 percent are Christians, and the remainder is Hindu.

Approximately 78 percent of the population live in urban settlements, the remainder in villages. Most of the rural inhabitants are Shiites.

Economy Pearl diving and trading were the major components of Bahrain's economy until the 1930s. This decreased in importance following the discovery of oil in the 1930s and because of the cultured pearls grown in Japan. In the 1960s, this sector ceased to operate altogether. Today, the economy is based on the production and export of refined oil products. Since Bahrain possesses only limited petroleum reserves, the country maintains a relatively low output, importing most of the oil for its refineries from Saudi Arabia.

In an attempt to diversify the economic base, resources have been directed over the years to other enterprises. An international center providing a variety of services to other countries in the region was established in the 1950s. Storage facilities (the first cold storage warehouses in the Persian Gulf) as well as an international airport serving Bahrain

Land Use, 1985

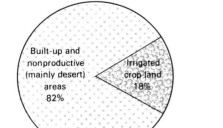

Built-up and nonproductive (mainly desert) areas 82%

Irrigated crop land 18%

Cultivated land 29,700 acres

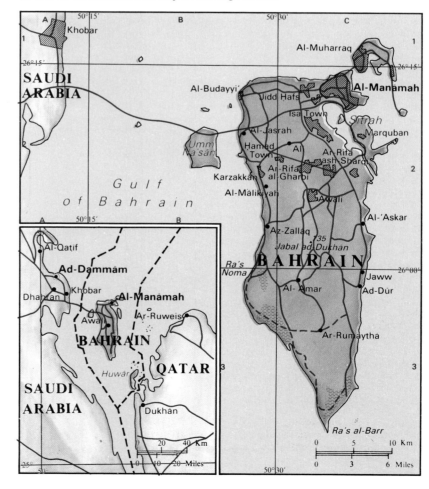

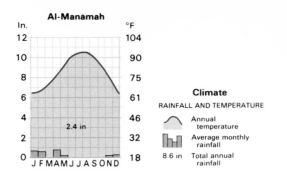

Al-Manāmah

Climate
RAINFALL AND TEMPERATURE

Annual temperature

Average monthly rainfall

8.6 in   Total annual rainfall

2.4 in

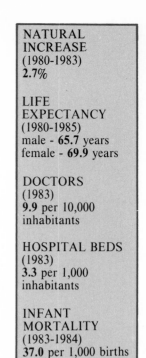

and its neighbors were constructed. Following the significant growth of oil revenues in the 1970s, resources were channeled in the direction of heavy industrial development. An international center of finance was also established.

Bahrain has suffered from an economic recession since the early 1980s, due to the decline in world oil prices. The recession, in turn, has led to a slowing down of economic activity within the country.

Bahrain and Saudi Arabia are involved in a number of joint industrial projects. Saudi Arabia finances much of Bahrain's economic ventures and has also assisted the country in overcoming the economic recession.

Agriculture The agricultural area is concentrated in a narrow strip along the northern coastline of the island of Bahrain. The agricultural sector covers nearly 30,000 acres irrigated by water from springs and wells. The principal crops are fruit, vegetables, and fodder. Advanced agricultural planning, coupled with a relatively small population, enables local agriculture to meet 75 percent of the local demand for fruit and vegetables, as well as part of its livestock requirements (meat and dairy products).

· Approximately 85 percent of the water comes from the pumping of groundwater, the remainder from ocean desalination plants. For a number of years, the groundwater level has been dropping. If this continues, most of the groundwater resources may become saline by the end of the century, preventing their use for irrigation.

Minerals Oil and gas are Bahrain's only mineral resources. An oilfield is located in the Awāli region, production having begun as early as 1935. The reserves at this field are approximately 41 million tons, having gradually decreased over the years. As a result, Bahrain began to reduce its output, producing only 2 million tons in 1985. Bahrain also produces oil from an offshore field (Abū Sa' Fah). This field is jointly owned by Bahrain and Saudi Arabia and the output is divided equally between the two.

Bahrain's refinery is located at Awāli. This was the first oil refinery to be constructed in the Persian Gulf, and it served most of the region during the early years of oil production. Following the establishment of refineries in most of the Persian Gulf countries, Saudi Arabia remained the major user of Bahrain's installation. Some of the Saudi oil, produced in fields near Bahrain, arrive by way of a pipeline. The annual production capacity of this refinery is 12 million tons, although the actual output in recent years has been approximately 10.5 million tons.

While the oil reserves have been decreasing, new gas fields have been discovered east of Bahrain. Gas reserves totaled 200 billion cubic meters in 1985.

Industry Until the 1970s, Bahrain's industrial

sector was composed of its refinery and a number of factories producing basic consumer goods. The increase in oil revenues enabled industry, particularly heavy industry, to undergo rapid development, often in cooperation with neighboring countries (Saudi Arabia and Kuwait). The main factories established were an aluminum manufacturing plant using locally produced natural gas, a gas liquidification plant, petrochemical factories, and a fertilizer plant. The development of heavy industry continued into the 1980s, during which period the construction of an iron and steel plant and a plant for gas products (propane, butane, and kerosene) were completed.

Since 1977, a shipyard has been in operation near the port of al-Manāmah, specializing in the repair of large bulk-cargo ships (up to 500,000 tons). The shipyard has experienced a recession in recent years.

History In 1783, tribesmen from the Arabian Peninsula conquered the island of Bahrain from the Persian rulers. The tribes were headed by sheiks from the al-Khalifa tribe, the descendants of whom have remained in control. During the eighteenth and early nineteenth centuries, internal power rivalries developed among the members of the ruling family. These rivalries resulted in sporadic acts of violence. The internal instability enabled external elements, especially Britain, to intervene in the country's affairs and reduce the independence of the local rulers. In 1820, Bahrain's rulers signed a treaty of friendship with Britain, while the country became a British protectorate in 1861. Within this framework, Britain took charge of the island's defense and foreign affairs. In practice, Britain

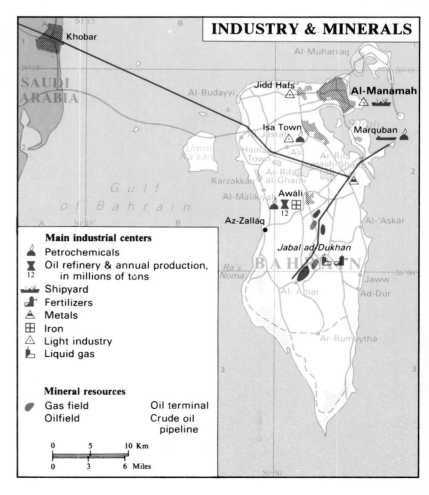

INDUSTRY & MINERALS

Main industrial centers
- Petrochemicals
- Oil refinery & annual production, in millions of tons
- Shipyard
- Fertilizers
- Metals
- Iron
- Light industry
- Liquid gas

Mineral resources
- Gas field
- Oilfield
- Oil terminal
- Crude oil pipeline

0   5   10 Km
0   3   6 Miles

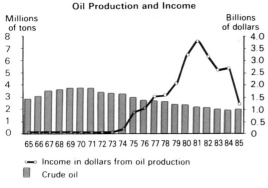

Oil Production and Income

Millions of tons / Billions of dollars

- ○—○ Income in dollars from oil production
- ▦ Crude oil

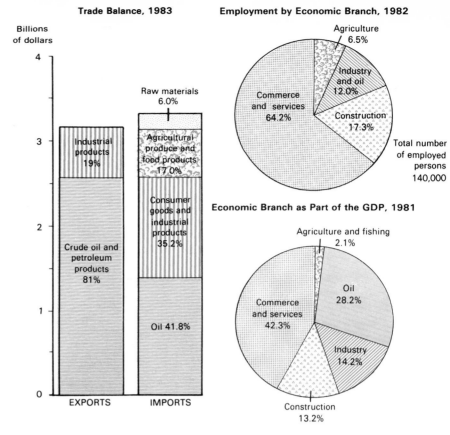

Trade Balance, 1983

Billions of dollars

EXPORTS:
- Industrial products 19%
- Crude oil and petroleum products 81%

IMPORTS:
- Raw materials 6.0%
- Agricultural produce and food products 17.0%
- Consumer goods and industrial products 35.2%
- Oil 41.8%

Employment by Economic Branch, 1982

- Agriculture 6.5%
- Industry and oil 12.0%
- Construction 17.3%
- Commerce and services 64.2%

Total number of employed persons 140,000

Economic Branch as Part of the GDP, 1981

- Agriculture and fishing 2.1%
- Oil 28.2%
- Industry 14.2%
- Construction 13.2%
- Commerce and services 42.3%

also had a major influence on the administration of the country's internal affairs.

Bahrain became the center for Britain's political and commercial activities in the Persian Gulf region. They constructed roads, established the infrastructure for a regular water supply, and set up educational and administration networks. In 1968, Britain decided to withdraw its forces from the Persian Gulf and to annul the protectorate treaties with the region's countries. Following the withdrawal in 1971, Bahrain became a fully independent state. The development and increase in general living standards, initiated by the British, continued during the 1970s thanks to the large oil revenues.

Government and Politics Bahrain is ruled by the al-Khalifa family who are Sunni Muslims. Since 1971, Sheik Issa ibn Salman has ruled the country. He possesses absolute power in all spheres of life, but is aided in daily administration by a government consisting of nineteen ministers, including representatives of the Shiite community. In accordance with the constitution, in force since 1973, there is also a legislature composed of forty-nine representatives. However, the sheik dissolved the legislative assembly in 1975, and it has not been reassembled.

Following the Islamic revolution in Iran in 1979, groups of Shiite opponents to the regime began to operate in Bahrain. These groups were supported by Iran. Iran claims sovereignty over the islands of Bahrain, basing its claim on Persian control in the seventeenth century. Between 1981 and 1984, there were a number of violent clashes between Shiite groups and the security forces.

There has been a long-term territorial dispute between Bahrain and Qatar over a number of small islands located between the two countries (especially the island of Huwār, which is held at present by Bahrain).

Bahrain has a defense pact with Saudi Arabia, assuring the former of military assistance in the face of any threat to its security or sovereignty.

Population by Age Group, 1981

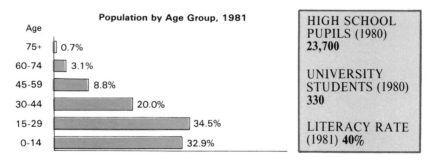

Age	
75+	0.7%
60-74	3.1%
45-59	8.8%
30-44	20.0%
15-29	34.5%
0-14	32.9%

HIGH SCHOOL PUPILS (1980) **23,700**

UNIVERSITY STUDENTS (1980) **330**

LITERACY RATE (1981) **40%**

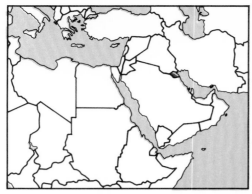

KUWAIT

Area **6,880 sq. miles (17,818 sq.km)**
Population (1985 census) **1,695,128**
Capital city **Kuwait**
Gross domestic product (GDP) per capita (1985) **$12,500**

Population in main cities **(1985 estimates)**	Kuwait 700,000 Al-Jahrah 90,000 Minā' al-Aḥmadi 60,000

NATURAL
INCREASE
(1980-1983)
2.9%

LIFE
EXPECTANCY
(1980-1985)
male - **68.0** years
female - **72.9** years

DOCTORS
(1983)
19.1 per 10,000
inhabitants

HOSPITAL BEDS
(1983)
4.6 per 1,000
inhabitants

INFANT
MORTALITY
(1983-1984)
30.3 per 1,000 births

Climate
RAINFALL AND TEMPERATURE

Annual temperature

Average monthly rainfall

8.6 in Total annual rainfall

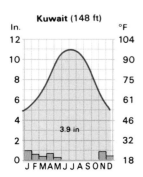

Kuwait is located on the northwestern shores of the Persian Gulf. Its territory comprises nine islands, covering an area of 350 sq. miles (900 sq.km) close to Kuwait's coast. Kuwait borders on Saudi Arabia and Iraq.

Topography Most of Kuwait is a low-lying desert area, not rising above 1,000 ft (300 meters). The northern part is covered mainly by gravel, the southern part with sandhills. In the southwest is a low undulating plateau, terminating in a steep escarpment descending to Wādī al-Bāṭin along which runs the border between Kuwait and Iraq. In the east, the Gulf of Kuwait penetrates for 20 miles (35 km) into the mainland. The city of Kuwait is located on the southern coast. The island of Būbiyān, completely covered by sand dunes, is the largest of Kuwait's islands.

Climate Kuwait has a hot arid climate, with extremely high summer temperatures and high humidity in the coastal region. The average July temperatures reach 95° F. (35° C.), while the maximum temperatures in the interior can reach 122° F. (50° C.). Sand and dust storms, coming from the desert in the northwest, are common occurrences in the summer. The winter is mild, with average temperatures of 55° F. (13° C.). In the interior of the country, the minimum winter temperatures occasionally fall to 32° F. (0° C.).

Rains fall in winter, between November and April. Precipitation is extremely limited and Kuwait suffers from a severe water shortage. Approximately 4.3 in (110 mm) of rain on the average fall along the coast, decreasing to 2 in (50 mm) in the interior.

Population According to the 1985 census, 1,695,128 people lived in Kuwait, of which 679,601 were citizens and 1,015,527 were foreign residents.

The present population size (1987) is three times greater than the 1965 total, mainly because of the immigration of foreigners who have come to work in the country. Their residence permits are

dependent on gainful employment. The largest foreign communities are Palestinians (mostly from Jordan), Iranians, Pakistanis, Indians, Egyptians, Syrians, and Iraqis.

Seventy-five percent of Kuwait's inhabitants are Arabs, 23 percent are Persians, and the remainder are Indians. Approximately 85 percent of the citizens are Sunni Muslims, 10 percent are Shiite Muslims, and the remainder are Hindus and Christians.

Kuwait's population is concentrated along the coast. According to the 1985 census, 95 percent of the population lived in urban settlements, the remainder residing in agricultural villages. There are a few thousand nomads.

Economy Until 1948, when the commercial marketing of oil began, most of Kuwait's inhabitants were engaged in fishing, pearl diving, and commerce. The center of economic activity was in the port city of Kuwait, serving as a site of commerce between India and the Middle East.

The discovery of oil led to a complete transformation of Kuwait's economic base. The petroleum industry, both its production and its export, gradually became the foundation for all economic activity. The growth of oil revenues, particularly after 1973, enabled the development of a high level of services and industry. In 1975, the Kuwaiti government decided to nationalize the petroleum industry, and by 1977 all the oil concessions had passed on to the government.

In an effort to diversify the economic activities and the sources of national revenue, Kuwait channeled some of the oil revenues into economic enterprises outside the country. Kuwait is a partner in a number of heavy industrial plants in neighboring countries (Bahrain, Saudi Arabia, and Qatar), in oil refineries and oil marketing companies in Europe, and also in commercial centers and airports in Africa, Europe, and the United States.

The decline in the demand for oil and the lower prices on the world market during the early 1980s resulted in a reduction in the country's oil revenues. Between 1981 and 1983, Kuwait experienced an economic recession. Since 1983, the economy has undergone a revival, partly because of the investments in foreign countries which began to pay sizable profits.

Despite Kuwait's proximity to the battlefront between Iraq and Iran, the war has had only a minor influence on the country's economy. The major effects have been an increased defense budget and a slight reduction in oil exports.

Agriculture The scarcity of water coupled with the difficult climatic conditions have prevented widespread agricultural cultivation. Kuwait is obliged to import a large proportion of its food, amounting to approximately 90 percent of grains,

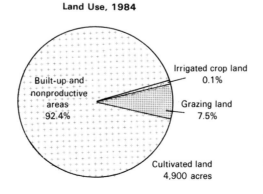

Land Use, 1984

Irrigated crop land 0.1%

Built-up and nonproductive areas 92.4%

Grazing land 7.5%

Cultivated land 4,900 acres

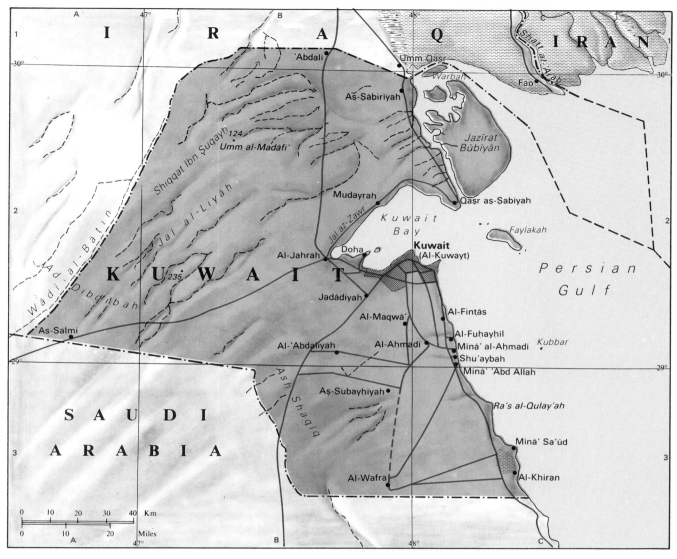

80 percent of meat, and 60 percent of vegetables. In 1984, only 4,000 people were employed in the agricultural sector, contributing only 1 percent to the GDP.

The agricultural area covers approximately 4,900 acres, mostly in the coastal region. All cultivation is irrigated, the principal crops being vegetables, dates, and fodder.

During the 1970s, the livestock economy underwent rapid development. In 1985, this sector comprised 90,000 head of cattle, 600,000 sheep, 310,000 goats, and a large amount of poultry.

Most of Kuwait's agricultural area is irrigated by desalinated sea water. Desalination was begun in the 1960s and now supplies 70 percent of domestic water consumption. The cost of desalination is relatively low, thanks to the use of local natural gas as an energy source.

Minerals Oil is Kuwait's principal, almost only, mineral resource. Production has continually increased since 1948, reaching a peak of 151 million tons in 1972. Since then, because of the large increase in oil prices, Kuwait has reduced its output. Following the decline in demand at the beginning of the 1980s, Kuwait reduced oil production even further, with an output of only 49 million tons in 1984. The known reserves stand at 12–13 billion tons (1985), with only Saudi Arabia and the Soviet Union having larger oil reserves.

The main oilfields are located in al-Burgan, south of the city of Kuwait, and in ar-Rawdhatayn, near the Iraqi border. A number of additional fields are located in the territorial waters, but their output is relatively small. The oil is transferred through pipes to three refineries near the city of Kuwait. In 1984, their annual production capacity equaled 28 million tons.

Gas is produced as a supplementary product of oil. No natural gas fields have, as yet, been discovered in Kuwait. In 1983, the output of gas was 4.5 million tons, with known gas reserves totaling 950 billion cubic meters in 1985.

Industry Kuwait's industry is based on oil refining and other petrochemical products. In 1984,

HIGH SCHOOL
PUPILS (1984)
75,000

UNIVERSITY
STUDENTS (1984)
14,000

LITERACY RATE
(1985) **80%**

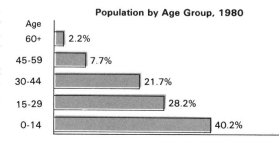

Population by Age Group, 1980

Age	
60+	2.2%
45-59	7.7%
30-44	21.7%
15-29	28.2%
0-14	40.2%

INDUSTRY & MINERALS

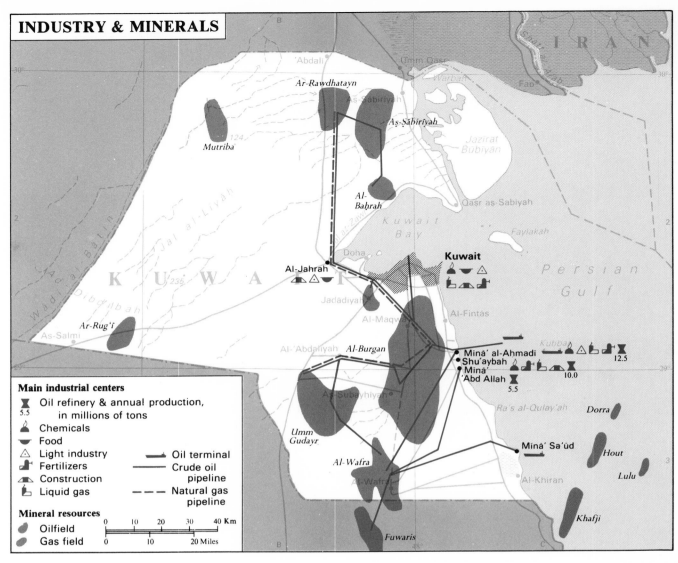

Main industrial centers

⊠ Oil refinery & annual production,
5.5   in millions of tons
⚗ Chemicals
◥ Food
△ Light industry
⚒ Fertilizers
⛰ Construction
⛽ Liquid gas

━━ Oil terminal
━━━ Crude oil
       pipeline
─ ─ ─ Natural gas
       pipeline

Mineral resources

◗ Oilfield
◖ Gas field

0 10 20 30 40 Km
0   10   20 Miles

oil and its associated products contributed 95.6 percent of the export revenues. Since the early 1970s, Kuwait has invested large amounts of money in the development of other industries apart from petrochemicals. The contribution of these industries to the GDP has grown from 3 percent at the beginning of the 1970s to 7.6 percent in 1984.

Substantial resources have been invested in the development of heavy industry, mainly in factories that use oil and gas as raw materials (liquid gas manufacture and other petrochemical products). Most of the industrial plants are concentrated in three industrial centers at Shu'aybah, Shuwaykh, and Mīnā' al-Aḥmadī.

Other industrial enterprises in Kuwait include factories for the manufacture of construction materials (especially cement), aluminum processing, food products, beverages, paper, and other consumer products.

History For hundreds of years, Kuwait's territory was a seasonal feeding ground for a number of Bedouin tribes. The area was included within the Ottoman Empire from the sixteenth century. At the beginning of the eighteenth century, a number of Bedouin families from the 'Anizah tribe, headed by the Sabah family, settled in Kuwait. They established a settlement along the coast of the Persian Gulf, which they named Kuwait (small fortress). Kuwait's location — on the coast of

the Gulf and on an important land route from the Arabian Peninsula to Mesopotamia — helped transform the place into a successful commercial center. The British-owned East India Company transported some of its merchandise by way of Kuwait. Kuwait also became a center for pearl trading, the pearls being fished along the coast.

The Ottoman Empire exercised only minor control in its administration of this area. In reality, the region was administered by local sheiks, headed by the Sabah family. In 1899, the head of the Sabah family, Sheik Mubarak, signed a defense treaty with Britain. According to this treaty, Britain was empowered to administer Kuwait's foreign affairs.

Following the collapse of the Ottoman Empire during World War I, Kuwait became, in reality, a British protectorate. The local leadership was retained by the al-Sabah family, from among whom the country's ruler was chosen.

Kuwait obtained its independence in 1961. At the same time, Iraq made a claim for sovereignty over Kuwait. Britain dispatched military forces to the country in order to protect its independence. Following the change of government in Iraq in 1963, the threat was removed.

During the 1960s, Kuwait's rulers spent substantial amounts of the oil revenues on the development of the country, especially the infrastructure and social services. Despite these activities, there was

Oil Production and Income

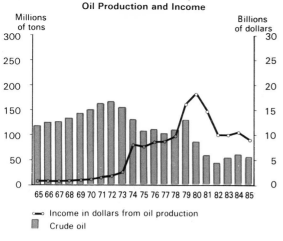

Millions of tons / Billions of dollars

- Income in dollars from oil production
- Crude oil

65 66 67 68 69 70 71 72 73 74 75 76 77 78 79 80 81 82 83 84 85

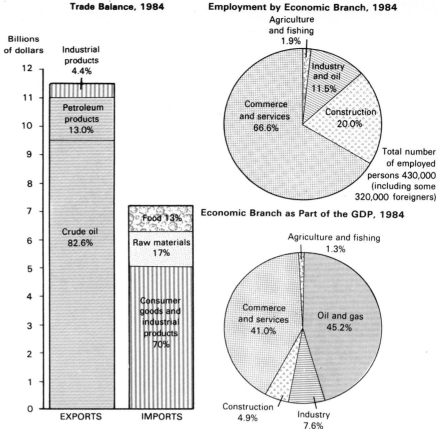

Trade Balance, 1984

Billions of dollars

EXPORTS
- Industrial products 4.4%
- Petroleum products 13.0%
- Crude oil 82.6%

IMPORTS
- Food 13%
- Raw materials 17%
- Consumer goods and industrial products 70%

Employment by Economic Branch, 1984

- Agriculture and fishing 1.9%
- Industry and oil 11.5%
- Construction 20.0%
- Commerce and services 66.6%

Total number of employed persons 430,000 (including some 320,000 foreigners)

Economic Branch as Part of the GDP, 1984

- Agriculture and fishing 1.3%
- Oil and gas 45.2%
- Commerce and services 41.0%
- Construction 4.9%
- Industry 7.6%

much criticism from the country's inhabitants concerning the use of oil revenues by the ruling family. This criticism was voiced in the legislative council, which succeeded in bringing about a change of government in 1965. Emir 'Abdullah, who had ruled Kuwait since 1950, died in the same year, and his place was taken by Salem Sabah.

Like his predecessor, Sabah adopted a neutral foreign policy. Kuwait functioned as a mediator in a number of inter-Arab conflicts (such as the civil war in Yemen and disputes between Syria and Iraq). Kuwait's great wealth enabled the country to grant financial aid to a number of Middle Eastern countries. Large sums of money were given to the frontline countries in the Arab–Israeli conflict. Following the Arab–Israeli war of 1967, Kuwait supported the imposition of an oil embargo on the United States and Britain, while in the aftermath of the 1973 war Kuwait was one of the countries who placed an oil embargo on the Western world and was among the leaders of those supporting a rise in oil prices.

Since the outbreak of the Iran–Iraq war in September 1980, Kuwait has been a major source of aid for Iraq. Kuwait permits Iraq to export oil via oil terminals in Kuwait, while many goods destined for Iraq are imported through Kuwait's ports. Kuwait's support of Iraq made it a target for attacks by Iran. In 1981, Iran bombed a Kuwaiti oil installation close to the border with Iraq. Since 1983, a pro-Iranian terrorist organization — operating within Kuwaiti territory — has been responsible for a number of attacks on oil installations and civilian targets. There was also an attempt on the life of Emir Jaber al-Sabah.

Government and Politics The emir possesses wide-ranging and absolute powers. A government whose leader and ministers are appointed by the emir works alongside him. All senior government posts are in the hands of members of the Sabah family.

In 1962, a constitution came into force, which led to the establishment of a legislature (parliament) comprising fifty representatives. Its powers are limited, but it does serve as a forum for public criticism of the government and the ruling family. The emir possesses the authority to dissolve the legislative assembly.

In the elections to the assembly of 1985, the franchise was extended to all male Kuwaiti citizens over the age of 21 who had resided in the country since 1970. These limitations meant that only 57,000 people had the right to vote. The emir dissolved the elected assembly in 1986, and no new assembly has taken its place.

Approximately 60 percent of Kuwait's inhabitants are foreigners who are not permitted to take part in political activities or to occupy important administrative and political posts. This discrimination has caused many of them to oppose the monarchy. A number of violent antigovernment groups are active in the country, of whom the most prominent are Iranian-backed Shiite groups.

There is a territorial dispute between Kuwait and Iraq over the islands of Būbiyān and Warbah, situated opposite the entrance to the Iraqi port at Umm Qaṣr. Despite this dispute, Kuwait has allowed Iraq to use the islands for military purposes since 1980.

In 1969, the neutral territory between Kuwait and Saudi Arabia — existing since 1922 — was finally divided, with the present boundary running through the center of this area.

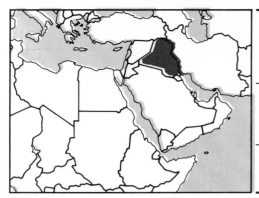

IRAQ

Area **169,284 sq. miles (438,446 sq.km)**
Population (1985 estimate) **15,000,000**
Capital city **Baghdād**
Gross domestic product (GDP) per capita (1984) **$2,185**

Population in main cities (1980 estimates)	Baghdād 4,000,000 Al-Baṣrah 750,000 Mosul 600,000	Kirkūk 500,000 Arbīl 380,000 An-Najaf 250,000	Karbalā' 150,000 Sulaymānīyah 140,000

Iraq lies in the ancient region of Mesopotamia (the Land Between the Rivers). The Euphrates and Tigris rivers flow through the country. Iraq shares borders with Iran, Turkey, Syria, Jordan, Saudi Arabia, and Kuwait, and has a short coastline — 31 miles (50 km) — in the Persian Gulf.

Topography Iraq consists of three geographical regions: (1) the desert; (2) the Euphrates and Tigris valleys; and (3) the Kurdistan mountains.

1. The desert region in the south and the west of the country occupies 60 percent of Iraq's land surface. This area rises gently toward the northwest where an upland area covered by thick beds of volcanic rock reaches an altitude of nearly 3,280 ft (1,000 meters). The desert consists of three subregions: the southern section, the western section, and al-Jazīrah (the Island).

The southern section is covered mostly by dunes, gravel, and bare limestone and chalk. This region has very few if any water resources and is the most arid part of Iraq.

The western section of the desert is largely covered by *ḥammada* (a bare rock-strewn desert surface), which was formed from limestone. In this region, there are numerous dry *wādīs* (riverbeds), which carry flash floods several times each year. This area is known as al-Wādiyah. Groundwater and vegetation can be found in some of the *wādīs*, providing nomads with grazing ground and water. Large basalt flows cover the westernmost part of this region.

The area lying between the Euphrates and the Tigris in northern Iraq (and northern Syria) is known as the Jazīrah. This is an arid, low-lying plateau, sloping very gently from northwest to southeast. It includes a number of north–south depressions, the largest being Wādī ath-Tharthār with a length of 125 miles (200 km).

2. The Euphrates and Tigris valleys may be divided into two parts: in their upper sections, which cross the Jazīrah, both rivers flow through narrow, deep valleys up to 2.5 miles (4 km) wide. Approximately 62 miles (100 km) north of Baghdād, the rivers enter a wide, almost flat plain, which extends down to the Persian Gulf. It is covered by a thick layer of fine silt deposited by the rivers. From the northern edge of this plain to the shores of the Persian Gulf, a distance of over 500 miles (800 km), the rivers descend only 130 ft (40 meters). This extremely gentle gradient results in a slow, meandering flow, with the riverbeds only a few yards below the surface of the plain itself. As a result, large areas are flooded during periods of high water and huge swamps can be found throughout the region.

3. The Kurdistan mountains, stretching through the northwestern part of Iraq, are a part of the Zagros mountain system, most of which lies in Iran. The mountainous region consists of several parallel ranges, separated by long deep valleys drained by rivers that flow into the Tigris. In the border region with Iran, the mountains are very rugged, their peaks reaching heights of over 9,750 ft (3,000 meters). They are deeply dissected by narrow precipitous valleys. Low rounded foothills cover much of the area between these mountains and the Tigris valley. The Kurdistan mountains are built mainly of thick beds of limestone, dolomite, and sandstone.

Climate Iraq's climate is arid. The summer is hot and the winter is cool. There is only limited rainfall throughout most of the country.

High summer temperatures prevail in the lowlands with an average July temperature in Baghdād of 96° F. (35° C.) and an average midday temperature for the same month of 112° F. (44° C.). During the summer, there is a constant hot and dry northwesterly wind known as the *shamāl*. Winter temperatures are relatively low with an average January temperature in Baghdād of 50° F. (10° C.) and occasional groundfrost. In Kurdistan, the summer is more mild while the winter is cold. The average January temperature is 41° F. (5° C.).

Rain falls in the winter months, from November to April. Precipitation decreases southward. In some of the higher places in the Kurdistan mountains, the average annual precipitation rises above 40 in (1,000 mm), mostly in the form of snow. Most of Iraq experiences only small amounts of annual precipitation, approximating 6 in (150 mm). Differences in precipitation can vary greatly from one year to the next.

The Euphrates and Tigris Rivers The Euphrates and Tigris rivers are the major source of water for agriculture in Iraq. The length of the Tigris in Iraq is 886 miles (1,418 km), that of the Euphrates 758 miles (1,213 km). The average annual discharge of the Euphrates at the point of entrance into Iraq is 26.5 billion cubic meters, that of the Tigris south of Baghdād 42 billion cubic meters. The Euphrates gets most of its water supply from precipitation that falls on the highlands of northeastern and eastern Turkey, while the Tigris derives most of its flow from the highlands of western Kurdistan. The Euphrates has no constant tributaries in Iraq, whereas the discharge of the Tigris in Iraq is greatly reinforced by a number of rivers coming from the east. The largest of these tributaries — the Great Zab, the Little Zab, the 'Uzaym, and the Diyālā — have their sources in the Kurdistan mountains and provide the Tigris with most of its water. Systems of dams for regulating the flow have been constructed on both rivers.

The confluence of the Euphrates and Tigris into a single watercourse, known as the Shatt al-'Arab which stretches for 112 miles (180 km), takes place

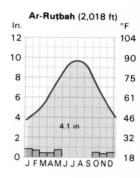

Ar-Ruṭbah (2,018 ft)
4.1 in

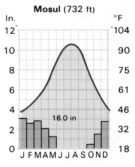

Mosul (732 ft)
16.0 in

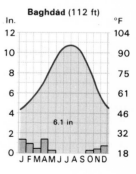

Baghdād (112 ft)
6.1 in

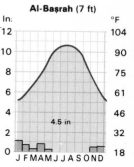

Al-Baṣrah (7 ft)
4.5 in

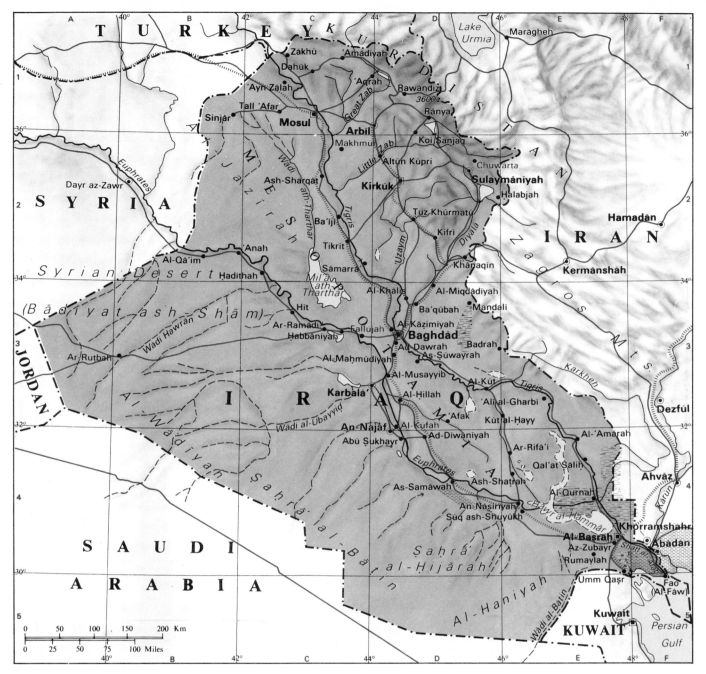

in the vicinity of the town of al-Qurnah. Due to the fact that a substantial amount of the water from both rivers is lost in large areas of swamps, only 6 billion cubic meters of water annually reaches the confluence of the rivers. However, the Shatt al-'Arab is reinforced by the Kārūn, which drains a large area in southwest Iran and provides three-quarters of the water that the Shatt al-'Arab carries to the sea.

Population Ninety-four percent of Iraq's inhabitants are Muslim. Nevertheless, the population is not homogeneous and is divided along religious and ethnic lines. Some 51 percent of the total population are Shiite Muslims, concentrated in the south of the country, where they constitute the large majority of the population and where their holy cities of an-Najaf, Karbalā', and as-Samāwah are located. Some 43 percent of the population are Sunni Muslims, mostly residing in the central and northern parts of the country. About 4 percent

of the population are Christians belonging to various sects, including Chaldeans, Assyrians, and Nestorians. There are some 80,000 Yazīdis (pagans), concentrated around Sinjār. There are also Mandeans, Bahais, and Jews in Iraq.

The largest ethnic minority in Iraq are the Kurds, who are Sunnis, numbering an estimated 2.5 million and constituting 17 percent of the total population. The Kurds are concentrated in the north and northeast of the country where they constitute 90 percent of the population. Since the 1970s, the Iraqi government has attempted to promote the migration of Kurds to the southern parts of the country. Other national minorities are Turkmen, concentrated in and around Kirkūk (330,000), Iranians (220,000), and tens of thousands of Armenians.

Since the 1950s there has been significant migration to the cities. The percentage of the urban population increased from 39 percent in 1957 to 70

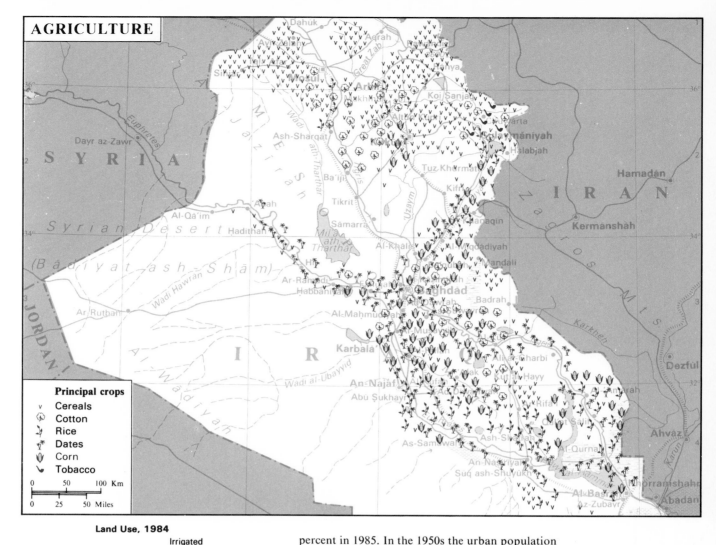

AGRICULTURE

Principal crops
- v   Cereals
- ⊛   Cotton
- ⚘   Rice
- �🌿   Dates
- ⚘   Corn
- ⚘   Tobacco

0   50   100 Km

0   25   50 Miles

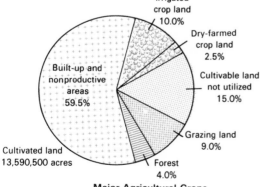

Land Use, 1984

Irrigated crop land 10.0%

Dry-farmed crop land 2.5%

Cultivable land not utilized 15.0%

Built-up and nonproductive areas 59.5%

Grazing land 9.0%

Cultivated land 13,590,500 acres

Forest 4.0%

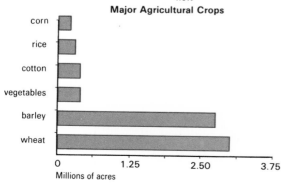

Major Agricultural Crops

corn
rice
cotton
vegetables
barley
wheat

0   1.25   2.50   3.75

Millions of acres

There are some 22 million palm trees in Iraq.

percent in 1985. In the 1950s the urban population totaled 5.4 million; this figure rose to 10.5 million by the mid-1980s. Most of Iraq's nomads have settled in villages and only a small minority still continue to lead a nomadic way of life, principally in the deserts in the west of the country.

Economy For thousands of years, the fertile plains between the Euphrates and the Tigris (Mesopotamia) constituted the richest agricultural lands in the Middle East. Agriculture, which relied principally on water from the rivers, served as a strong economic base for the region's inhabitants. In recent times, the importance of agriculture in the country's economy has declined, particularly following the rise of petroleum as the most important factor in the national economy. During the 1980s the war with Iran severely affected Iraq's economy as substantial financial resources were diverted to the war effort and many of the country's workers were conscripted into the army.

Agriculture Some 31.25 million acres, 28 percent of the total land area of Iraq, is suitable for cultivation, but 13.6 million acres carry crops each year (80 percent of which by irrigation). The nonexploitation of more than half of the arable land is due to the use of outdated and inefficient methods of cultivation and irrigation, as well as a lack of fertilizer to improve the soil quality. The inefficiency of the agricultural sector has led to its decrease in economic importance and a reduction in the number of workers in this sector. Official programs for developing and modernizing

HIGH SCHOOL PUPILS (1982) **974,000**

UNIVERSITY STUDENTS (1982) **85,573**

LITERACY RATE (1982) **40%**

Population by Ethnic Group

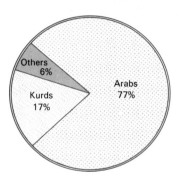

Others 6%
Kurds 17%
Arabs 77%

Population by Religion

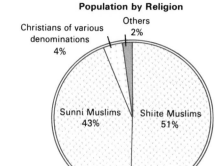

Others 2%
Christians of various denominations 4%
Sunni Muslims 43%
Shiite Muslims 51%

agriculture have met with only limited success.

Since 1980, the war with Iran has had further detrimental effects on agriculture and has resulted in an increase in food imports, totaling some $2.9 billion in 1983 (15 percent of total imports). However, the increased income from petroleum exports since 1984 has enabled new investment in agricultural development, evidenced by an expansion of the major agricultural crops such as rice, barley, wheat, corn, cotton, potatoes, and sugar cane. Financial and technological resources have also been invested to expand the poultry branch (especially egg production) and to develop livestock.

Iraqi agriculture is known for its date palms. For many years dates constituted the principal agricultural export. Because date palms thrive on saturated soil, brackish water, and extremely hot temperatures the tree has proliferated in southern Iraq. The main concentrations are in the Shatt al-'Arab region and alongside the large canals in the river valleys. The dates also provide the raw material for various industries — alcohol, vinegar, sugar, and protein concentrate — all of which use 175,000 tons of dates annually.

Minerals   Oil is the principal mineral resource of Iraq. The large oilfields are located in the north around Kirkūk and Mosul, and in the south near al-Baṣrah and east of Baghdād. Additional small oilfields are dispersed throughout the east of the country, in the frontier area with Iran. The proven petroleum reserves of Iraq total 6 billion tons, an amount exceeded in the Middle East only by Saudi Arabia and Iran.

Oil production in Iraq began in 1927. In the early years, the annual production was about 4 million tons (1938). Output rose following World War II, reaching 30 million tons in 1954. Output continued to increase, reaching a peak of 171 million tons in 1979. The war with Iran resulted in a substantial decrease in output. Only 44 million tons were produced in 1981. Despite the fact that some of the oil installations were destroyed in the war, Iraq succeeded in increasing the output to 75 million tons by 1985.

The construction of new oil pipelines has enabled Iraq to increase its oil exports. The large oilfields are connected by pipelines to ports on the Mediterranean Sea and the Persian Gulf. Two pipes link the Kirkūk region to the coast of Iskenderun in Turkey. The annual flow capacity in these pipes is 70 million tons. An additional pipeline from Kirkūk passes by way of the southern oilfields of Rumaylah and az-Zubayr to the port of Fao on the Persian Gulf. This pipeline has an annual capacity of 50 million tons. There is also a pipeline connecting Kirkūk to Bāniyās in Syria and Tripoli in Lebanon, but this as well as the terminal at Fao

have not been in use since the outbreak of the Iran–Iraq war. Iraq is planning the construction of additional pipelines, two of which link the Rumaylah oilfields to the oil terminal in Yanbu' on the Red Sea in Saudi Arabia. An additional pipeline will link Kirkūk to Iskenderun in Turkey, while yet another will bring oil to the port of 'Aqaba in Jordan.

There are eight oil refineries in Iraq. Before the war with Iran their annual output totaled 9 million tons of refined oil. During the war a number of the refineries were put out of action and thus there has been a substantial decrease in output.

Besides oil, Iraq exploits sulfur and phosphate deposits. Other mineral deposits, not all of which are tapped, include copper, chromite, lead, zinc, iron, gypsum, and coal.

Industry   The petroleum industry is the mainstay of Iraq's economy. It was nationalized in 1973, following which all the oil concessions, until then in foreign hands, were taken over by the state. Despite the fact that only 0.8 percent of the work force is employed in the petroleum industry, this sector contributes 67 percent to the GDP and 90 percent of total government income. Petroleum royalties were estimated at $10 billion in 1984.

Iraq's remaining industry is limited. According to the Five-Year Plan for 1976–1980, industry was to have undergone accelerated development with the ultimate objective being the supply of a wider range of goods locally. Substantial sums were diverted to the food, textile, and construction industries. Factories for the production of fertilizers, chemicals, pesticides, liquid gas, and other products were also established. At the outset of the Iran–Iraq war (1980), the industrial sector employed 13 percent of the work force, contributing 6 percent to the GDP.

History   The region in which Iraq is located has a long history, beginning over five thousand years ago. The fertile soil and abundance of water resources turned Mesopotamia into the cradle of civilization in the Near East. Many invaders were

Population by Age Group, 1982

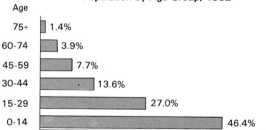

Age	
75+	1.4%
60-74	3.9%
45-59	7.7%
30-44	13.6%
15-29	27.0%
0-14	46.4%

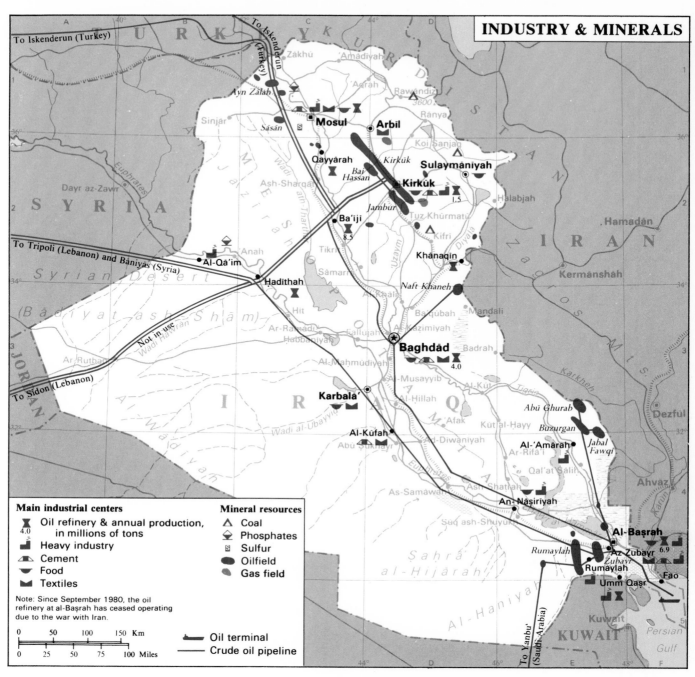

Main industrial centers

- ⚒ Oil refinery & annual production, in millions of tons
  4.0
- ⬛ Heavy industry
- ⛰ Cement
- ▽ Food
- ⋈ Textiles

Note: Since September 1980, the oil refinery at al-Başrah has ceased operating due to the war with Iran.

0   50   100   150 Km
0   25   50   75   100 Miles

Mineral resources

- △ Coal
- ⬠ Phosphates
- Ⓢ Sulfur
- ⬤ Oilfield
- ◗ Gas field

⚓ Oil terminal
— Crude oil pipeline

attracted to the region, and all left their indelible stamp on the local population. Among the most notable invaders were Arabs from the Arabian Peninsula, Mongols from Central Asia, and Ottoman Turks from Asia Minor.

The modern era in Iraq began with World War I, when the area was conquered by the British from the Ottoman Empire. The victorious nations of World War I entrusted Iraq to Britain under a mandate. This resulted in much discontent and unrest in Iraq since the Iraqis had hoped to attain independence. Britain partially acceded to these aspirations in 1921 when it appointed Emir Feisal to rule Iraq. In reality, they installed British advisers to govern the country. The British mandate was terminated on August 3, 1932, and Iraq attained its independence. Britain continued to maintain military forces in Iraq until 1947.

The first years following independence were characterized by a lack of political stability and a struggle against continued British intervention in Iraq. A number of revolutions took place and the post of prime minister passed from hand to hand. In 1942, Rashīd 'Ali al-Kilani rebelled against the pro-British government by siding with Nazi Germany. The British intervened and suppressed the rebellion by force. They returned the government to the royal regent, 'Abd-ul-Ilah, and to the pro-Western prime minister Nuri al-Sa'id, who remained in this post until 1958.

On July 14, 1958, the government was overthrown by a leftist nationalist military coup, headed by General 'Abd-ul-Karim Qassem. King Feisal II, the regent, 'Abd-ul-Ilah, and Nuri al-Sa'id were all killed during the revolution. The House of Legislature was dispersed and the royal constitution of 1925 was annulled.

In February 1963, another group of army officers, members of the Ba'th (Arab revival) party, took control of the government. This party had

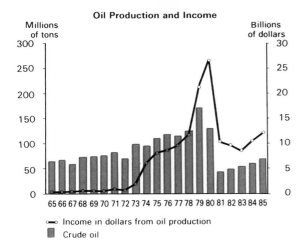

Oil Production and Income

Millions of tons / Billions of dollars

- ○— Income in dollars from oil production
- ■ Crude oil

Government and Politics Since July 17, 1968, the government in Iraq has been in the hands of the Ba'th party, headed since 1969 by President Saddam Hussein. The president possesses wide-ranging powers that give him complete freedom of action. He heads the Revolutionary Council of nine members. This council determines both internal and foreign policy. There is a legislature (the National Assembly) with 250 members, elected once every four years in general elections. The legislature's powers are limited. In the elections to the National Assembly in 1984, the Ba'th party obtained 73 percent of the seats. The remaining seats went to representatives of small parties, Kurds, communists, and some independent candidates.

Since Iraq attained independence, political leadership has always been in the hands of the Sunnis. The fact that the Shiite Muslims constitute the majority of the population is not reflected in the composition of the government and its institutions. This situation has resulted in a constant struggle between the Shiites and the Iraqi government. In recent years the attitude toward the Shiites has been modified, as witnessed by their greater participation in government.

Since the end of the Kurdish rebellion in 1975, the Kurds have waged their struggle for autonomy on the political front. Talks between the Patriotic Union for Kurdistan headed by Jalal Talibani and the leaders of the Ba'th party have been underway for a number of years. At the same time, the Kurdish underground organization Pesh Marjah has continued to wage a guerrilla war against the Iraqi army.

been founded in Syria as the promoter of socialism and inter-Arab nationalism. During the coup, General Qassem was murdered, and 'Abd-ul-Salam 'Aref was appointed president. His regime annulled the military law which had been in operation since 1958, and appointed a civilian government. 'Aref was killed in an airplane crash in 1966 and his position was taken over by his brother 'Abd-ul-Rahman 'Aref. He was himself deposed in July 1968 by leaders of the Ba'th party; a new president, General Ahmad Hassan al-Bakr, was appointed. Al-Bakr retained his position until July 16, 1969, when he retired. In his place, General Saddam Hussein — who until then had been the strongman behind the government — was appointed president.

During the period of al-Bakr's rule, the Kurdish rebellion, which had begun in 1961 and has continued sporadically ever since, slackened. Under the leadership of Mustafa Barzani, the Kurds demanded autonomy in those areas in which they made up the majority of the population. In 1970, a treaty was signed, according to which the Kurds would attain autonomy in a number of regions in return for which they would cease their military activities against the Iraqi army. However, differences of opinion arose between the Kurds and the Iraqi government concerning the boundaries of the autonomous areas and the percentage of revenue to be received by the Kurds from the oilfields in Kirkūk. As a result, the rebellion was renewed in 1974.

In March 1975, Iraq and Iran signed a treaty determining the boundary line between the two countries along the Shatt al-'Arab waterway. The treaty also included the settlement of other territorial claims by the two countries, and included Iran's commitment to cease its support of the Kurdish rebels. This withdrawal of support resulted in the collapse of the Kurdish revolt.

Following 1975, Iraq has lodged numerous complaints against Iran's violation of the treaty. Tension between the two countries rose following the revolution in Iran (1979) and the seizure of power by Ayatollah Khomeini. Iraq saw this religious Shiite government as posing a threat to its security, not least because 51 percent of its own population are Shiites. Iran, for its part, accused Iraq of causing unrest among the Arab population within its territory (in the Khuzestān region). During 1979, localized military skirmishes took place along Iraq's border with Iran. This resulted in an Iraqi military invasion of Iranian territory on September 22, 1980, commencing the war that has so far shown no signs of ending.

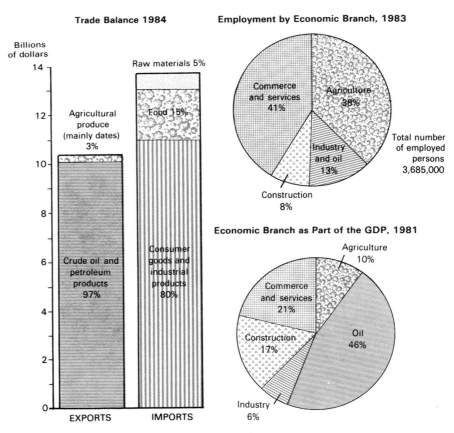

Trade Balance 1984

Billions of dollars

Exports: Crude oil and petroleum products 97%; Agricultural produce (mainly dates) 3%

Imports: Consumer goods and industrial products 80%; Food 15%; Raw materials 5%

EXPORTS   IMPORTS

Employment by Economic Branch, 1983

Commerce and services 41%; Agriculture 38%; Industry and oil 13%; Construction 8%

Total number of employed persons 3,685,000

Economic Branch as Part of the GDP, 1981

Agriculture 10%; Oil 46%; Industry 6%; Construction 17%; Commerce and services 21%

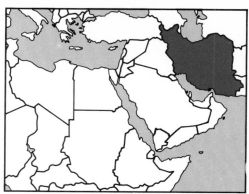

IRAN

Area 636,293 sq. miles (1,648,000 sq.km)
Population (1985 estimate) **48,000,000**
Capital city **Tehrān**
Gross domestic product (GDP) per capita (1984) **$ 3,747**

Population in main cities (1985 estimates)			
Tehran 5,800,000	Tabrīz 720,000	Kermānshah 350,000
Esfahan 850,000	Shīrāz 530,000	Qom 320,000
Mashhad 830,000	Ahvaz 350,000	

Iran borders on Iraq, Turkey, the Soviet Union, Afghanistan, and Pakistan. In the south, the Persian Gulf and the Gulf of Oman separate Iran from the Arabian Peninsula. Part of the Caspian Sea's southern coastline (375 miles [600 km]) lies in northern Iran.

Topography Iran's geographical structure is dominated by mountain ranges, plateaus, and basins. The Iranian Plateau occupies the interior of the country. It is surrounded by mountain ranges formed mainly by folding processes of the earth's crust. The most rugged relief is to be found in northwest Iran, where the Iranian and the eastern Turkey mountain ranges meet.

The mountain ranges surrounding the Iranian Plateau are the Zagros mountains, Makran mountains, eastern Iranian mountains, and the Elburz mountains.

The Zagros mountains, with a northwest-southeast alignment, are the largest mountain system in Iran. They reach a width of 250 miles (400 km), consisting of parallel mountain ranges. Some of the peaks reach heights of over 13,100 ft (4,000 meters). The Zagros mountains are mostly built of limestone beds, with occasional sandstone or chalk. Only a few of the streams that drain the region flow into the sea, much of the area draining into internal basins. In the south, in the vicinity of the Persian Gulf, most of the streams are often dry.

The Makran mountains are the southeast extension of the Zagros ridges. They lie parallel to the Gulf of Oman and the Indian Ocean. Their peaks are lower than those of the Zagros mountains, reaching heights of 6,560 ft (2,000 meters). In the south, along the Gulf of Oman, most of the mountain slopes reach the coastline. The coastal plain is narrow, reaching widths of only 6–12 miles (10–20 km).

The mountain ranges in eastern Iran are aligned along a north–south axis. The highest mountain in the region — Kūh-e Taftān at 12,930 ft (3,941 meters) — is near the border with Pakistan. Between the mountain ranges there are numerous internal basins, the most important being the Sistan Basin with extensive salt pans.

The Elburz and the Alādāgh mountains make up the northern highlands of Iran. The Elburz mountains consist of a narrow series of folds. They include a volcanic massif, Mount Damāvand, whose peak (18,600 ft [5,670 meters]), the highest in the Middle East, overlooks the city of Tehrān. A 15–20 mile (25–35 km) wide coastal plain separates the Elburz mountains from the shores of the Caspian Sea.

Most of Iran is occupied by the largely barren Iranian Plateau, with an average elevation of 3,600 ft (1,000 meters). The plateau contains a series of large enclosed basins, separated from each other by mountain ranges.

Dasht-e Kavir (the Salt Desert), covered by salt marshes and waterlogged mud, forms the northeast part of the Iranian Plateau. This desert is characterized by extremely harsh ground and climatic conditions, making human habitation or transit virtually impossible.

South of this salt desert is the Dasht-e Lut (Lut Desert), mostly covered by low mobile dunes. Much of the area is occupied by dry salt flats.

The Rud mountain range separates smaller western basins of the Iranian Plateau from the main deserts. Some of these basins are also partly covered by sands and salt pans. However, since the upper reaches of the Rud mountains receive a relatively high amount of precipitation (20–24

in [500–600 mm] per year on the average), fresh water collects at the foot of the mountains.

The southernmost basin is Jaz Mūriān, partially covered by salt pans. Fertile alluvial soils are to be found in parts of the Jaz Mūriān, especially in the flood plain of the Bampūr river, which drains into this basin.

The Āzārbāïjān and the Khuzestān regions complete Iran's topographical structure. These areas are physically separate regions.

Āzārbāïjān in northwest Iran stretches from the north of the Qezel Owzan river to Iran's borders with the Soviet Union and Turkey. It consists mainly of a plateau with several peaks, the highest being Mount Sabalan at an elevation of 15,784 ft (4,811 meters). There are a number of basins within the plateau, one of which contains Lake Urmia.

The Khuzestān region is a wide plain stretching from the plain of Mesopotamia across the border with Iraq to the foothills of the Zagros mountains. The lower course of the Kārūn river flows through the region. Part of Khuzestān is covered by swamps.

Climate Land–climate conditions prevail throughout most of Iran, affected by the high relief of the mountains enclosing the interior plateau. Most of the country's regions experience high temperatures in the summer months (June–September) and low temperatures in the winter months (November–April). In general, winter temperatures are much lower than average temperatures for this season at similar latitudes.

The average daily temperature in the hottest month (July) rises to 97° F. (36° C.) in Tehrān and to 113° F. (45° C.) in the lower southern parts of the plateau interior and in parts of the Persian Gulf coastal area. In the mountains surrounding the plateau, above 5,900 ft (1,800 meters), summer temperatures are less extreme, with the average daily temperature ranging between 77–81° F. (25–27° C.).

The temperatures in most regions are extremely low during the winter. Only in the southern regions are the temperatures relatively moderate. In the interior plateau, the temperatures often fall well below 32° F. (0° C.). In the mountains, above elevations of 5,900 ft (1,800 meters), temperatures are constantly below 32° F. (0° C.) during much of the winter, occasionally falling to as low as –5° F. (–20° C.). The most difficult winter conditions prevail in the northwest of the country, in the Kurdistan mountains. At heights above 8,200 ft (2,500 meters), temperatures of –22° F. (–30° C.) and even lower are occasionally recorded.

Rain-bearing air masses arrive from the Mediterranean in the west and from the Caspian Sea to the north. The rains mostly fall in the winter months. Summer rains fall only in the north of the Elburz mountains and along the Caspian coast. The northern slopes of the Elburz mountains receive an average of 52 in (1,300 mm) of rain per year, increasing to 79 in (2,000 mm) in the mountain uplands.

Winds from the Mediterranean Sea bring rain to the Kurdistan and Zagros mountains. Up to 40 in (1,000 mm) per year fall in the Kurdistan mountains and the northern parts of the Zagros mountains. In the Zagros mountains, the amount of precipitation decreases as one goes south.

In the interior plateau, barred from the influence of rain-bearing winds by the mountains, precipitation is below 8 in (200 mm) on the average, while in the southeast of the country, annual rainfall is less than 4 in (100 mm).

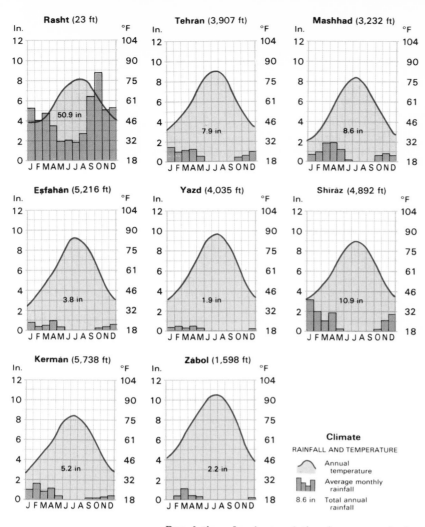

Rasht (23 ft)
In. / °F — 50.9 in — J F M A M J J A S O N D

Tehrān (3,907 ft)
In. / °F — 7.9 in — J F M A M J J A S O N D

Mashhad (3,232 ft)
In. / °F — 8.6 in — J F M A M J J A S O N D

Eṣfahān (5,216 ft)
In. / °F — 3.8 in — J F M A M J J A S O N D

Yazd (4,035 ft)
In. / °F — 1.9 in — J F M A M J J A S O N D

Shirāz (4,892 ft)
In. / °F — 10.9 in — J F M A M J J A S O N D

Kermān (5,738 ft)
In. / °F — 5.2 in — J F M A M J J A S O N D

Zābol (1,598 ft)
In. / °F — 2.2 in — J F M A M J J A S O N D

Climate
RAINFALL AND TEMPERATURE
— Annual temperature
— Average monthly rainfall
8.6 in — Total annual rainfall

Population Iran's population is composed of many ethnic groups. Approximately 71 percent of the inhabitants are Iranians, speaking dialects of Persian. The largest ethnic minority are the Azerbaijanis, making up 11 percent of the population. They speak Turkish and mostly live in the northwest of the country, in the vicinity of the Soviet and Turkish borders. The second largest ethnic minority are the Kurds, who make up approximately 7 percent of the population. The Kurds are concentrated in northwest Iran, between the Urmia Basin and the surroundings of Kermānshāh. Arabs make up 5 percent of the population. They mostly reside in the Khuzestān region and along the Persian Gulf and speak Arabic.

Other ethnic groups are Turkmen (1.5 percent of the population) southeast of the Caspian Sea; Bakhtiars (1.4%) who live in the Zagros mountains; Lurs (1.3%) who are seminomadic and live in the central part of the Zagros mountains; Uzbeks and Tajiks, in the northeast close to the Soviet border; Qashqā'ī in western Iran; Hazara tribes in the south of the country; and the Baluchis, originating in Pakistan and living in the southeast of the country. Armenian communities live in the large cities, particularly Tehrān, Eṣfahān, and Tabrīz.

The religious composition of Iran's population is relatively homogeneous, approximately 88 percent being Shiite Muslims. Approximately 10 percent are Sunni Muslims (the Kurds, Turkmen, some of the Arabs, the Baluchis, and others).

The majority of Iran's Christians are Armenian, the remainder being Catholic, Protestant, and Orthodox, especially Russian Orthodox. Small communities of Chaldean and Assyrian Christians, belonging to the ancient Eastern churches, are also to be found in Iran. Other communities in Iran are the Bahais and Jews.

According to the 1986 census, 54 percent of the country's inhabitants live in cities. With the exception of some 250,000 nomads, the remainder of the population live in villages.

Economy Iran's modern economy has its roots in the early 1930s. At the beginning of the 1950s, agriculture was still the major economic branch both in terms of its contribution to the GDP (30%) and the number of employees (65% of the work force). Industry, particularly the petroleum industry, was as yet undeveloped. Following the nationalization of the petroleum industry in 1951, revenue increased substantially. From the middle of the 1950s, this money was channeled into the development of industry, agriculture, and services.

Rapid economic growth took place from the middle of the 1960s until 1977. The principal features of this process were the implementation of the agrarian reform, completed in 1965; the signing of a cooperation agreement with the Soviet Union (the latter receiving natural gas and in return providing aid for the establishment of heavy industry); and the increase in revenues from the export of oil and natural gas.

As a result of the decrease in oil revenues, development slowed down in 1977, coming to a halt in 1978. There was also growing dissatisfaction with the economic and political policies of the shah. Internal unrest led to numerous strikes, which particularly affected the industrial sector. The rise to power of Ayatollah Khomeini in 1979 and the war with Iraq, which began in 1980, resulted in a worsening of the economic crisis, especially because of the substantial decrease in revenue from oil exports. In 1979, oil revenues amounted to $19.1 billion, while by 1981 this had fallen to $8.6 billion. The continuation of the war paralyzed many industrial enterprises and caused the departure of many foreign investors, entrepreneurs, specialists, and technicians.

Despite the cost of the war — one-third of the national budget — the Iranian government has endeavored, since 1983, to return the economy to its prewar standing. These efforts have encountered many obstacles, due to the scarcity of raw materials, spare parts, and professional manpower (part of which has been diverted to the war effort). The paralysis of so much of the country's economic activities has led to an increasing dependence on oil revenues.

Agriculture Since the 1950s, the importance of agriculture has declined. At the beginning of the 1950s, 65 percent of the country's work force was employed in agriculture, contributing approximately 30 percent to the GDP. By 1984, only 34 percent of the labor force was employed in this sector, contributing 16 percent to the GDP. Since 1984, Iran has invested substantial resources in agricultural development, aimed at reducing the country's dependence on agricultural imports — 20 percent of the total import bill in 1984. It is estimated that the cultivable area in Iran occupies 47.5 million acres, or 11.5 percent of the total area. Approximately 28.4 million acres are cultivated each year, of which 9 million acres are irrigated. Dry-farming areas are concentrated on the northern slopes of the Elburz mountains, in the coastal plain of the Caspian Sea, in the basins of Āzārbāījān, and the western parts of the Zagros mountains. Other dry-farming areas are

Population by Religion

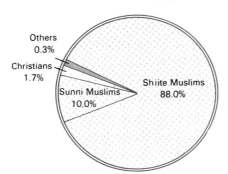

Others 0.3%
Christians 1.7%
Sunni Muslims 10.0%
Shiite Muslims 88.0%

Population by Ethnic Group

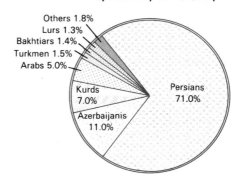

Others 1.8%
Lurs 1.3%
Bakhtiars 1.4%
Turkmen 1.5%
Arabs 5.0%
Kurds 7.0%
Azerbaijanis 11.0%
Persians 71.0%

scattered throughout the Kopet-Dag and Alādāgh highlands in the northeast of the country, in the Zagros highlands, and the southern sections of the Rud mountains.

Until the beginning of the 1960s, irrigated areas were confined to the river valleys — their water coming from the melting snows — and strips of land at the foot of the mountains, irrigation taking place by means of *qanats* (underground channels bringing groundwater to the surface). As a result of the construction of over thirty dams and water reservoirs along the country's rivers, additional irrigated areas were gradually brought under cultivation during the 1960s and the first half of the 1970s. Most of these additional lands are in the southwest of the country in the Khuzestān region and in the Caspian Sea coastal plain in the north. Smaller irrigated areas were brought under cultivation south of Tehrān, in the vicinity of Shīrāz and Eṣfahān, south of Lake Urmia, and south of the Rud mountains.

Much of the agricultural area is devoted to wheat (approximately 15 million acres in 1984). Barley covers approximately 3.5 million acres, and rice, 750,000 acres. Fruit, tobacco, grapes, and vegetables are grown mainly in the north and northwest of the country and in the Khuzestān region. Date cultivation is widespread in the south. Other crops in Iran are cotton, sugar cane, corn, and sugar beet.

Extensive areas are used for pasture, mainly sheep (35 million), goats (14 million), and cattle (8.5 million). The livestock sector is limited, providing for only part of the domestic milk, meat, and egg consumption.

Minerals The most important mineral resources in Iran are oil and gas. Iran's first oilfield was discovered in 1908. Since then, numerous additional oilfields have been discovered in the country and offshore. The large oilfields are located in the Khuzestān region and along the eastern coast of the Persian Gulf, in territorial waters, and in the Qom region. Oil output continually increased, reaching 10 million tons in 1938, and 301 million tons in 1974. The Islamic revolution and the war with Iraq resulted in a substantial decline in output, 66 million tons being produced in 1981. Output again increased after 1981, reaching 110 million tons in 1985. Iran's proven oil reserves total 7 billion tons (1985).

Six refineries, with a maximum capacity of 30 million tons, are in operation. Until 1980, nearly all of the oil refining took place at the Ābādān refinery — one of the largest refineries in the world with an annual production capacity of 30 million tons. In 1980, this refinery was damaged by Iraqi forces and in 1982 it ceased to operate. The refineries in Eṣfahān and Tabrīz were also

damaged in the war, bringing about a reduction in their production capacity.

Most of the oil is exported. For this purpose, a large oil terminal was constructed on the island of Khārg, 19 miles (30 km) from the Iranian coast. The island houses huge storage tanks with a capacity of 1.7 million tons. Until the outbreak of the war with Iraq, most of the oil was exported through this port. As a result of hostilities, much of the oil was transferred to terminals around the Strait of Hormuz, located at a considerable distance from the battlefront. The principal oil terminal in this region was constructed on the island of Sīrrī.

Iran holds 14 percent (13.6 trillion cubic meters) of the world's proven natural gas reserves. The major natural gas fields are in the Qom region and the Laristan district in the south of the country. Gas was produced in relatively small quantities until the increase in oil prices in 1974. Output progressively increased, reaching 40 billion cubic meters in 1979. Part of the gas was exported to the Soviet Union through a pipeline connecting the gas fields at Laristan to Astārā on the Iran–Soviet border. Following the overthrow of the shah, gas output declined and the pipeline ceased to function in 1981. In its final year of operation (1980), 5.3 billion cubic meters of natural gas (30 percent of Iran's total gas output) was exported to the Soviet Union. In 1985, gas production reached 13.6 billion cubic meters, all of which was used for domestic consumption.

There are many other minerals in Iran, but only a few are exploited. In 1985, mining activities accounted for 440,000 tons of iron ore, 1.5 million tons of coal, 55,000 tons of chromium ore, 1,800 tons of copper, 36,000 tons of zinc, and 20,000 tons of lead. Small amounts of sulfur, manganese, nickel, asbestos, phosphates, salt, and gold were also produced.

Industry Industrial development began in the 1930s. Initially, this sector consisted mainly of textiles and food processing, making use of local agricultural raw materials. Industrial expansion took a turn in the 1950s, with the establishment of fac-

Population by Age Group, 1982

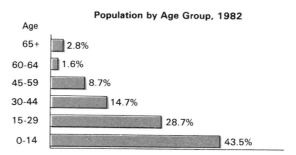

Age
65+ 2.8%
60-64 1.6%
45-59 8.7%
30-44 14.7%
15-29 28.7%
0-14 43.5%

tories for fertilizer, cement, and building materials. The main phase of development took place during the 1960s and the early 1970s. During this period, heavy industry plants were established, including iron and steel plants, petrochemical factories, car assembly plants, and factories for the manufacture of agricultural and industrial machinery. Copper production increased with the construction of a copper processing plant. In addition, factories for the production of aluminum, pharmaceutical products, paper, and other consumer goods were established during this period.

Despite the diversified nature of Iran's industrial sector, the oil industry has remained the most important in terms of export revenues (95% in 1984). The remaining industrial products are mostly destined for the local market, contributing only 3 percent to export revenues in 1984.

History Until the modern era, Iran (known as Persia until 1935) was controlled for long periods by foreign empires — Arab, Seljuk, and Mongol. At the same time, the Persian royal families succeeded in establishing independent kingdoms and even empires from which they controlled areas outside Iran. Among the most prominent families were the Sasanians, the Safavids, and the Qajars.

During the nineteenth century, Persia was ruled by kings of the Qajar family. The dominant powers of the time — Britain, Russia, Turkey, and France — all attempted to bring their influence to bear on Persia. Parts of northern Persia were conquered by Russia and subsequently annexed, while in 1907 Britain and Russia agreed to the division of Persia into respective areas of influence.

In the mid-nineteenth century, there was much internal unrest, due to the corruption in the royal household. The 1905 revolution in Russia led to an intensification of the internal disquiet, resulting in a struggle between the supporters of a constitutional monarchy (the traders and the priests) and the shah (king) and his supporters, who were opposed to a constitution. The struggle was accompanied by a worsening economy and an increase in foreign intervention. Despite the opposition of Shah Muzaffar ad-Din, the parliament met in October 1906 and drew up a constitution for the eventual transformation of Persia into a constitutional monarchy.

Following the death of the shah in 1906, his son Muhammad 'Ali inherited the throne. The new shah opposed the constitution and the existence of the parliament. A violent struggle broke out between the shah and his opponents. In 1909, the nationalist forces (the supporters of the constitution) succeeded in overthrowing the shah and placing his son Ahmad on the throne.

Despite Persia's declaration of neutrality during World War I, Turkish and Russian forces invaded the northwest of the country while British forces captured territory in the south. In areas that remained unconquered, rebellions broke out between tribes, which the central government was unable to suppress. By 1921, the Russian forces had withdrawn from Iran's territory.

In 1921, due to the weakness of the shah and the corruption of his regime, the government was overthrown by Reza Khan (later Reza Shah), a senior officer in the Persian army. He appointed himself prime minister. Four years later, in 1925, the Persian parliament deposed Shah Ahmad and appointed Reza Shah in his place. He adopted the name Pahlevi for the new royal family.

Reza Shah was a totalitarian ruler, ruthlessly suppressing any opposition to his regime. At the same time, he made efforts to modernize society and began to develop the economic infrastructure. In foreign policy, he aspired to free Iran from the influence of the great powers and the country's dependence on outsiders.

Iran declared its neutrality during World War II, but the shah supported Nazi Germany. The German invasion of the Soviet Union in 1941 and the shah's refusal to permit the transfer of supplies to the Soviet Union through Iran's territory served as an excuse for both Britain and the Soviet Union to invade Iran and to depose Reza Shah, who was exiled to South Africa. He was replaced by his son, Muhammad Reza. Following the termination of the war, the British and Soviet forces withdrew from Iranian territory.

In April 1951, Iran nationalized the petroleum industry, which until then had been in British hands. As a result of this step, a worldwide embargo was imposed on Iranian oil, and the country was thrown into an economic crisis. In March of the same year, Muhammad Musaddeq was appointed prime minister. He had previously filled a number of important governmental positions, and was the leader of the groups supporting nationalization. During his period of office Musaddeq attempted, with the support of large sectors of the population, to reduce the extent of the shah's authority. His efforts ended in failure in August 1953 when the shah, aided by the army, arrested him and forced him out of office. A military regime was subsequently established, remaining in control until 1957.

At the beginning of the 1960s, aided by the oil revenues, the shah began to introduce comprehensive social and economic changes. Within the framework of the "White Revolution" an agrarian reform was implemented. This included the requisition of large holdings and their subsequent distribution to farmers and the nationalization

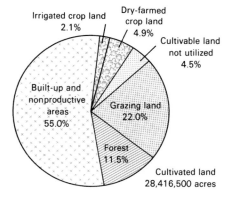

Land Use, 1984

Irrigated crop land 2.1%
Dry-farmed crop land 4.9%
Cultivable land not utilized 4.5%
Built-up and nonproductive areas 55.0%
Grazing land 22.0%
Forest 11.5%
Cultivated land 28,416,500 acres

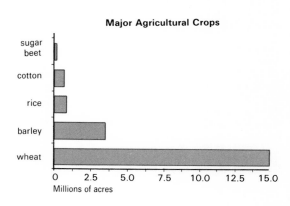

Major Agricultural Crops

sugar beet
cotton
rice
barley
wheat

0   2.5   5.0   7.5   10.0   12.5   15.0
Millions of acres

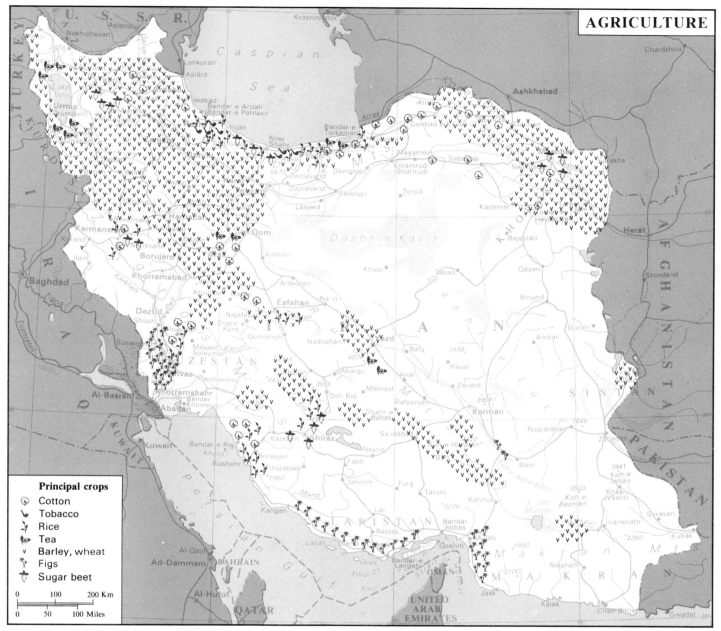

AGRICULTURE

Principal crops

- 🌀 Cotton
- ⬎ Tobacco
- ⸙ Rice
- ⬙ Tea
- v Barley, wheat
- ⸸ Figs
- ⸶ Sugar beet

```
0        100      200 Km
0    50      100 Miles
```

of water resources, pasture lands, and forests. In addition, money was channeled into industrial investment, while health and education services were expanded. The reforms were opposed by the religious leaders, arguing that they contradicted the principles of religious belief (among the religious leaders was Ayatollah Khomeini who was exiled to Iraq in 1963). In its foreign policy, Iran continued its neutral status, developing close relations with the United States as well as with the Soviet Union.

The modernization and rapid development continued during the early 1970s, thanks to the greatly increased oil revenues. Political stability also prevailed. The shah concentrated wide-ranging powers in his own hands, assisted by the security police (the Savak) in the suppression of his opponents. During this period, the army was strengthened and upgraded, mainly through aid from the United States.

During 1976, there were fresh demands for greater democracy and participation in political life. These demands arose in the wake of the economic recession brought about by the substantial

reduction in oil revenues. The religious leaders called for a return to the principles of Islam, which, they claimed, had been neglected by the shah and his regime.

During 1977–1979, dissension increased, finding its expression in violent demonstrations and demands for the shah's deposition and the abolishment of the monarchy. Severe setbacks in the country's economy were caused by strikes. All attempts at restoring order failed. In January 1979, the shah was obliged to leave Iran. The efforts of Prime Minister Shapur Bakhtiar to channel the revolution into a democratic outcome were unsuccessful. The religious zealots increased their power. Their leader — Ayatollah Khomeini — returned from exile in April 1979 and declared the establishment of an Islamic republic in Iran.

The consolidation of the new regime was achieved through the execution of many of the revolution's leaders and the regime's opponents. With the election of Sa'id 'Ali Khamani in October 1981 as president, partial political stability was restored, and this has so far been maintained. The

91

Main industrial centers

- ⚒ Oil refinery & annual production, in millions of tons
- ⊞ Steel and iron
- ▲▲ Machine assembly
- ✸ Metals
- ♠ Petrochemicals
- ⬤ Fertilizers
- ⬤ Liquid gas
- ▽ Food
- ⩗ Textiles
- ⬥ Cement

Mineral resources

- ⬛ Oilfield
- ⬛ Gas field
- △ Coal
- S Sulfur
- Cr Chromium
- Fe Iron
- Cu Copper
- Zn Zinc
- Pb Lead

- ▬ Oil terminal
- —— Crude oil pipeline
- - - - Natural gas
- ·········· Product pipeline

rise of Khomeini to power and the reintroduction of Shiite Muslim principles as the guiding force behind the Iranian republic led to changes in the political situation in neighboring countries, especially in the Persian Gulf.

Iraq, which viewed the Islamic revolution as a threat to its own sovereignty and security, attempted to exploit the unsettled situation in Iran following the revolution and attempted to make good on its territorial claims. In September 1980, the Iraqi army invaded Iranian territory. The war has continued until the present time (1988).

For many years, relations between Iran and Iraq had been tense. According to a treaty signed in

1975, Iran would cease its support of the Kurdish rebels and a boundary line along the Shatt al-'Arab was demarcated. The treaty also included the determination of the countries' respective territorial claims.

In subsequent years, Iraq lodged many complaints against Iran for violations of the treaty. The tension between the two countries increased after the rise to power of Ayatollah Khomeini. Iraq viewed this extreme Shiite regime as a threat to its own security, not least because approximately 51 percent of Iraq's population is Shiite.

For its part, Iran accused Iraq of stirring up internal unrest and of supporting the Arab residents

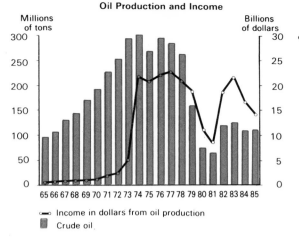

Oil Production and Income

Millions of tons / Billions of dollars

○—○ Income in dollars from oil production
▪ Crude oil

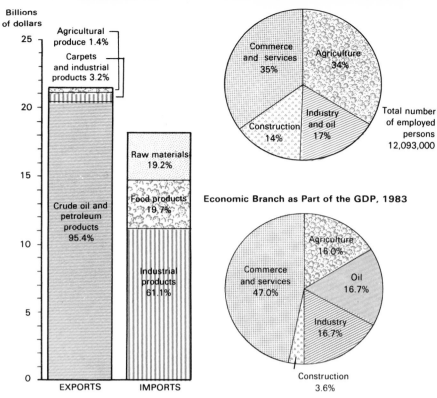

Trade Balance, 1984

Billions of dollars

EXPORTS:
- Agricultural produce 1.4%
- Carpets and industrial products 3.2%
- Crude oil and petroleum products 95.4%

IMPORTS:
- Raw materials 19.2%
- Food products 19.7%
- Industrial products 61.1%

Employment by Economic Branch, 1984

- Commerce and services 35%
- Agriculture 34%
- Industry and oil 17%
- Construction 14%

Total number of employed persons 12,093,000

Economic Branch as Part of the GDP, 1983

- Commerce and services 47.0%
- Agriculture 16.0%
- Oil 16.7%
- Industry 16.7%
- Construction 3.6%

of the Khuzestān region in their struggle for autonomy.

During 1979, a number of military skirmishes took place along the border between Iraq and Iran. These incidents eventually led to the eruption of full-scale warfare in September 1980.

Government and Politics Iran is a theocratic state, headed since 1979 by Ayatollah Khomeini, who bears the title of Supreme Religious Leader for life. He is assisted by a Supervisory Council consisting of twelve representatives — six religious experts and six lawyers. This council determines the country's laws in accordance with Islamic religious principles, presenting them to the Parliament for ratification.

The executive branch is headed by a president who is elected in general elections every four years. In 1985, 'Ali Khamani, who obtained over 70 percent of the vote, was elected for a second term.

The president appoints the prime minister and the cabinet officers, these appointments being subject to parliamentary authorization. The Parliament is composed of 270 representatives, also elected every four years in general elections. With the exception of the Islamic Republican party, which represents the views of the Supreme Religious Leader, all other political organizations have been banned. Over half of the members of Parliament belong to the Islamic Republican party, the remainder being unaffiliated religious personalities.

The existence of many ethnic minorities and their demands for autonomy pose a problem for the central government. The most prominent struggle is that of the Kurds (Sunnis by religion) who demand autonomy in the northwest of the country, where they make up a majority of the population. In addition, the Baluchis in the southeast of the country and the Turkmen and Azerbaijanis in the northeast and northwest have similar claims. The problem of the minorities has increased since the revolution, with occasional military skirmishes taking place between the government and the minority groups.

Dissatisfaction among the population with the continuing Iran–Iraq war is not publicly expressed. At the same time, a number of civilian groups — most notably the Communist party (Tudeh) — have come into conflict with the regime. The rise to power of Khomeini and his policies, which aspire to the imposition of Shiite principles beyond the country's borders, have resulted in a worsening of relations with most Middle Eastern countries.

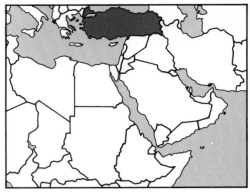

TURKEY

Area **300,946 sq. miles (779,450 sq.km)**
Population (1985 census) **51,400,000**
Capital city **Ankara**
Gross domestic product (GDP) per capita (1984) **$1,000**

Population in main cities (1985 census)			
	Istanbul 2,900,000	Adana 636,000	Konya 385,000
	Ankara 2,300,000	Bursa 510,000	Eskişehir 340,000
	Izmir 832,000	Gaziantep 420,000	Kayseri 330,000

Turkey extends over the peninsula known as Asia Minor as well as much of the mountainous region east of it. A small part of the country, to the west of the Bosporus and Dardanelles Straits, is in Europe. The country is mostly mountainous, with lowlands accounting for only 10 percent of the area. Turkey borders on the Soviet Union, Iran, Iraq, Syria, Greece, and Bulgaria.

Topography Turkey has been subject to folding, faulting, and much volcanic activity. These processes gave rise to a physical structure that is composed of three parallel east–west regions, with two further regions in the east and west of the

country. The Anatolian Plateau lies between the Pontus mountain range in the north and the Taurus mountain range in the south. The two mountain systems converge in eastern Turkey, forming the Armenian and Kurdistan mountains. In western Turkey are the Aegean and Marmara coastlands.

1. The Pontus mountain system extends for 680 miles (1,100 km) with an average width of 60–95 miles (100–150 km), parallel to the Black Sea coast. The highest peaks are in the east, reaching 13,000 ft (4,000 meters). The mountains are incised by valleys, running parallel to the folded mountain ranges with an east–west alignment. The Black Sea

coastal strip is mostly narrow, reaching widths of only up to 1 mile (1–2 km).

2. The Anatolian Plateau, with an average elevation of 2,950 ft (900 meters), is built mostly of limestone beds. The plateau consists of fertile alluvial internal basins, separated from each other by hills and extinct volcanic mountains. The southeastern section of Anatolia has salt lakes and pans and is lower than the rest of the region.

3. The Taurus mountain system extends in the south for 930 miles (1,500 km) with an average width of 95 miles (150 km) parallel to the Mediterranean coast. The mountains comprise a number of parallel ranges, built principally of limestone beds. In most places, the mountains reach the coast. The rugged landscape makes passage from the Mediterranean coast to the Anatolian Plateau difficult.

4. The Kurdistan and Armenian mountains, in the east of Turkey, were formed as a result of the convergence of two fold systems, the Taurus and Pontus mountains. The region has many volcanic mountains, which have left the surface with a mantle of volcanic material. Most of the area lies above 6,560 ft (2,000 meters), with peaks rising above 9,840 ft (3,000 meters), the highest point being Mount Ararat (16,945 ft [5,165 meters]). The thick volcanic mantle has led to the formation of fertile areas between the ranges. Lake Van — into which an internal basin drains — is located near the Iranian border. Most of the Kurdistan and Armenian mountains are drained by the Euphrates and Tigris rivers. Part of the country is drained by the Aras river, which flows into the Caspian Sea. Part of the upper section of the Aras forms the border with the Soviet Union. The southern part of Kurdistan is relatively low (2,300 ft [700 meters]).

5. The Aegean and Marmara coastal region is bounded on the east by a dissected plateau ranging from 2,300–3,000 ft (700–1,000 meters) in height. This plateau is drained westward by numerous rivers, the largest of which have formed wide valleys. The Aegean coastline is extremely indented. These indentations, as well as the Bosporus and Dardanelles Straits, are submerged ancient river valleys.

Climate Due to the country's complex topographical structure, climatic conditions vary according to the region.

1. The Taurus mountains and the Aegean coast — These regions experience Mediterranean conditions, with a hot, dry summer and a mild, rainy winter. The temperature for the hottest month (July) is 77–84° F. (25–29° C.), decreasing to 45–50° F. (7–10° C.) in the coldest month (January). Rain falls only in winter, precipitation ranging from 20 in (500 mm) per year in the Aegean Sea region to 80 in (2,000 mm) annually on some of the southern and western slopes of the Taurus mountains.

2. The Pontus mountains — This region is characterized by a cool climate with rains falling throughout the year. In the winter, the region is exposed to cold air from the north. The average sea-level temperature in the hottest month (July) is 72–77° F. (22–25° C.), decreasing to 30–43° F. (–1–6° C.) in the coldest month (January). Precipitation approximates 24 in (600 mm) on the western coast and the central region, increasing to 100 in (2,500 mm) in the northeastern region.

3. Anatolian Plateau — Substantial differences in both temperature and amount of precipitation are evident in Anatolia's subregions. The average temperature in the hottest month is 73–79° F. (23–26° C.), decreasing to 25–36° F. (–4–2° C.) in the coldest month. There is a large diurnal temperature range. The southeastern area, in the vicinity of Lake Tuz, is hot and more arid. Throughout the plateau, rains fall in the winter, with some summer rains in the north. The plateau, cut off from rain-bearing winds by the surrounding mountains, has low precipitation totals — 16–24 in (400–600 mm) in the west and north, 10 in (250 mm) in the arid southeast.

4. A dry mountain climate prevails in the Kurdistan and Armenian mountains. The altitude and the topography have a major influence on the climate. The summer is cool, while the winter is extremely cold. The average temperature in the hottest month, at an altitude of 4,900–5,900 ft (1,500–1,800 meters), is 64–70° F. (18–21° C.), decreasing to 21–50° F. (–6–10° C.) in the coldest month. Extremely low temperatures of –22° F. (–30° C.) have been recorded. There is a large diurnal temperature range. Precipitation falls in winter, mostly in the form of snow.

Annual precipitation varies from place to place. The amount is dependent on the topography as well as the extent to which the mountains are exposed to rain-bearing winds. The largest amount — 60 in (1,500 mm) — falls south of Lake Van, and the smallest — 12 in (300 mm) — in the Aras valley.

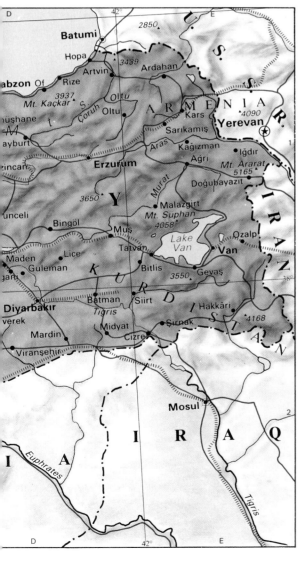

| NATURAL INCREASE (1980-1983) 2.6% |
| LIFE EXPECTANCY (1980-1985) male - 60.3 years female - 64.9 years |
| DOCTORS (1985) 8.0 per 10,000 inhabitants |
| HOSPITAL BEDS (1985) 2.05 per 1,000 inhabitants |
| INFANT MORTALITY (1983) 110.0 per 1,000 births |

| HIGH SCHOOL PUPILS (1984) 2,000,000 |
| UNIVERSITY STUDENTS (1984) 323,000 |
| LITERACY RATE (1980) 70% |

5. The Kurdistan Plateau is exposed to the influence of the Syrian and Arabian Peninsula deserts, resulting in a hot semi-arid climate. The average temperature in the hottest month, at an altitude of 1,970–2,630 ft (600–800 meters), is 82–90° F. (28–32° C.), decreasing to 36–39° F. (2–4° C.) in the coldest month. Hot, dry winds cause extreme temperatures, especially in early summer and autumn. Temperatures of over 104° F. (40° C.) are frequently recorded, while there is a large diurnal temperature range.

Average annual precipitation decreases from 24 in (600 mm) in the north of the plateau to 12 in (300 mm) in the south.

Population Approximately 91 percent of the population are Turkish Sunni Muslims. The largest ethnic minority are the Kurds — who are also Sunni Muslims — comprising approximately 7.5 percent (3.8 million people) of the population. The Kurds live in the east and southeast of the country. Arabs constitute 1 percent (500,000 people) of the population and are concentrated in the south and southeast of the country, close to the Syrian border. They are particularly numerous in the Hatay and Adana districts.

Other ethnic minorities — accounting for only a small proportion of the population — include Laz (originating in the Caucasus), Circassians and Georgians in the northeast of the country, and tens of thousands of Greeks in Istanbul and the surrounding area.

Until World War I, the religious minorities formed one-fourth of the Turkish population with-

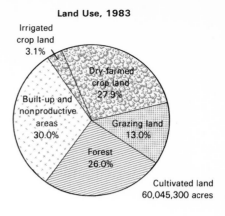

Land Use, 1983

Irrigated crop land 3.1%

Dry-farmed crop land 27.9%

Built-up and nonproductive areas 30.0%

Grazing land 13.0%

Forest 26.0%

Cultivated land 60,045,300 acres

in its present boundaries. The largest minorities were 2.5 million Greeks (Orthodox Christians) and 1.2 million Armenians (Armenian Orthodox Christians). During 1915–1916, the Turks caused the death of nearly half of the Armenian community, most of the remainder being forced to leave the country. During the 1920s, Greece and Turkey agreed to a population transfer, as a result of which most of the Greeks left the country. Today, the Turkish population is religiously homogeneous. Approximately 99 percent of the population are Muslims, nearly all of them Sunni. The country's small Shiite community lives in the southeast of the country. There are approximately 200,000 Christians in Turkey (1983), of whom 76,000 are Orthodox Christians, 64,000 Armenian Orthodox, 29,000 Catholics, and 23,000 Protestants. There are also 30,000 Jews in Turkey. The majority of the Christians and Jews live in the Istanbul region.

Population and settlement dispersal is not uniform. Most of the inhabitants live in the west of the country, along the northern coast and part of the southern coast. In much of the Anatolian Plateau and in the eastern mountains, population is sparse. Since the beginning of the 1950s, Turkey has undergone a rapid urbanization process. In 1950, 75 percent of the population lived in some 36,000 rural settlements. By 1984, the proportion of the rural population had decreased to 49 percent, while the urban population had doubled from 25 to 51 percent. Rural–urban migration has been due to the industrial development in the large cities, on the one hand, and the lack of employment opportunities and low living standards in the villages, on the other.

Economy Turkey's economy has developed at a rapid pace since the end of World War II. Among the contributing factors were the participation of private enterprise — mostly local residents — in the industrial development process, and the substantial amount of foreign aid received, mostly from the United States.

Development slowed down in the 1970s, principally because of the rise in oil prices in 1973. As a result of the new economic policy, which was implemented by the civilian (democratically elected) government, a gradual improvement in Turkey's economy began to take place at the beginning of the 1980s.

Agriculture Agriculture is a major constituent of the country's economy, employing 49 percent of the work force and contributing 19.3 percent to the GDP (1984). Agricultural output is sufficient to meet domestic consumption requirements and Turkey is obliged to import only small quantities of foodstuffs, mainly oil seed. Since the early 1970s, there has been a significant increase in agri-

Climate

RAINFALL AND TEMPERATURE

Annual temperature

Average monthly rainfall

8.6 in   Total annual rainfall

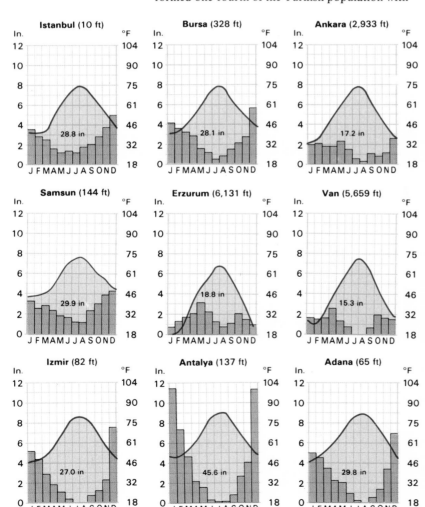

Istanbul (10 ft)   28.8 in

Bursa (328 ft)   28.1 in

Ankara (2,933 ft)   17.2 in

Samsun (144 ft)   29.9 in

Erzurum (6,131 ft)   18.8 in

Van (5,659 ft)   15.3 in

Izmir (82 ft)   27.0 in

Antalya (137 ft)   45.6 in

Adana (65 ft)   29.8 in

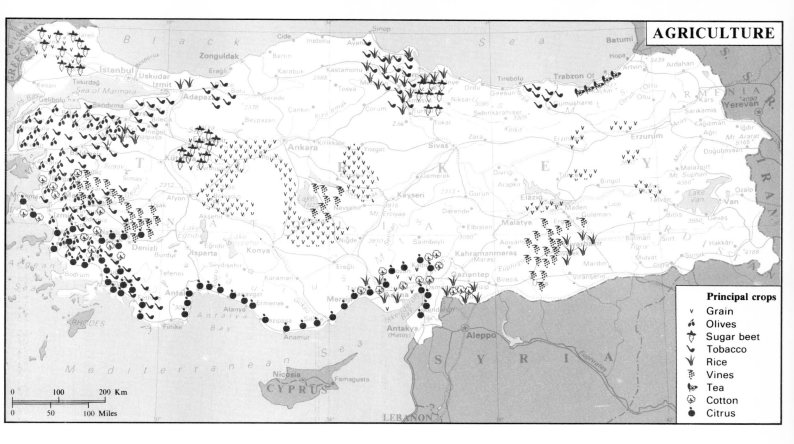

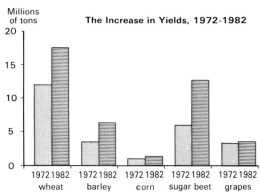

The Increase in Yields, 1972-1982

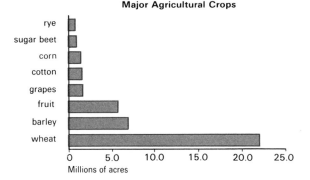

Major Agricultural Crops

cultural output as a result of improved cultivation techniques and the increased use of high-quality seeds, fertilizers, pesticides, and agricultural mechanization.

Approximately 61 million acres — 31 percent of the country's area — are arable. Of this area, approximately 80 percent is cultivated, the remainder lying fallow. Ninety percent of the agricultural area is devoted to dry-farming, the remaining 10 percent being under irrigation. The principal agricultural crop in Turkey is wheat, taking up 45 percent (22 million acres) of the cultivated area (1983). Wheat cultivation is dispersed throughout the country, but is concentrated in the Anatolian Plateau. Barley is also grown over an extensive area (7 million acres), especially in the Anatolian Plateau. The most important commercial crop is cotton (1.5 million acres), which is grown under irrigation, in the coastal plain near Adana and in the Aegean region. Also of considerable commercial importance is tobacco, one of Turkey's traditional crops. Tobacco cultivation takes up approximately 450,000 acres, especially in the Black

Sea and Aegean coastlands. Other important crops include rye, oats, sugar beet, poppies (for opium production), tea, and rice.

Turkey has a large livestock economy, which supplies most of the domestic meat and milk requirements.

Minerals Deposits of approximately twenty different metals are found in Turkey. Despite this diversity, mining contributed only 3 percent to exports in 1984.

In export terms, the most important mineral is chromium. Approximately 500,000 tons of chromium ore are mined annually (1981–1985) from three mines, the largest one being at Guleman west of Lake Van. Additional mines are in the Eskişehir region, in northwest and west Anatolia. High-quality iron ore (a mixture of 60–66 percent iron in the ore) is mined in the vicinity of Divriği, between Sivas and Erzurum. There are good coal mines in the northwest close to the city of Zonguldak. In 1984, 7.1 million tons of coal were mined, most of which was used in the nearby steel industries at Karabük and Ereğli. Brown coal (lignite), used

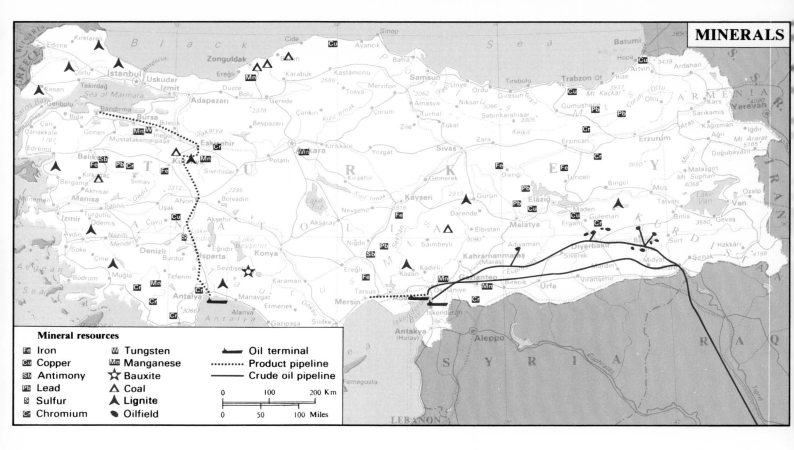

mainly in the production of electricity, is mined in western Anatolia.

Copper was produced in Turkey in ancient times. Present-day mining is concentrated in the northeast of the country. Manganese deposits, used in the iron and steel industry, are scattered throughout Turkey but are mined only in the west of the country, in the Eskişehir region and around Ereğli. The only bauxite mine in the country is near Seydişehir (northeast of Antalya). This mine provides the raw material for a nearby aluminum plant.

Oilfields are located in the southeast. These are an extension of the oilfields in Iraq. Annual output was 2.1 million tons in 1985. The proven oil reserves total only 40 million tons, as a result of which output has been reduced (in 1973, ouput was 3.5 million tons). Oil is processed in four refineries, with a total annual production capacity of 22 million tons. Other minerals, produced in small quantities, include lead, graphite, asbestos, salt, mercury, zinc, phosphates, wolfram, and antimony.

Industry The industrial sector employed 12.5 percent (2 million people) of the work force in 1984, contributing approximately 25 percent to the GDP. Industrial development was based on three factors: the large-scale and diverse agricultural produce, the existence of many minerals, and the large population.

The most widespread industry is textiles and clothing. Locally produced cotton and wool provide the raw materials for the many factories dispersed throughout the country. The food industry is the second largest branch, with important factories for the manufacture of sugar (annual output of 1.8 million tons) and preserved foodstuffs. Cement production is also important, with 29 factories dispersed throughout the country, producing

Important Minerals — Annual Production and Proven Reserves

Mineral	Annual production in tons		Proven reserves in tons, 1985
Chromite	500,000	(1980-1985)	No figures
Iron	3,900,000	(1980)	28,000,000
Coal	7,100,000	(1984)	No figures
Lignite	28,000,000	(1984)	6,000,000,000
Copper	30,000	(1984)	90,000,000
Manganese (refined)	17,000	(1984)	No figures
Bauxite	130,000	(1984)	30,000,000
Oil	2,100,000	(1985)	40,000,000

14 million tons in 1984. The steel industry, which is largely dependent on the local supply of coal and iron, is concentrated in Karabük and Ereğli and in Iskenderun. Annual steel production is 2.7 million tons.

In the 1970s and 1980s, fertilizer and petrochemical industries were developed in Turkey. The main fertilizer factory was constructed at Kutahya in the west of the country, producing 6.9 million tons of fertilizer per year. Other fertilizer factories were established in Samsun, Elâzığ, Mersin, and Iskenderun. A petrochemical factory was established in Izmit, using raw materials from the local refinery. In addition, there are 23 car assembly plants in Turkey (in 1984, 23,000 lorries, 8,700 buses, and 41,800 tractors were assembled). Other important industries in Turkey include the manufacture of paper, electrical appliances, and general consumer goods.

History Turkey's history has ancient roots. The Hittite Empire, whose center was in the Anatolian Plateau, reached its peak in the middle of the second century BCE. Between the years 330–1453, Constantinople (Istanbul) was the capital of the Byzantine Empire. The Islamic religion and the

Turkish language were brought to the region by the Seljuks in the eleventh century. The Ottoman nation began to develop in the thirteenth century, growing into a large empire which at its zenith included North Africa and most of the Middle East.

Turkey's modern history began after the dissolution of the Ottoman Empire during World War I. Turkey lost control of all territories lying outside Asia Minor. Some areas fell under the influence of Britain and France. In 1919, the Greeks — with the approval of Britain and France — invaded Anatolia. The sultan's government was left helpless, but there was much opposition to this external intervention among the country's inhabitants.

In April 1920, Mustafa Kemal — a soldier in the Ottoman army — established a nationalist government in opposition to the sultan. Kemal succeeded in driving out the Greeks (August 1922) after a number of battles. In 1923, his government signed an agreement with the allied powers in which most of Turkey's current borders were demarcated.

In October 1923, Turkey was declared a republic and Kemal (who named himself Atatürk — father of the Turks) was elected president. His regime was ruthless, his own political party — the Republican People's party — being the only one allowed to exist. His absolute powers enabled him to impose social, economic, and political reforms, the intention being to transform Turkey into a modern European state. The religious legal system was replaced by a secular system, Turkish script was replaced by Latin script, and women were granted full rights. Following Kemal's death in 1938, Ismet İnönü was elected president.

During World War II, Turkey maintained a position of neutrality. Following the war, a policy of liberalization was carried out, with political parties being granted the right to organize. In May 1950, free elections took place with the Democratic party emerging victorious. Celâl Bayar was elected president, and Adnan Menderes, prime minister. They initiated economic development in every sector of the economy — especially industry — and brought about an economic boom that continued until the mid-1950s. At the same time, the government continued to impose limitations on any opposition activity. These limitations, together with the economic recession in the late 1950s, resulted in a military coup in 1960, headed by General Gamal Gürsel.

New elections took place in October 1961, following which the military regime transferred power to a civilian government headed by Ismet İnönü. This government succeeded in mustering only narrow support during its four years in power and was therefore unable to implement its social and economic policies.

In the elections of 1965, the right-wing party headed by Suleiman Demirel was victorious. Demirel's government was unable to meet the economic and social challenges, resulting in increased strife between the right- and left-wing factions. The internal unrest led to demonstrations, disruption of law and order, strikes, and physical violence between citizens. Following pressure from military leaders, Demirel resigned, and a new government — which in reality was headed by military personnel — was formed in December 1971. Following two years of a military government, elections were held in October 1973 with Bulent Ecevit emerging as the victor.

In July 1974, the Turkish army invaded Cyprus following the overthrow of the Cypriot government by Greek officers. The Turkish invasion was intended to prevent the new Cypriot regime from implementing Greek aspirations for a union of Cyprus with Greece. A large number of military units took part in the invasion, with Turkey controlling 40 percent of the island. The invasion and the continued military presence in Cyprus resulted

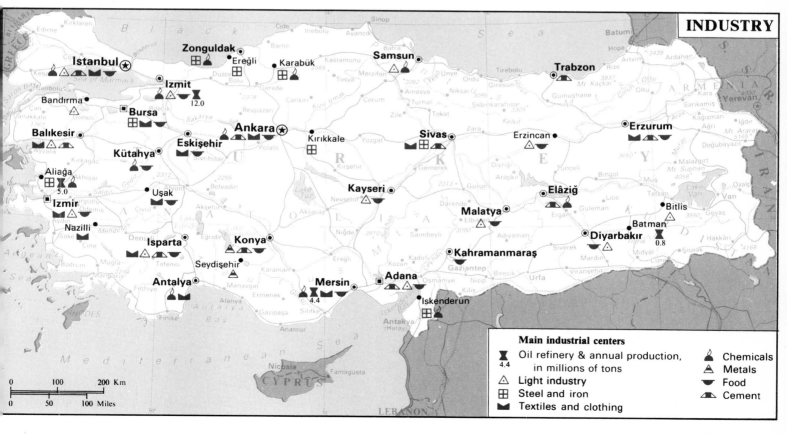

INDUSTRY

Main industrial centers

⚒ Oil refinery & annual production, in millions of tons	♨ Chemicals
△ Light industry	△ Metals
⊞ Steel and iron	▼ Food
◣ Textiles and clothing	⛰ Cement

in much strife within Ecevit's government, eventually bringing about its dissolution.

Over the next six years, a number of governments failed in their attempts to revive the country's economy. A scarcity of raw materials and food products, widespread unemployment, and high inflation spread internal unrest throughout the country. As a result of the weakness displayed by both government and security services, violent incidents and terrorist activities between rival groups became a common occurrence.

In September 1980, General Kenan Evren seized power following a bloody military coup. The military managed the affairs of state by imposing strict limitations on freedom and individual rights. These limitations brought about internal rest and stability, despite strong international criticism.

In November 1983, under military agreement, general elections were held. Turgut Özal was elected as prime minister. Since holding office, Özal has worked successfully to improve the economic situation, and to gradually reduce the limitations that were imposed by martial law.

Government and Politics At the head of the Turkish republic is a president possessing wide-ranging powers. The president is elected by the Turkish National Assembly for one term of seven years. He also serves as the military commander-in-chief and is empowered to appoint members of the national legislature responsible for the daily administration of state affairs.

There are 400 representatives in the legislature (the National Assembly), elected in free elections every five years. In the elections held in 1987, the Homeland party headed by Turgut Özal was victorious.

Turkey is divided into 67 provinces, each of which is controlled by a governor who is appointed directly by the president.

Most of Turkey's borders were determined by the Lausanne Agreement of 1923. In 1926, the boundary line in the Mosul region was fixed, while in 1939 Turkey annexed the Hatay district which until then had been under Syrian (French mandatory) control. In February 1974, Greece discovered oilfields in the Aegean Sea. This discovery led to a conflict between Turkey and Greece over the boundaries of the two countries' respective territorial waters and the rights of oil exploitation in the Aegean Sea. Turkey also has dormant border disputes with Syria and the Soviet Union.

Since the end of World War II, Turkey has strengthened its ties with the Western world. The most obvious expression of this has been Turkey's membership in NATO.

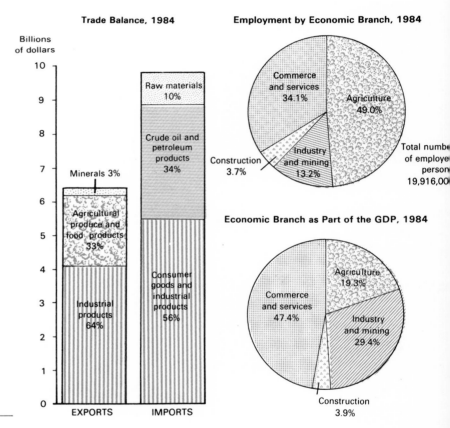

Population by Age Group, 1980

Age

65+	4.8%
60-64	1.8%
45-59	11.2%
30-44	16.0%
15-29	27.7%
0-14	38.5%

Trade Balance, 1984

Billions of dollars

EXPORTS
- Minerals 3%
- Agricultural produce and food products 33%
- Industrial products 64%

IMPORTS
- Raw materials 10%
- Crude oil and petroleum products 34%
- Consumer goods and industrial products 56%

Employment by Economic Branch, 1984

- Commerce and services 34.1%
- Agriculture 49.0%
- Construction 3.7%
- Industry and mining 13.2%

Total number of employed persons 19,916,000

Economic Branch as Part of the GDP, 1984

- Commerce and services 47.4%
- Agriculture 19.3%
- Industry and mining 29.4%
- Construction 3.9%

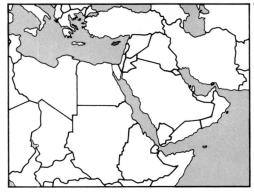

CYPRUS

Area **3,572 sq. miles (9,251 sq.km)**
Population (1981 estimate) **660,000**
Capital city **Nicosia**
Gross domestic product (GDP) per capita
Greek sector (1983) **$3,193**   Turkish sector (1983) **$1,050**

Population in main cities (1982 estimates)	Nicosia 250,000	Larnaca 48,300
	Limassol 107,000	Famagusta 39,500

The island of Cyprus lies in the eastern Mediterranean, 45 miles (70 km) south of Turkey and 55 miles (90 km) west of Syria.

Topography   Cyprus is a residual of a mountain system that was once part of the Taurus mountains in southern Turkey. As a result of intensive tectonic activity and the submergence of part of the Taurus system, the area of the island was separated from the mainland. On the island, there are three distinct landscapes: the Troödos mountain massif in the south, the Kyrenia mountains in the north, and the Mesaöria Plain in the center.

The Troödos mountains occupy approximately half of the island's area and are built of three principal rock formations. The center of the mountain massif consists of hard crystalline rocks which are exposed in the uplands (above 2,600 ft [800 meters]). This massif contains the highest peak in Cyprus — Mount Olympus (6,400 ft [1,951 meters]). The erosion of these hard rocks has formed precipitous slopes with deeply incised narrow valleys. A narrow belt of volcanic rock forms an area that surrounds the crystalline massif at an altitude of approximately 2,600 ft (800 meters). The lower outer belt of the massif is built mainly of soft limestone formations into which wide valleys have been formed by river erosion.

The Kyrenia range and its continuation to the east, the Karpas mountains, are a sharp narrow fold 4–5 miles (6–8 km) wide, and reaching a height of 3,280 ft (1,000 meters). The ridge has sharp peaks with steep northern slopes. The Kyrenia mountain ridge is made up of large blocks incised by narrow valleys that cross from north to south. The Karpas range is lower than the Kyrenia range and has a gentler relief.

The Mesaöria Plain separates the Kyrenia mountains from the Troödos range. The plain has a series of low hills which reach the sea in both the east and the west. Between the hills, there are plains covered by thick layers of sediment. The plain is crossed by a number of streams, the largest of which is the Pedieas river.

Cyprus's coastline stretches for 470 miles (755

S.B.A.: U.K. Sovereign Base Area

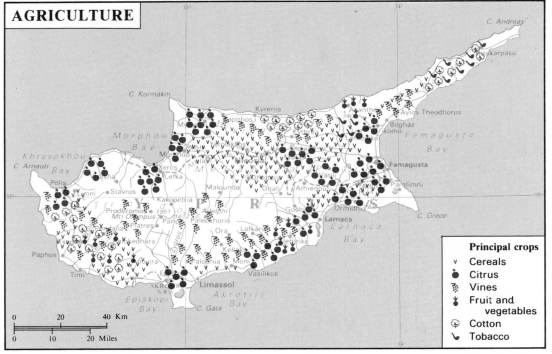

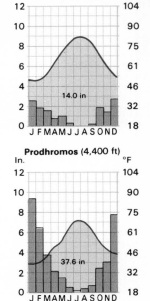

Nicosia (722 ft)

14.0 in

Prodhromos (4,400 ft)

37.6 in

Principal crops

v Cereals
🍋 Citrus
🌿 Vines
🍇 Fruit and vegetables
🌸 Cotton
🌾 Tobacco

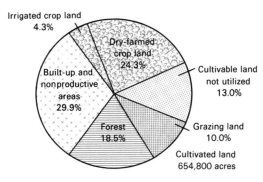

Land Use, 1984

Irrigated crop land 4.3%
Dry-farmed crop land 24.3%
Built-up and nonproductive areas 29.9%
Cultivable land not utilized 13.0%
Forest 18.5%
Grazing land 10.0%
Cultivated land 654,800 acres

km). To the south and southwest, the edges of the Troödos mountains reach all the way to the coast. Throughout the rest of the country, the coastal strip is approximately up to 2 miles (1–3 km) wide.

Climate Cyprus experiences typical Mediterranean conditions. The Troödos mountain massif in the south and the Kyrenian mountain range in the north obstruct the influence of the sea from reaching the Mesaöria Plain. The summer is hot and dry throughout most of the island, while the winter (October–March) is wet and temperate.

In the mountain regions, the average maximum temperature in the hottest month (August) is 81° F. (27° C.), decreasing to an average minimum of 39° F. (4° C.) in the coldest month (January). The Mesaöria Plain is extremely hot in summer, with temperatures occasionally reaching 104° F. (40° C.). The average temperature in Nicosia is 97° F. (36° C.) in August, descending to an average of 41–43° F. (5–6° C.) in January.

Rains fall in the winter months. Precipitation distribution varies according to the topography. In the Troödos mountains, rain falls mostly on the southwestern slopes which are exposed to the sea winds. In this region, the average annual precipitation reaches 40 in (1,000 mm) per year. Winter snows fall at altitudes of above 3,280 ft (1,000 meters). In the Masaöria Plain, the average annual

precipitation is approximately 14.5 in (370 mm).

Population There are two ethnic communities in Cyprus — Greeks and Turks. The Greeks comprise 81 percent of the population, the overwhelming majority of which follow the Greek Orthodox Church. The Turks, who make up 18 percent of the population, are Sunni Muslims. The remaining inhabitants are Armenians (Christians), Arabs (Maronite Christians), and Europeans. Since 1974, nearly all of the Turkish Cypriots have resided in the northern section of the island, occupying 40 percent of the total area. Approximately 60 percent of the country's inhabitants live in towns, the remainder in villages.

Economy Until the partition of the country in 1974, Cyprus's economy was based mostly on agriculture. During the early 1970s, this sector contributed approximately 23 percent to the GDP, employing 40 percent of the country's work force. Industry was the second most important sector, contributing approximately 15 percent to the GDP. Additional sources of revenues were tourism, the British army bases on the island, and the export of mineral resources (copper, iron pyrites, chromium, and asbestos).

After 1975, two separate economic systems were created. During the first years following partition, the economy of both zones experienced a recession as a result of the destruction caused by the civil war. The partition of the island also created a refugee problem, imposing a further burden on the scarce resources.

The Turkish section (the north) of the island contains approximately two-thirds of the cultivable area, or 962,000 acres. It has most of the citrus orchards, all of the tobacco plantations, a large number of the tourist facilities, and one-third of the industrial plants.

The Economy of the Greek Zone Since many of the economic resources remained in the Turkish section, the Greek Cypriot government has made efforts to develop a new economic infrastructure based on agriculture, industry, and services (especially tourism).

Agriculture Most of the cultivated area is

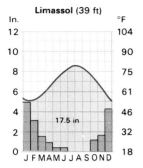

Limassol (39 ft)

Climate
RAINFALL AND TEMPERATURE

 Annual
temperature

Average monthly
rainfall

8.6 in Total annual
rainfall

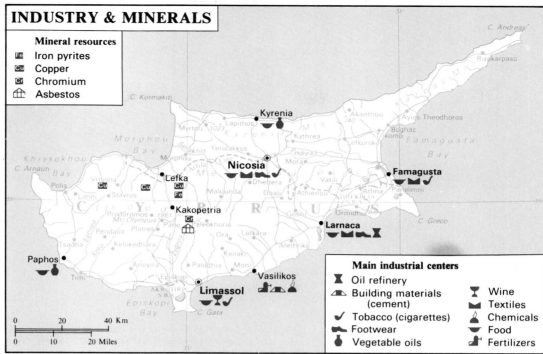

INDUSTRY & MINERALS

Mineral resources
- Fe Iron pyrites
- Cu Copper
- Cr Chromium
- Asbestos

Main industrial centers
- Oil refinery
- Building materials (cement)
- Tobacco (cigarettes)
- Footwear
- Vegetable oils
- Wine
- Textiles
- Chemicals
- Food
- Fertilizers

NATURAL
INCREASE
(1980-1983)
1.3%

LIFE
EXPECTANCY
(1980-1985)
male - **72.3** years
female - **76.0** years

DOCTORS
(1982)
12.2 per 10,000
inhabitants

HOSPITAL BEDS
(1982)
6.8 per 1,000
inhabitants

INFANT
MORTALITY
(1983-1984)
17.2 per 1,000 births

HIGH SCHOOL
PUPILS
(1985-1986)
46,000

LITERACY RATE
(1982) **89%**

devoted to dry-farming, although extensive resources are being invested in the development of irrigation. Four new dams have been constructed for this purpose, three of which were completed in 1984, with the fourth to be ready by 1989. These dams will enable an increase in the irrigated area by 40 percent (from 100,000 to 140,000 acres). The principal agricultural crops are potatoes, which make up most of the agricultural exports, vegetables, and flowers. Other crops include vines, olives, citrus fruit, deciduous fruit, and cereals. In 1984, agriculture contributed 10 percent to the GDP and provided employment for approximately 20 percent of the work force.

Minerals Cyprus contains few mineral resources, most of which are concentrated in the Troödos mountains in the Greek zone. At present, the copper deposits, copper and iron pyrites, and asbestos are all being mined. Chromium was also mined until 1983. In recent years, the deposits have dwindled and their output has decreased.

Industry Since the partition of the island, the industrial sector has undergone substantial development. Before partition, the factories in the Greek section included a small refinery at Larnaca and a large cement plant at Vasilikos. Many small factories have since been established, specializing in clothing and footwear, food products, beverages (including wine), chemical products, fertilizers, and metal goods.

Tourism This sector has also experienced substantial development since partition. Hotels, tourist facilities, an airport at Larnaca, and seaports at Lanarca and Limassol (the large port at Famagusta remained under Turkish control) have all been constructed. As a result of these projects, the number of tourists visiting the Greek zone increased from 216,000 in 1978 to 740,000 in 1984.

The Economy of the Turkish Zone The Turkish zone is less developed than its Greek counterpart. The development of the economy has been hindered by the lack of capital investment and professional manpower as well as by limited export markets. In recent years, the Turkish government has financed approximately 50 percent of this region's budget.

Agriculture Agriculture is the major economic sector, contributing approximately 20 percent to the GDP and providing employment for 40 percent of the work force. The most important agricultural crop is citrus fruit, accounting for most of the agricultural exports. Other crops include tobacco, cereals, vegetables, and deciduous fruit.

Minerals Mineral resources in the Turkish zone are very limited, consisting of a few small copper mines in the northern fringes of the Troödos mountains. In recent years, the copper reserves have dwindled and mining has ceased.

Industry Industry is backward, providing employment for only 5 percent of the work force. Industrial plants are small, specializing in tobacco processing, cigarette manufacture, oil, food, and clothing.

Tourism Despite the fact that 60 percent of the country's tourist facilities remained in the Turkish zone following partition, the number of tourists has declined. In 1984, only 87,000 tourists visited the northern region of the island, 80 percent of whom came from Turkey.

History Until Cyprus attained independence in 1960, the island had been under foreign rule. From the sixth century until 1878, Cyprus was part of the Ottoman Empire. It was during this period that the Turks first settled on the island. In 1878, the Ottomans transferred power to Britain, in exchange for Britain's support of Turkey at the Berlin Congress. During World War I, Britain annexed the island, declaring it a crown colony in 1925.

Population by Age Group, 1983

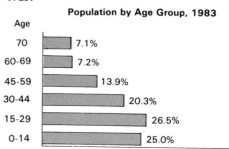

Age	
70	7.1%
60-69	7.2%
45-59	13.9%
30-44	20.3%
15-29	26.5%
0-14	25.0%

103

The movement for the liberation of Cyprus from foreign rule was formed as early as the beginning of the twentieth century, during which period there was a struggle for independence within Greece. The Greek Cypriots aspired to unification with Greece. Serious disturbances broke out in 1931, but these were suppressed by the British. The struggle continued in subsequent years, and in 1955 the underground National Organization of Cypriot Struggle was formed. This group was responsible for terrorist and other violent activities. Turkey opposed any form of Greek annexation of the island, and this led to a deterioration in relations between the two countries. When it was apparent that Greek annexation was not a realistic option, the Greek leader, Archbishop Makarios, proposed the granting of independence to the island. In February 1959, the leaders of Greece and Turkey approved this proposal and made arrangements for an equitable ethnic division of power within the government. The Turkish Cypriots (composing 18 percent of the population) received 30 percent of the parliamentary seats as well as the position of vice president.

After independence in 1960 both communities began opposing the power-sharing arrangements. The Greeks argued that the Turks had a larger representation in Parliament than their numbers justified, while the Turks complained that the Greek-dominated government discriminated against them. The joint government was dissolved at the end of 1963, resulting in a civil war. In March 1964, a United Nations force was dispatched to the island, bringing about an end to the violence. The UN force remained on the island to maintain order.

The Turkish Cypriots — who no longer participated in the government — created their own institutions, effectively partitioning the island. Despite ongoing negotiations between the leaders of the two communities during 1964–1974, the gap between their respective claims became more deeply entrenched. The Turks desired the establishment of a federation on the island, while the Greeks — headed by Cypriot President Makarios — supported the establishment of a single national unit. Makarios was opposed to énosis (union with Greece), despite the fact that this stance contrasted with that of the Greek military junta. In response, the Greek government organized a coup in which Makarios was deposed. He was replaced by Nikos Sampson, who was an ardent supporter of énosis. Turkey, which now suspected a Greek move to annex Cyprus, invaded the island and conquered the northern section. Approximately 200,000 Greeks who lived in this area became refugees and were obliged to migrate to the Greek-controlled south. Approximately 30,000 Turkish Cypriots migrated from the Greek zone to the Turkish-controlled north. Following five months of exile, Makarios returned to power, serving as president of the Greek section until his death in 1977.

In February 1975, the Greeks and Turks fixed a boundary line (the Attila line), in effect partitioning the island into two separate political entities. The boundary passes through the city of Nicosia, dividing it into two sections.

On November 15, 1983, the Turkish leader, Rauf Denktash, declared the establishment of an independent Turkish state in the north of the island. Only Turkey formally recognizes the existence of this new state, and it is not represented in any international forum.

Government and Politics Cyprus was estab-

lished in 1960 as a republic, headed by a president who appoints the government. According to the constitution, the president has to be a member of the Greek community, while his deputy has to come from the Turkish community. The government is supposed to consist of seven Greek ministers and three Turkish ministers. A legislative assembly was also established, comprising 35 Greek representatives and 15 Turkish representatives. The president and the legislature are elected in general elections held every five years. Ever since the Turkish representatives left the government in 1963, the constitution has been redundant. In effect, there are two governments in existence.

The Greek section is headed by a president, elected for a term of five years, working in conjunction with a government that is responsible for the administration of the country's affairs. Spyros Kyprianou, president from 1977 until February 1988, has been succeeded by Georgios Vassiliou. The elected assembly consists of 80 representatives.

A similar system of government exists in the Turkish zone. A president is elected every five years, working in conjunction with a government. The elected assembly consists of 40 representatives.

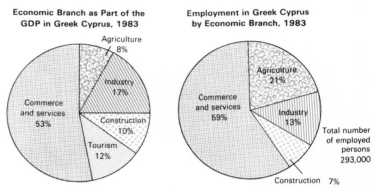

Economic Branch as Part of the GDP in Greek Cyprus, 1983

Agriculture 8%
Industry 17%
Construction 10%
Tourism 12%
Commerce and services 53%

Employment in Greek Cyprus by Economic Branch, 1983

Agriculture 21%
Industry 13%
Construction 7%
Commerce and services 59%
Total number of employed persons 293,000

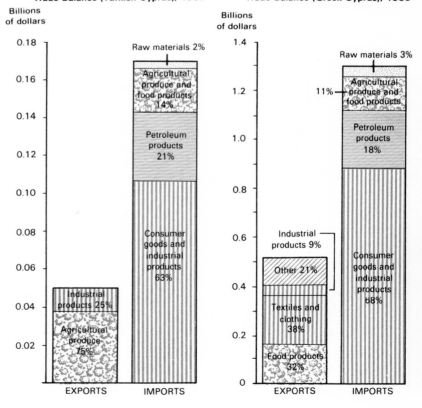

Trade Balance (Turkish Cyprus), 1983

Billions of dollars

EXPORTS
Industrial products 25%
Agricultural produce 75%

IMPORTS
Raw materials 2%
Agricultural produce and food products 14%
Petroleum products 21%
Consumer goods and industrial products 63%

Trade Balance (Greek Cyprus), 1983

Billions of dollars

EXPORTS
Industrial products 9%
Other 21%
Textiles and clothing 38%
Food products 32%

IMPORTS
Raw materials 3%
Agricultural produce and food products 11%
Petroleum products 18%
Consumer goods and industrial products 68%

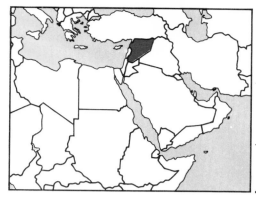

SYRIA

Area **71,498 sq. mi. (185,180 sq. kms.)**
Population (1986 estimate) **10,960,000**
Capital city **Damascus**
Gross domestic product (GDP) per capita (1984) **$ 2,400**

Population in main cities (1984 estimates)		
Damascus 1,180,000	Latakia 225,000
Aleppo 1,100,000	Ḥamāh 190,000
Homs 406,000	

Syria is the northernmost country on the eastern shores of the Mediterranean. It is bordered by Turkey in the north, Lebanon and Israel in the west, Jordan in the south, and Iraq in the east.

Topography Syria's physical features consist of a chain of mountains in the west running parallel to the coastline; to the east of the mountains, running in a north–south direction, is a deep valley which forms part of the Syrian-African Rift. Another highland area then rises and slopes gently eastward to the Syrian Desert.

The Nuṣayrīyah mountains, fronting the Mediterranean coast in the north of Syria, are an extension of the Lebanon mountains. These mountains, built of limestone, have an average width of 25 miles (40 km). The highest point is 5,125 ft (1,562 meters). The western flank of the ridge slopes gradually to the sea; but in the east it drops sharply to the part of the Syrian-African Rift known as the Ghāb Depression.

The Orontes river flows northward through the Ghāb Depression. In the past, the river flooded the surrounding area each winter, leaving large swamps. The drainage of these swamps and the control of the Orontes flow was one of the first major development projects to be carried out in Syria. The Ghāb Depression has since become a fertile agricultural region.

A large, semi-arid plateau, composed of limestone and chalk, lies to the east of the rift valley.

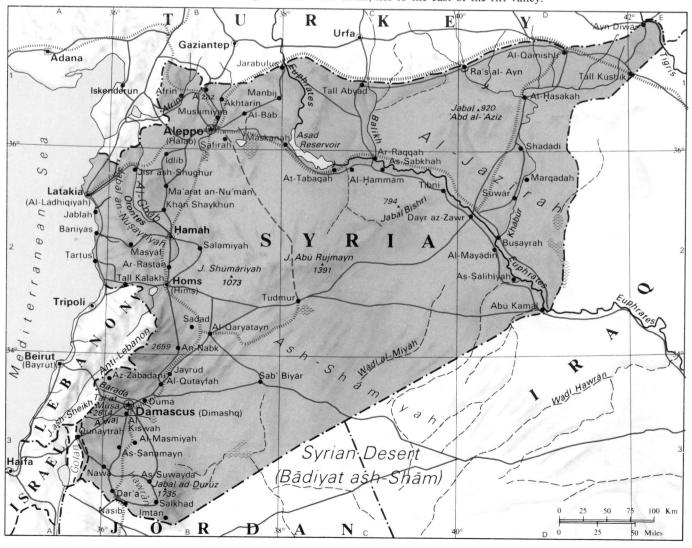

The plateau, gently sloping towards the Euphrates river valley, has a mean height of 980–1,310 ft (300–400 meters). A number of mountains rises above the plateau, most prominent of which are Jabal Abū Rujmayn (4,565 ft [1,391 meters]) and Jabal Shūmāriyah (3,520 ft [1,073 meters]). The plateau has a number of enclosed basins, some of which are filled with salt marshes. The river Euphrates flows through Syria for a distance of 310 miles (500 km), and crosses a narrow, deep valley approximately 330 ft (100 meters) below the surface level of the plateau. The river meanders over the entire width of the valley.

The arid plateau extends east of the Euphrates, to and beyond the valley of the Tigris river in Iraq. The low plateau between the two rivers is known as the Jazīrah (island in Arabic). This is an arid, undulating area, elevated in the center by the 'Abd al-'Azīz hills, which reach a peak of 3,020 ft (920 meters). The north of the Jazīrah is partly covered by volcanic rock formations and fertile soil. The rivers Balīkh and Khābūr, tributaries of the Euphrates, flow through the Syrian Jazīrah.

The southern part of Syria is separated from the sea by the Lebanon mountains. The eastern slopes of the Anti-Lebanon range are in Syria, with the highest point located at Tal'at Mūsa (8,626 ft [2,629 meters]). The Syrian Desert, a southern continuation of the plateau, extends to the eastern foot of the Anti-Lebanon range. This area includes the Damascus basin, an oasis which receives its waters from the rivers Baradā and 'Awaj, descending from the Anti-Lebanon. An extensive, arid region southeast of Damascus is covered by thick basalt formations, making it extremely difficult to traverse. Jabal ad-Durūz (5,690 ft [1,735 meters]) — near the Jordanian border — is also comprised of basalt. To the west of Jabal ad-Durūz lies the Hawrān Plain, covered by fertile volcanic soil.

Climate Syria has three climatic regions: the Mediterranean, the steppe, and the desert. Mediterranean conditions, with a hot summer and mild winter, prevail along the coast and on the western

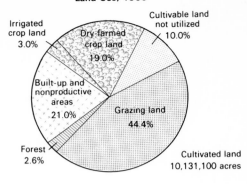

Land Use, 1983

- Irrigated crop land 3.0%
- Dry-farmed crop land 19.0%
- Cultivable land not utilized 10.0%
- Built-up and nonproductive areas 21.0%
- Grazing land 44.4%
- Forest 2.6%
- Cultivated land 10,131,100 acres

slopes of the Nuṣayrīyah mountains. The average high temperature on the Mediterranean coast (in Latakia) for the hottest month, August, is 84° F. (29° C.), while the average low temperature in the coldest month, January, is 50° F. (10° C.). On the Nuṣayrīyah mountains, altitude greatly reduces the average and absolute temperatures.

Both the Nuṣayrīyah and the Lebanon mountains restrict the tempering and humid effects of the sea on areas to the east, resulting in arid steppe conditions. The average high temperature in August in the Damascus region is 99° F. (37° C.), decreasing to 36° F. (2° C.) in January.

A desert climate prevails in east and southeast Syria. There are large differences between both summer and winter and diurnal temperatures. The average high August temperature in Tudmur is 110° F. (43° C.), decreasing to an average low of 36° F. (2° C.) in January.

Precipitation falls in the winter months between November and April. Along the coast (at Latakia) average annual rainfall totals 24 in (600 mm). Precipitation reaches 51 in (1,300 mm) in the Nuṣayrīyah highlands. The steppe and the desert regions, located in the rain shadow, receive only small and irregular amounts of rainfall. In the north (in the Jazīrah), 10 in (250 mm) of rain falls, decreasing to 4 in (100 mm) in the south (the Syrian Desert). The Damascus basin, located at the edge of the desert, receives 5 in (130 mm). Because of its high elevation, Jabal ad-Durūz receives up to 20 in (500 mm) of rain.

Population Syria's population is ethnically and religiously heterogeneous. Approximately 89 percent of the inhabitants are Arabs, mostly Muslims with Christian and Druze minorities. Ethnic minorities include Kurds, Turkmen, and Circassians (all Sunni Muslim), Armenians (Christians, most of whom belong to the Armenian Orthodox Church), and approximately 1,500 Jews.

Many Palestinians have resided in Syria since 1948. Some live in refugee camps while others are settled in towns and villages.

Most of the Muslims (86 percent of the population) are members of the Sunni sect. The remainder are 'Alawites, Shiites and Ismā'ilites. Approximately 2.8 percent of the inhabitants are Druze, practicing their own unique form of religion.

Some 11 percent of the population are Christian, a third of whom are Greek Orthodox. The remainder are Armenian Orthodox, Armenian Catholic, Greek Catholic, Maronites, Jacobites, and Assyrians.

Most of Syria's ethnic minorities live at the country's periphery: the Kurds in the northeast, near the border with Iraq and Turkey; the Druze in Jabal ad-Durūz, near the border with Jordan; the Turkmen north of Aleppo, near the border

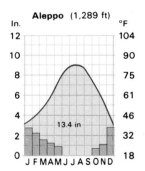

Aleppo (1,289 ft)
13.4 in

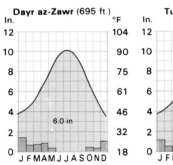

Dayr az-Zawr (695 ft.)
6.0 in

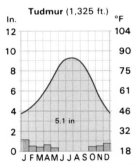

Tudmur (1,325 ft.)
5.1 in

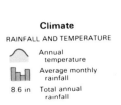

Climate
RAINFALL AND TEMPERATURE

- Annual temperature
- Average monthly rainfall
- 8.6 in Total annual rainfall

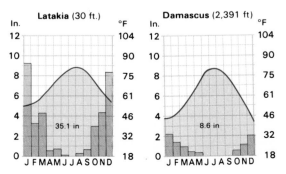

Latakia (30 ft.)
35.1 in

Damascus (2,391 ft)
8.6 in

AGRICULTURE

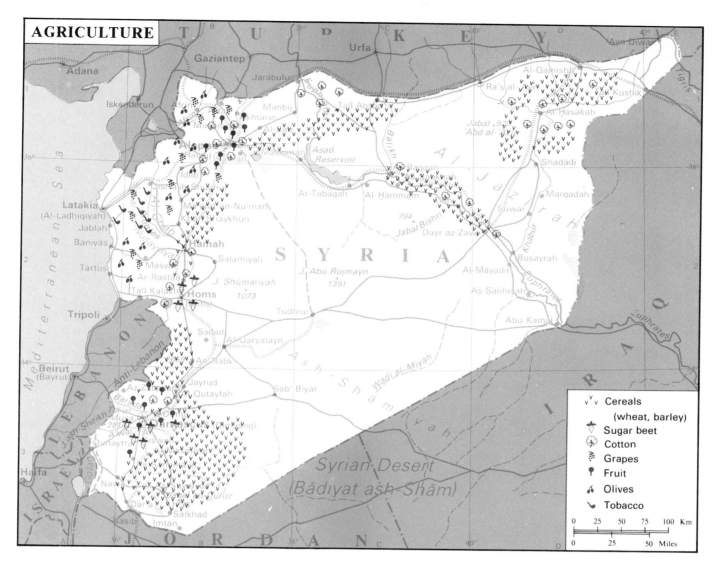

with Turkey; the Circassians in the Jazīrah region; the Jews in Damascus and Aleppo.

Seventy-eight percent of the country's inhabitants are concentrated in a belt running from Aleppo in the north, to Ḥamāh, Homs, and Damascus, and along the coastal region from Latakia to Ṭarṭūs. The rest of the country is sparsely populated. Approximately half of the country's population live in urban settlements. The few thousand nomads who dwell in the northeast of the country are gradually undergoing sedentation.

Economy Until well into the 1960s, agriculture was the country's principal source of income. It provided the greatest employment and contributed most to the GDP. Industry was mainly confined to the processing of agricultural produce.

A gradual change began to take place at the end of the 1960s. In 1968, oil production and export began, resulting in an increase in national revenue and an improvement in the trade balance. Relative to other Middle Eastern countries, Syria is only a minor exporter of petroleum. National revenue also derived from the export of phosphates which began in 1972, when high prices were attained in the world market. Income also accrued from the main Iraqi oil pipeline, that crosses Syria. The added revenue was used for economic development, especially in the industrial sector and the oil branch in particular.

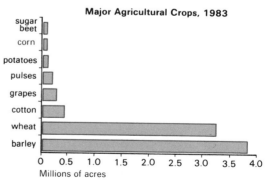

After 1977, the development process gradually slowed down. This was due to the decrease in revenues resulting from the decline in both world oil and phosphate prices and the closing of the oil pipeline from Iraq in 1981. Moreover, the cost of maintaining the Syrian forces in Lebanon after 1976 took up a significant part of the nation's financial resources.

Syria has suffered an economic recession since the early 1980s. This is reflected in the shortage of foodstuffs and other basic commodities, a scarcity of spare parts for machinery, and irregular electricity supply. Growing unemployment resulted from

INDUSTRY & MINERALS

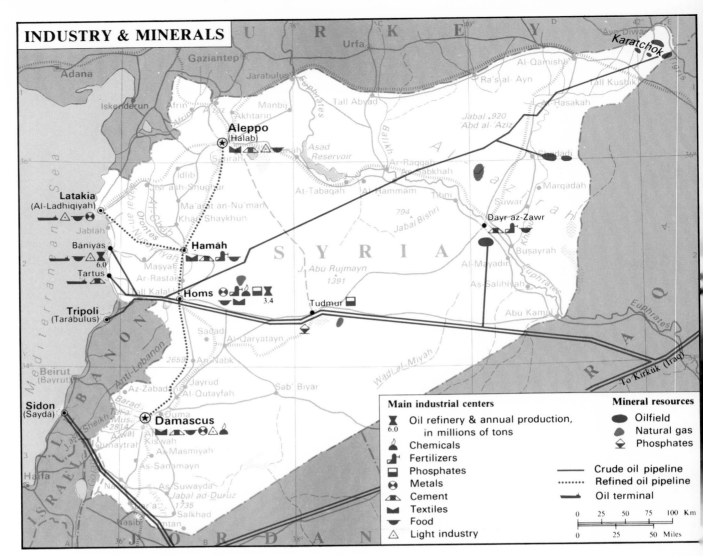

Main industrial centers

- ✕ Oil refinery & annual production, in millions of tons — 6.0
- ♨ Chemicals
- ⚒ Fertilizers
- ▭ Phosphates
- ⊗ Metals
- ▲ Cement
- ⊻ Textiles
- ▽ Food
- △ Light industry

Mineral resources

- ⬤ Oilfield
- ◖ Natural gas
- ⬦ Phosphates

—— Crude oil pipeline
········· Refined oil pipeline
⊢► Oil terminal

0 25 50 75 100 Km
0   25   50 Miles

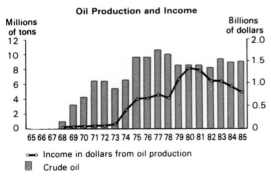

Oil Production and Income

Millions of tons — Billions of dollars

65 66 67 68 69 70 71 72 73 74 75 76 77 78 79 80 81 82 83 84 85

○— Income in dollars from oil production
▨ Crude oil

the paralysis of factories lacking the necessary funds for maintenance. Syria's support of Iran in the Iraq–Iran war caused the rich Arab oil states to end financial assistance. As a result, the economic and military dependency of Syria on the Soviet Union has greatly increased.

Agriculture The role of agriculture has declined in recent years. In 1965, agriculture contributed 32 percent to the GDP, employing 53 percent of the labor force. By 1985, the contribution to the GDP had decreased to 20 percent, with only 30 percent of the work force employed in agriculture.

The cultivable area stands at 15 million acres, or 32 percent of the country's land surface. Yields are largely dependent on rainfall due to the high percentage of dry-farming (90 percent of cultivated land). The agricultural lands are concentrated in a 62 mile (100 km) wide strip in the west, stretching from Damascus in the south to Aleppo in the north, and over much of the Syrian Jazīrah. The irrigated lands are mainly concentrated in the Damascus and Aleppo basins, the rift valley and the Jazīrah, where cultivation takes place along the Euphrates, Balīkh and Khābūr river valleys.

In recent years, Syria has attempted to extend the irrigated area. The construction of the at-Ṭabaqah Dam on the Euphrates river was completed in 1976. According to the five-year plan for 1986–1990, three additional dams are planned for the Khābūr river as well as a further dam on the Euphrates. Following their completion, it is estimated that the irrigated area in the Jazīrah will increase from 162,500 acres to 1,500,000 acres.

As a result of these efforts, production has indeed increased. However, it remains insufficient to meet the requirements of the domestic market. Syria is obliged to import agricultural produce, particularly grains and vegetables.

Most of Syria's cultivated area is devoted to wheat and barley crops. The most profitable commercial crop is cotton. In recent years, the area devoted to cotton cultivation has been expanded and efforts have been made to increase output (the output per unit area is now three times greater than in the early 1970s).

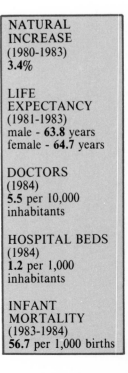

NATURAL INCREASE (1980–1983)
3.4%

LIFE EXPECTANCY (1981–1983)
male - **63.8** years
female - **64.7** years

DOCTORS (1984)
5.5 per 10,000 inhabitants

HOSPITAL BEDS (1984)
1.2 per 1,000 inhabitants

INFANT MORTALITY (1983–1984)
56.7 per 1,000 births

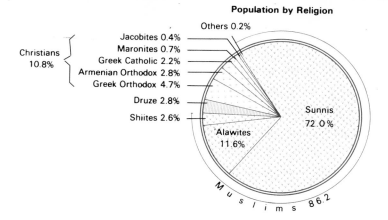

Population by Religion

Christians 10.8%
- Jacobites 0.4%
- Maronites 0.7%
- Greek Catholic 2.2%
- Armenian Orthodox 2.8%
- Greek Orthodox 4.7%

Druze 2.8%
Shiites 2.6%
Alawites 11.6%
Sunnis 72.0%
Others 0.2%

Muslims 86.2

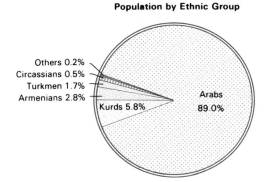

Population by Ethnic Group

- Others 0.2%
- Circassians 0.5%
- Turkmen 1.7%
- Armenians 2.8%
- Kurds 5.8%
- Arabs 89.0%

Sugar beet is another important crop. Sugar consumption per capita in Syria is among the highest in the world. Other important crops are grapes, beans, corn, potatoes, and tobacco.

Animal husbandry contributes to one-third of the total value of agricultural production and supplies most of the meat and dairy products to the local market. Extensive pasture areas are devoted to grazing. The livestock consists of sheep (13.5 million), cattle (770,000), and goats (1.2 million).

Minerals Syria has few minerals of commercial value, apart from petroleum. Oil production began in the Karatchok region in the northeast of the country in 1968. In the early 1980s, approximately 9 million tons of crude oil per year were produced from these fields. The quality of the oil is poor and is unsuitable for processing without the blend of higher-grade oil. Syria is therefore obliged to import the necessary oil for refining from Iran and the Persian Gulf countries.

In 1984, purer oil was discovered in the Dayr az-Zawr region in the east of the country. The reserves were estimated at 1.5 billion tons. Production at this field began in 1986 and it is estimated that eventually 7 million tons of crude oil per year will be produced. This will meet the domestic needs, leaving a surplus for export.

In the Jazīrah and Tudmur regions, natural gas reserves are estimated at 35 billion cubic meters. The gas produced from these fields — 135 million cubic meters per year — is used by local industry.

Since 1971, phosphates, used principally for the production of fertilizers, have been extracted at three locations in the Tudmur region. Reserves are estimated at 1 billion tons. In 1984, 1.5 million tons of phosphates were mined, most of which was exported.

Other minerals in Syria include salt deposits and natural asphalt, with annual outputs of 50,000 and 75,000 tons, respectively.

Industry Since the beginning of the 1970s, industry has played an increasingly important role in the country's economy. The proportion of the industrial work force has grown from 12 percent at the beginning of the 1960s to 25 percent in 1982. Since 1964, Syria has nationalized the large factories, leaving the smaller ones in private hands.

The most important industrial branch is oil refining. Approximately 9 million tons of refined products were produced at the refineries at Homs and Bāniyās in 1983. In the same year, the export of refined and crude oil accounted for $1.5 billion (75 percent of total exports) in revenue.

The processing of phosphates is the second most important industrial branch in terms of export revenues. The phosphate plants, located near the mines at Tudmur, have an annual production capacity of 1.2 million tons.

The traditional textile industry uses local cotton, producing goods mostly for the home market. Food processing of local agricultural produce takes place throughout the country. There are seven factories for sugar production (206,000 tons in 1983) and factories for the manufacture of vegetable oils.

Other industries include: cement manufacture, steel and iron, agricultural machinery, pesticides, paper, tobacco, and various consumer goods.

History Throughout most of its history, Syria had been within the sphere of large empires and states. In the seventh century, the 'Umayyad dynasty ruled in Syria, establishing its capital at Damascus.

Syria was part of the Ottoman Empire until the end of World War I. In 1918, Syria was conquered by the British army. In accordance with the decisions taken by the Allied forces at the San Remo Conference in 1920, Syria was transferred to French rule. The French attempted to modernize Syria, but were resisted by the country's nationalists. The constant tension between the French and Syrians occasionally erupted into violence.

After the surrender of France to Germany early in World War II, Syria was controlled by the pro-German Vichy government. This brought about the invasion of Syria by British and Free French forces. Following their conquest of Syria, control was transferred to the Free French government which granted Syria its independence. The French regime, however, continued to intervene in affairs of state. When at last parliamentary elections were held in 1943, the National Bloc triumphed, and its leader, Shukri al-Kuwatli, was elected president. The French left Syria in April 1946.

In 1948–1949, Syria — together with Lebanon, Jordan, Iraq, and Egypt — went to war against Israel. In 1949, two military coups took place

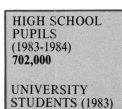

HIGH SCHOOL PUPILS (1983-1984) **702,000**

UNIVERSITY STUDENTS (1983) **113,000**

LITERACY RATE (1983) **50%**

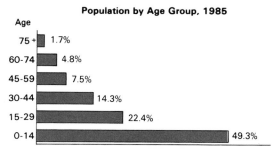

Population by Age Group, 1985

Age
- 75+ : 1.7%
- 60-74 : 4.8%
- 45-59 : 7.5%
- 30-44 : 14.3%
- 15-29 : 22.4%
- 0-14 : 49.3%

in Syria, the second of which resulted in the imposition of a tyrannical regime led by Adib ash-Shishakli. He dissolved all parties except his own. Shishakli was deposed in 1954 by a group of army officers who reestablished civilian government and renewed party activity.

Early in 1958, the country's leaders, members of the Ba'th party (proponents of pan-Arab unity) signed a resolution in favor of union with Egypt. (Yemen also joined as a minor partner.) This union was known as the United Arab Republic. It proved a bitter disappointment, particularly among nationalist groups who saw Egypt gaining control of Syria's internal affairs. In 1961, the government was overthrown by a military coup and the unification treaty was abolished.

Syria continued to suffer from political instability. In 1962 and 1963, two more revolts took place. Yet another coup in 1966 resulted in the overthrow of the veteran leadership of the Ba'th party. It was replaced by an extreme leftist faction of the party headed by General Salah al-Jadid.

In June 1967, following a year of tension along the border, war again broke out between Syria and Israel. The Syrian army was defeated and was forced to retreat from the "Golan Heights" to a line 40 miles (65 km) from Damascus. The military defeat led to internal political struggles, eventually bringing the 'Alawite General Hafiz al-Asad to power. He removed his opponents from all positions of control and influence.

In March 1971, Asad was elected Syria's president. In his new role, Asad worked to improve the country's economy and to bring about political stability. Income from petroleum and phosphate exports contributed greatly to industrial and agricultural development, as well as to the expansion of the country's infrastructure and the general improvement in living standards.

In October 1973, Syria — in coordination with Egypt — again went to war with Israel. Despite some initial military gains, Syria was unsuccessful in its attempt to recover the "Golan Heights,"
conquered by Israel in 1967.

In June 1976, President Asad dispatched Syrian forces to Lebanon following appeals from the Lebanese president, Suleiman Franjiyeh, to help end the civil war in his country. The Syrian army has remained in Lebanon since, with the Syrian government involved in Lebanon's multifactional disputes, as mediator or as supporter of one of the factions.

Since 1976, unrest has increased between the majority Sunni population and the minority 'Alawite government headed by Asad. The conflict between the religious communities is focused on the mixed residential areas in Latakia, Homs, Ḥamāh, Aleppo, and Damascus. Between 1977 and 1982, the 'Alawites were attacked, causing military reaction against the Sunni population. The repression of the Sunnis came to a head in February 1982, when thousands of Sunni Muslims — many of whom were members of the Muslim Brotherhood — were murdered in Ḥamāh. At the beginning of 1985, the Sunni unrest was diffused following presidential permission to return hundreds of the Muslim Brotherhood supporters to Syria.

The Israeli invasion of Lebanon in 1982 led to military clashes between Syria and Israel on Lebanon's territory. Following three months of sporadic fighting, the Syrian army was obliged to withdraw to a confined area in northeast and north Lebanon. Following Israel's withdrawal from most of Lebanon, the Syrian army returned to the areas it had occupied prior to June 1982.

Government and Politics At the head of government stands the president who is elected by a referendum every seven years. The president has unlimited powers and is assisted by three deputies, all of whom are appointed by him. The president also appoints the government ministers who are responsible for the daily administration of state affairs. In February 1985, Hafiz al-Asad was elected by absolute majority to serve for a third term as president. There is a legislative chamber (the People's Council) comprising 195 representatives who are elected in general elections every four years. In practice, the People's Council serves as a rubber stamp for decisions already taken by the country's leaders. Members of the People's Council theoretically represent the whole spectrum of political parties operating in the country. At the elections to the People's Council in March 1986, however, the Ba'th party won 129 seats, the remaining 66 mandates being divided among the other parties.

Asad's regime is based on support from the 'Alawi community. Members of this sect occupy important leadership positions in the government, the Ba'th party, the army, and the security services.

Syria's relations with her neighbors — Jordan, Turkey, and Iraq — have a tendency to shift and remain unstable. There has been a continuous dispute between the Syrian Ba'th party and the Ba'th party in Iraq over ideological issues as well as over the exploitation of waters from the river Euphrates. Syria also has a dispute with Turkey regarding territorial claims and water resources.

Since May 1974, quiet has prevailed along the cease-fire line between Syria and Israel. Syria's support of Iran in its war with Iraq had led to a worsening of relations with some of the Arab states in the Persian Gulf. As a result, the amount of financial aid to Syria has been reduced.

Syria's ties with the Soviet Union are strong. Since 1955, the Soviet Union has consistently supplied Syria with substantial military aid, and has become its major economic and political backer.

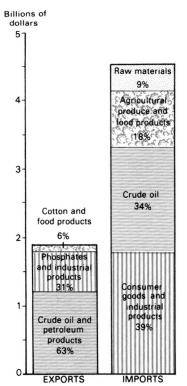

Trade Balance, 1983

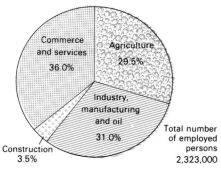

Employment by Economic Branch, 1983

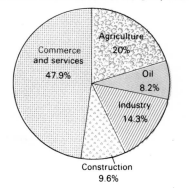

Economic Branch as Part of the GDP, 1985

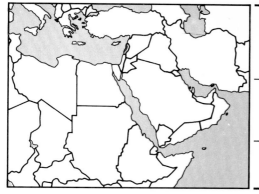

LEBANON

Area **4,035 sq. miles (10,452 sq.km)**
Population (1985 estimate) **2,750,000**
Capital city **Beirut**
Gross domestic product (GDP) per capita (1984) **$1,500**

Population in main cities (1984 estimates)	Beirut 800,000 Tripoli 160,000 Sidon 100,000	Zahlah 45,000

Lebanon's name derives from Mount Lebanon, the principal geographical feature in the country. Lebanon is on the East Mediterranean coast, and borders on Syria to the east and north and Israel to the south.

Topography Lebanon is part of the "Levant" geographical region, together with Syria and Israel. The country comprises four parallel natural regions with a north–south alignment: the coastal strip, the western mountains, the Lebanon (Beqa'a) valley (part of the Syrian-African Rift) and the eastern mountains.

The coastal strip is mostly narrow, the width ranging from only hundreds of feet to 6 miles (10 km). There are fertile alluvial soils in the wider sections of the coastal strip. Along the coast are a number of capes which penetrate into the sea. The cities of Beirut and Tripoli are located on two of these capes. The town of Tyre is located on an island that has become connected to the mainland.

The western mountains consist of two mountain ranges. The northern section — the Mount Lebanon range — occupies most of the country's land surface, stretching from the al-Kabīr river (at Lebanon's northern border with Syria) to the Litāni river in the south. The mountain ridge, which is mostly built of limestone, is a plateau above which rise high peaks (the highest being at Qurnat as-Sawdā (10,130 ft [3,087 meters]). The western slopes of Mount Lebanon have a gentle gradient and are rich in water resources.

The southern section — the Lebanon Galilee — stretches south of the Litāni river to the border with Israel. This region is lower than Mount Lebanon and is incised by many small streams. Geographically, this region is an extension of the Israeli Galilee. The highest peak is Marūn ar-Ra's (3,050 ft [930 meters]) in the southeast of the region, near the border with Israel.

The Lebanon valley (the Beqa'a) is the highest

section of the Syrian-African Rift valley in the Levant area, with an average width of 6–12 miles (10–20 km). Although heights reach 3,675 ft (1,120 meters) near Ba'albek, this region is 3,280 ft (1,000 meters) lower than the surrounding mountains, which enclose the valley with their steep slopes. Part of the Beqa'a is an undulating plain, but most of the region is hilly. The main watershed of the Lebanon valley is near Ba'albek. From this point, the al-'Asi river begins its northward course, while the river Litāni flows in a southerly direction. The southern section of the Beqa'a receives more precipitation than the northern region; it has many springs and fertile soils.

The eastern mountain region consists of the western slopes of the Anti-Lebanon and the Mount Hermon slopes. These two mountain ranges are separated from each other by the Zabadāni valley, which is crossed by the Baradā river flowing toward Damascus. The peaks of both the Anti-Lebanon and the Hermon are in Syria.

Climate Lebanon has a Mediterranean climate, with a hot summer and temperate winter. In the coastal plain the average temperature in the hottest month (August) is 77° F. (25° C.), decreasing to 55° F. (13° C.) in the coldest month (January). In Mount Lebanon, temperatures are influenced by the altitude. At heights of 6,560 ft (2,000 meters), the average August temperature is 61° F. (16° C.), declining to 39° F. (4° C.) in January. The Beqa'a valley is hotter, with an average August temperature of 72° F. (22° C.), declining to 45° F. (7° C.) in January.

The rainy season lasts from October until April. Annual precipitation totals 20 in (500 mm) in the coastal strip. The western mountains receive 50 in (1,200 mm) of rain, increasing to 67–80 in (1,700–2,000 mm) at the peaks. The Beqa'a valley receives from 10 in (250 mm) in the north and approximately 23 in (580 mm) in the south. On the peaks of the Hermon and the Anti-Lebanon, which are not protected from the westerly rain-bearing winds, annual precipitation totals 31–40 in (800–1,000 mm). The eastern slopes of these mountains are arid.

Population Because of the highly sensitive nature of demographic issues and the balance between communities, no population census has been carried out in Lebanon since 1932. Population data are therefore based on estimates. Approximately 51 percent of the inhabitants are Muslims and 42 percent are Christians. In ethnic terms, 90 percent of the population are Arabs; 6 percent, Armenians; 1.5 percent Kurds, and the remainder Circassians and Europeans.

In terms of the religious composition, Lebanon's population is fragmented to a greater extent than any other country in the Middle East. There is much antagonism between the communities, often

Land Use, 1984

Irrigated crop land 8.1%

Built-up and non productive areas 63.6%

Dry-farmed crop land 20.5%

Grazing land 1.0%

Cultivated land 736,400 acres

Forest 6.8%

Climate

RAINFALL AND TEMPERATURE

Annual temperature

Average monthly rainfall

8.6 in — Total annual rainfall

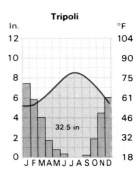

Tripoli

32.5 in

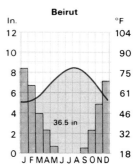

Beirut

36.5 in

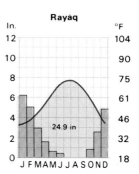

Rayāq

24.9 in

erupting in violent clashes. Until the 1970s, the Christian communities formed a majority of the population. But as a result of the higher birthrate among the Muslim inhabitants and the extensive outmigration of Christians leaving Lebanon, the Muslims have become the largest religious community.

The Muslim population is divided into Shiite (28 percent of the total population) and Sunni Muslims (23 percent). The Christian community includes Maronites (25 percent), Greek Orthodox (7 percent), Greek Catholics (3 percent), Armenian Orthodox (5 percent), Armenian Catholics (1 percent), and a small number of Protestants and Assyrian Christians. The Druze form an additional religious community with 6 percent of the population. There are also a few hundred Jews and Bahais.

Approximately 250,000 inhabitants are Pales-

tinian refugees who do not possess Lebanese citizenship. These refugees, mostly Sunni Muslims, arrived in Lebanon in 1948. The large majority are concentrated in refugee camps throughout the country, while a minority live in towns and villages.

Most of the communities are concentrated within well-defined geographical areas. The Shiites reside mostly in the south, in the north of the Beqa'a valley, in the towns of Tripoli and Sidon, and in West Beirut. Most of the Maronites live in the north of Mount Lebanon, while most of the Sunnis are concentrated in the north of the country, especially in the coastal cities, particularly Tripoli. Most of the Druze are concentrated in the southern half of Mount Lebanon and in the Mount Hermon area. The Armenian, Greek Catholic, Greek Orthodox, and other Christian communities are all concentrated in the large cities.

Since the mid-1970s, there has been an unceasing

NATURAL
INCREASE
(1980–1983)
2.2%

LIFE
EXPECTANCY
(1980–1985)
male - **65.0** years
female - **68.9** years

DOCTORS
(1982)
11.3 per 10,000
inhabitants

HOSPITAL BEDS
(1982)
4.3 per 1,000
inhabitants

INFANT
MORTALITY
(1983–1984)
48.0 per 1,000 births

flow of migrants leaving the country. It is estimated that between 1980 and 1985, Lebanon's population decreased by approximately 300,000.

Economy Lebanon's economy is based on the service sector, which contributes approximately 70 percent to the GDP. Until the outbreak of the civil war in 1975, Lebanon — and especially the city of Beirut — was the most important financial center of the Arab Middle East. A large portion of the oil revenues from the Persian Gulf countries passed through Lebanon's highly developed banking system. The free trade area of Beirut attracted capital and commerce from the Middle East and the rest of the world. Until 1975, Beirut's sea and air ports were the most important transport nodes in the region. Tourism was also an important economic activity. The liberal atmosphere and the mountainous topography, suited to both summer and winter tourism, made Lebanon the holiday and entertainment center of the whole Arab world. Approximately 2 million tourists annually visited Lebanon.

To a certain extent, Lebanon's economy was successful because of the weakness of the central government, whose intervention in economic affairs was minimal. This situation enabled the private sector to control the country's economy.

The civil war led to an economic recession which has continued until the present time (1988). The service sector has been particularly damaged. The city of Beirut has been destroyed, the tourism and entertainment centers have collapsed, the Beirut port has been paralyzed and the airport has lost its importance. Thousands of inhabitants who previously administered the country's commercial, banking, and other financial services have left the country.

Agriculture Despite the fact that most of the country receives enough rain for dry-farming, only 29 percent of the total area, approximately 736,400 acres, are cultivated. Of this, 210,000 acres are irrigated. This is largely due to the mountainous nature of the country; cultivation takes place only where the gradient of the slopes is gentle or by means of terracing. Because of the large differences in height, agricultural produce is extremely varied. In the coastal plain, citrus fruit, subtropical fruit, cotton, sugar cane, and fodder are grown. In the mountain lowlands, olives, tobacco, and grapes are the principal crops, while in the upland areas apples, pears, and cherries are grown. Most of the area devoted to fodder crops is in the Beqa'a valley, where grapes and fruit trees are also cultivated.

Until 1975, Lebanon exported much of its agricultural produce to Middle Eastern countries, especially to Syria and Saudi Arabia. Following the outbreak of the civil war, this export ceased, but a limited amount of agricultural products is again being exported.

Minerals Few natural mineral resources have been discovered in Lebanon. Iron ore is produced

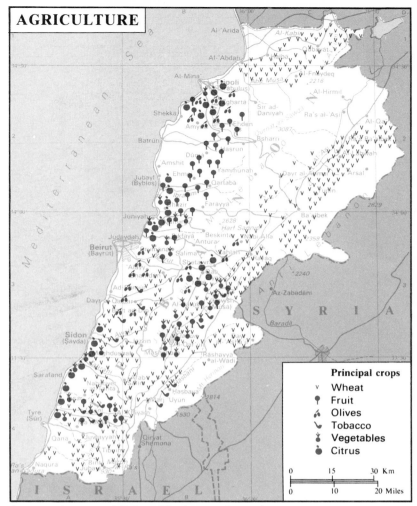

AGRICULTURE

Principal crops
- v Wheat
- Fruit
- Olives
- Tobacco
- Vegetables
- Citrus

| 0 | 15 | 30 Km |
| 0 | 10 | 20 Miles |

from a mine east of Beirut. The low-grade ore is processed in a factory near Beirut. Other minerals, which are not economically viable, include brown coal (lignite), copper, asphalt, phosphates, and additional iron ore deposits.

Industry The lack of local raw materials has limited any widespread industrial development. Heavy industry includes two oil refineries (at Tripoli and in the Zahrani delta near Sidon) and cement plants. The refinery at Tripoli receives crude oil through pipelines from Iraq and Syria. The refinery at Zahrani receives oil from an ocean-based oil terminal. The maximum production capacity of both refineries is 2.5 million tons per year, destined for local consumption. The cement manufacturing plants and other components of the construction industry were developed during the economic boom that existed before 1975. The cement industry is the only sector to use local raw materials. Lebanon also has textiles, clothing, food, cigarette, wood, leather, and plastic factories. Factories specializing in the production of paper, cosmetics, and medicines were established in the 1980s.

Approximately 80 percent of the industrial enterprises are concentrated in Beirut and its environs, with the remainder in Tripoli, Sidon, and ad-Damūr. The civil war severely damaged the industrial infrastructure, resulting in the destruction of one-third of the factories. During the war and its immediate aftermath, tens of thousands of industrial workers migrated to the oil-rich Persian Gulf states. There was also a decline in the amount of capital investment in industry.

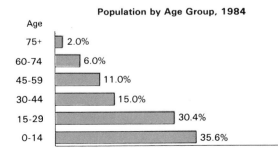

Population by Age Group, 1984

Age
- 75+ : 2.0%
- 60-74 : 6.0%
- 45-59 : 11.0%
- 30-44 : 15.0%
- 15-29 : 30.4%
- 0-14 : 35.6%

HIGH SCHOOL PUPILS (1981-1982) **254,000**

UNIVERSITY STUDENTS (1981) **70,000**

LITERACY RATE (1980) **79%**

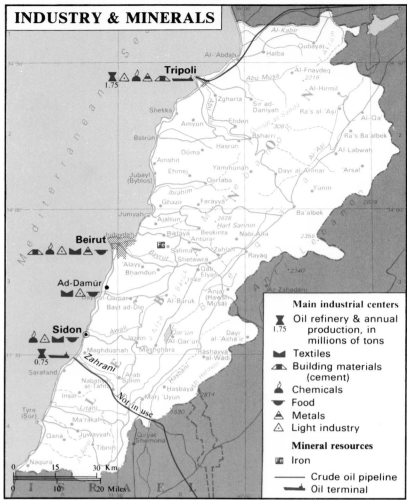

Main industrial centers

⊠ Oil refinery & annual production, in millions of tons
1.75

◰ Textiles

◭ Building materials (cement)

⬙ Chemicals

▼ Food

△ Metals

△ Light industry

Mineral resources

Fe Iron

—— Crude oil pipeline

⊷ Oil terminal

History Lebanon's independent status has its roots in the autonomous district that existed within the Ottoman Empire between 1861 and 1914. This district was created as a result of the favorable response by the Turks to the requests by Britain, France, Austria, and Prussia to grant autonomy to the Mount Lebanon region because of the Maronite Christian majority. Autonomy was designed to bring an end to the ceaseless bloodshed between Christians and Druze during 1837–1858. This district became known as Little Lebanon and was ruled by a governor who was appointed by the Ottoman government.

At the termination of World War I, Lebanon was conquered by the British army. At the San Remo Conference in 1920, Lebanon and Syria were transferred to French mandate control. The French established separate governments in Lebanon and Syria. Within Lebanon's territory they included the Tripoli region in the north, the Beqa'a valley in the east, the coastal plain (including Beirut) in the west and the area of south Lebanon. As a result of this territorial expansion, the Christian majority was greatly reduced. Large numbers of Muslims resided in the newly annexed regions. In 1926, Lebanon formulated a constitution, laying down the principle of community size as determinant of representation in the government institutions.

Under French rule, Lebanon's economy experienced a boom and Beirut began to establish itself as an important commercial center. The administrative networks were improved, the education system was expanded, and many new roads were built.

In July 1941, British and Free French forces captured Lebanon from the representatives of the Vichy regime (the French government that collaborated with Nazi Germany). The French promised to grant Lebanon its independence, but this was conditional on continued French intervention in security and foreign affairs. The Lebanese nationalists refused to accept these conditions, and the granting of independence was delayed until 1945–1946, when France withdrew its military forces from Lebanon.

In 1943, before independence, the leaders of the major communities — the Maronite Christians headed by Bishara al-Khouri and the Sunni Muslims headed by Riyad al-Sulh — reached an unwritten understanding concerning the principles for the establishment of an independent state. This agreement became known as the National Pact and determined the allocation of government posts according to the following key: president — Maronite; prime minister — Sunni Muslim; president of Parliament — Shiite Muslim. It was also determined that Lebanon constituted part of the Arab world. This was later reflected in Lebanon's role as a founder member of the Arab League in 1945 and its participation — together with Syria, Jordan, Iraq, and Egypt — in the war against Israel in 1948.

Between 1943 and 1952, Bishara al-Khouri served as president. Khouri did not initiate much development, and he was forced to resign in 1948. In his place, Camille Chamoun was elected as president. At first, Chamoun enjoyed widespread support among the various communities. Despite this, Lebanon became embroiled in an internal struggle and a civil war in 1958. This was due to Chamoun's pro-Western policy at a time when large sectors of the population — particularly the Muslims — were becoming increasingly pan-Arabic and anti-Western in their outlook. It became apparent that Lebanon's independence was in danger, and Chamoun turned to the United States for assistance to ensure the country's continued existence. America dispatched military forces to Lebanon and the civil war was terminated in September 1958. Subsequently, Chamoun and his supporters were deposed. In his place, the Lebanese commander-in-chief, General Fu'ad Shihab, was chosen as president.

Shihab's internal policy resulted in an increased role for the non-Christians in the administrative institutions and in the development of backward regions, especially the south of the country where the Shiite Muslims formed the large majority of the population. In 1964, Charles Hilou was elected as president. He continued to implement the policies of his predecessor. Internal political stability enabled Lebanon to become a commercial and financial center for the Arab Middle East during the 1960s. As part of the efforts to preserve internal stability, Lebanon refrained from participating in the Six-Day War of 1967 against Israel.

During the 1960s, Palestinian terrorist organizations began to take root in Lebanon. They refused to accept the authority of the central government, taking over the Palestinian refugee camps and transforming them into military bases. By the end of the 1960s, all of south Lebanon near the Israeli border was under their control. Their strength grew during 1970–1971 when the terrorists expelled from Jordan arrived in Lebanon. The Lebanese government did not implement a hardline policy to impose its rule on these groups, not least because it feared a hostile response from the Muslim population, which could result

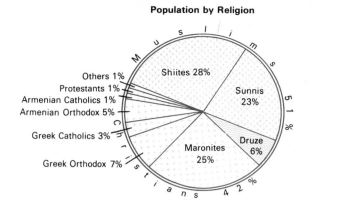

Population by Religion

Muslims 51%
Christians 42%

Shiites 28%
Sunnis 23%
Druze 6%
Maronites 25%
Greek Orthodox 7%
Greek Catholics 3%
Armenian Orthodox 5%
Armenian Catholics 1%
Protestants 1%
Others 1%

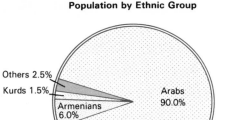

Population by Ethnic Group

Arabs 90.0%
Armenians 6.0%
Kurds 1.5%
Others 2.5%

in a weakening of internal stability. In addition to the terrorists, there were also armed militias who operated outside the government framework. In 1975, clashes between the terrorists and the Christian militias took place in Beirut. In January 1976, the fighting spread throughout the country, turning into a civil war during which Lebanon's social and economic infrastructure was destroyed.

In 1976, Syria intervened in the struggle in an attempt to bring an end to the fighting and to impose new political arrangements. The Syrian army conquered most of Lebanon's territory, except for the region near the border with Israel. Despite the subsequent calming down in the civil war, clashes between the terrorist organizations continued.

In March 1978, following an increase in terrorist operations against Israel, the latter invaded south Lebanon, advancing as far as the Lītānī river. After three months, the Israelis withdrew, being replaced by a United Nations force. A narrow strip along the Israeli border remained under the control of the local Christian residents, who were supported by Israel. Nevertheless, acts of terror against Israel continued to take place until, in July 1981, an informal cease-fire was reached between Israel and the terrorists.

In June 1982 Israel violated the cease-fire when it invaded Lebanon with the intention of destroying the extensive terrorist military infrastructure that threatened the border with Lebanon. Israel conquered south Lebanon as far as the Beirut-Damascus road. Beirut, in which thousands of terrorists were concentrated, was placed under siege. After two months of this siege, the terrorists were forced to evacuate Beirut and leave Lebanon altogether. During the siege, the Lebanese Parliament elected a new president, Bashir Jumayyil. Two weeks after his election, he was assassinated and was replaced by his brother, Amin Jumayyil. The Israeli army remained in Lebanon until June 1985. Israel continues to support the Christian forces who control the border strip.

The Israeli military presence in Lebanon did not prevent the continued intercommunity fighting. In April 1984, the fighting subsided and a national unity government, headed by Rashid Karameh, was formed. He filled the position of prime minister until he was assassinated in June 1987. The leaders of all the major communities and factions were represented in this government. With Syrian mediation, the government endeavored to attain internal political stability. But at present (1988), mutual terrorist operations continue to take place between the various militias in Beirut and elsewhere in the country.

Government and Politics The republic of Lebanon is headed by a president, who holds wide-ranging powers. He is assisted by a cabinet that he appoints. The president is chosen by the legislature every five years. The whole political system is based on the allocation of posts according to community affiliation. The president has to be a Maronite Christian, the prime minister a Sunni Muslim, and the president of Parliament a Shiite Muslim. The 99 representatives in the legislature are chosen in constituency elections held every four years. The allocation of seats in the Parliament is also carried out according to the relative power of the communities: Maronites — 30; Sunni Muslims — 20; Shiite Muslims — 19; Greek Orthodox — 11; Greek Catholics — 6; Druze — 6; Armenians — 4; Armenian Catholics, Protestants, and other communities — 1 representative each.

Since 1975, Lebanon has, to all intents and purposes, ceased to exist as an independent political unit. The country is split between the various communities who, in turn, are divided among themselves. The central government is, in effect, under Syrian protection and is unable to impose its authority on the population.

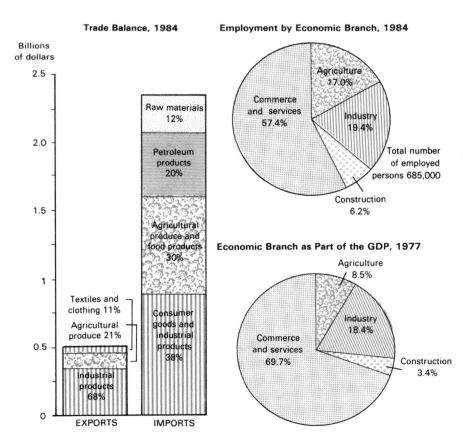

Trade Balance, 1984

Billions of dollars

EXPORTS:
Textiles and clothing 11%
Agricultural produce 21%
Industrial products 68%

IMPORTS:
Raw materials 12%
Petroleum products 20%
Agricultural produce and food products 30%
Consumer goods and industrial products 38%

Employment by Economic Branch, 1984

Commerce and services 57.4%
Agriculture 17.0%
Industry 19.4%
Construction 6.2%

Total number of employed persons 685,000

Economic Branch as Part of the GDP, 1977

Commerce and services 69.7%
Agriculture 8.5%
Industry 18.4%
Construction 3.4%

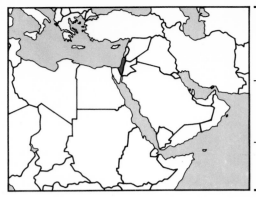

ISRAEL

Area 7,992 sq. miles (20,700 sq.km)
Population (1986 estimate) **4,423,000**
Capital city **Jerusalem**
Gross domestic product (GDP) per capita (1984) **$5,700**

Population in main cities (1986 estimates)	Jerusalem 457,000 Tel Aviv 322,000 Haifa 224,000	Holon 139,000 Bat Yam 131,000 Petah Tiqwa 129,000	Ramat Gan 116,000 Be'er Sheva' 115,000

Israel is bordered by the Mediterranean to the west, Lebanon to the north, Syria and Jordan to the east, and Egypt to the south. Israel also controls territories captured during the Six-Day War in 1967, including the Golan Heights captured from Syria (425 sq. miles [1,100 sq.km]), Judea and Samaria (the West Bank) captured from Jordan (2,297 sq. miles [5,950 sq.km]), and the Gaza Strip captured from Egypt (139 sq. miles [360 sq.km]). With the exception of East Jerusalem and the Golan Heights, these regions have not been formally annexed to Israel.

Topography Israel consists of three natural regions that extend in a north–south direction: the coastal plain, the highlands, and the Jordan and 'Arava valleys.

The coastal plain is 137 miles (220 km) long. The average width of this region is 25–31 miles (40–50 km) in the south, narrowing as one goes north. Near Mount Carmel and at Rosh HaNiqra, the mountains almost reach the coastline. The coastal plain is covered partly by sand dunes and partly by alluvial soils. Until the 1930s, large areas — particularly in the central coastal plain — were covered by swamps which were later drained by Jewish settlers.

The highlands extend over much of Israel. The mountains are built mainly of limestone and chalk. They are divided into three major sections, separated by valleys: the Galilee mountains in the

north; the Judea and Samaria mountains in the center; and the Negev hills in the south.

The average height of the Upper Galilee mountains in the north is approximately 2,950 ft (900 meters), descending to 1,640 ft (500 meters) in Lower Galilee to the south. The western slopes have a gentle gradient, while the eastern slopes have steep inclines. The Galilee is deeply dissected by valleys running east to west. Parts of eastern Galilee are covered by basalt.

The Jezreel valley, covered by a thick layer of fertile alluvial soil, lies between the Galilee and Samaria mountains. This valley affords easy access from the coastal plain to the Jordan valley. Mount Carmel, an extension of the Samarian mountains, rises steeply to the southwest of the Jezreel valley.

The Judea and Samaria mountains are actually one continuous mountain chain from north to south, 80 miles (130 km) long with an average width of 25–31 miles (40–50 km) and an average height of 2,460 ft (750 meters). The highest peak is Mount Ba'al Hazor at 3,333 ft (1,016 meters). The mountains are incised by many streams, most of which are often dry. As in the Galilee mountains to the north, the western slopes have a gentle incline, while the eastern slopes are steep. In the south, the Judean mountains slope toward the 'Arad and Be'er Sheva' valleys.

The Negev hills consist of a series of ranges with steep southeasterly slopes and gentle northwesterly

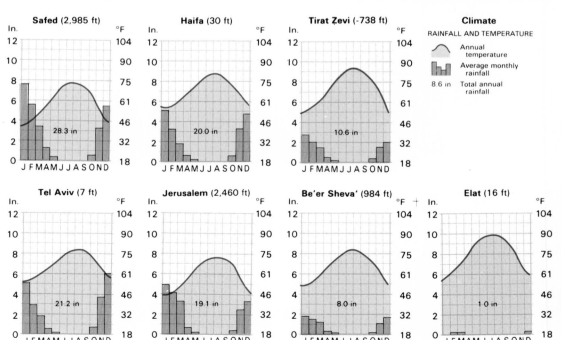

slopes. A unique geomorphological feature in this region is the craters that were formed by the erosion of upward-folded strata. The craters are approximately 6–19 miles (10–30 km) long and up to 3 miles (1–5 km) wide. They are surrounded on all sides by precipitous slopes. On their eastern side is an opening, through which the craters are drained into the 'Arava. Hard crystalline and metamorphic rocks, making up the northern margins of the Sinai Peninsula mountains, are exposed in the southern Negev. The Negev is a desert region and its streams have little if any water.

The Jordan and 'Arava valleys form the lowest part of the Syrian-African Rift valley. Much of this region is below sea level. The river Jordan flows through the Jordan valley from the Sea of Galilee (Lake Kinneret) in the north into the Dead Sea — the lowest point on earth (1,319 ft [402 meters] below sea level) — in the south.

The Golan Heights, in the northeast, are covered mostly by basalt. The steep western slopes descend to the Jordan valley. In the north is Mount Hermon, the peak of which is in Syria. The highest point of Mount Hermon within Israel is 7,218 ft (2,200 meters).

Climate Most of the country has a Mediterranean climate. Summers are hot, and the coastal region is very humid. Rain falls only in the winter, with temperate conditions in the coastal region and lower temperatures in the mountains.

The south of the country (the Negev and the 'Arava) experiences arid conditions. The summer is extremely hot while the winter is mild. In this area there is a large diurnal temperature range. There is limited rainfall in the winter months.

The average temperature in the hottest month (August) is 81° F. (27° C.) in the coastal plain, 73° F. (23° C.) in the mountains, 79° F. (26° C.) in the Negev, and 90° F. (32° C.) in the south and the 'Arava. The average temperatures in the coldest month (January) are 57° F. (14° C.) in the coastal plain, 46° F. (8° C.) in the mountains, 52° F. (11° C.) in the Negev, and 59° F. (15° C.) in Elat in the south.

The rainy season lasts from the beginning of October until May. Most of the rain falls between December and February. The average precipitation total is approximately 20 in (520 mm) per year in the coastal plain. In the highland region and the Jordan and 'Arava valleys, precipitation decreases toward the south. Approximately 28 in (700 mm) of rain falls in the Galilee, 20 in (500 mm) in Judea and Samaria, and less than 4 in (100 mm) in the Negev. The northern section of the Jordan valley receives approximately 16 in (400 mm) of rain, decreasing to less than 4 in (100 mm) in the 'Arava to the south. The Golan Heights receive 26 in (650 mm) of rain per year.

Population of Israel The overwhelming majority of Israel's citizens (82.5%) are Jewish, the remainder are mostly Arabs, and there is also a small Circassian community. The religious affiliations of the non-Jewish population are divided into three principal groups: Muslims, Christians, and Druze.

The Muslims, nearly all of whom are Sunni Muslims, make up 13.5 percent of the total population. The Christians comprise approximately 2.3 percent and are divided into a number of communities, the largest being the Greek Catholics, the Greek Orthodox, and the Roman Catholics. The Druze are the third largest religious community, comprising approximately 1.7 percent of the population. Most Druze live in eighteen villages in the Galilee and Mount Carmel, a minority re-

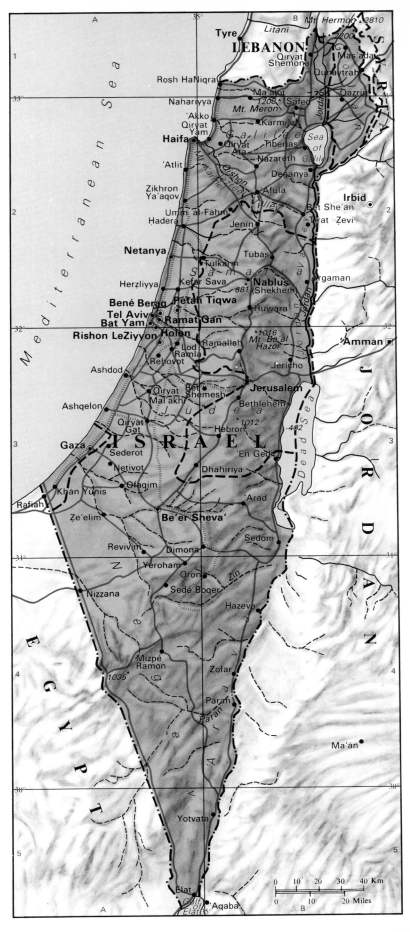

siding in four villages in the Golan Heights. There are also a few hundred Bahais and Samaritans (descendants of Israelites of the eighth century BCE who maintain their own ritual).

Approximately 89 percent of Israel's citizens live in urban settlements, 9.4 percent live in villages, and 1.6 percent are seminomads, belonging to 36 Bedouin tribes. Most of Israel's inhabitants (75 percent) are concentrated in the coastal plain.

Population of Judea, Samaria, and the Gaza Strip The inhabitants of Judea and Samaria who are not Israeli citizens numbered 813,400 in 1985, while the number of non-Israeli citizens living in the Gaza Strip totaled 525,500. Virtually all of them are Sunni Muslims. Since 1968, and especially since 1977, Jewish settlements have also been established in these areas, totaling 46,000 residents in 1985.

Economy Shortly following the establishment of the State of Israel, the country underwent rapid economic development. In 1955, the per capita GDP was $2,025, rising to $4,952 by 1972. The major factors for the rapid economic growth were the mass immigration, which included experienced professional workers and entrepreneurs with capital to invest; economic assistance from the United States and other countries; and the receipt of reparations from Germany as payment for the confiscation of Jewish property in Europe during World War II. The Six-Day War of 1967 resulted in further economic development, not least because of the economic link established between Israel and the territories captured during the war. Growth principally took place in industry, construction, and the service sector.

As a result of the Yom Kippur War of 1973 and the sharp rise in oil prices, economic development slowed down. Fewer resources were invested in development (especially in industry) while the national debt increased substantially.

Since 1985, there has been an improvement in the economic situation. The national debt has been reduced, the amount of capital channeled into development has increased, while public expenditure has declined. This improvement was partly due to the economic assistance Israel received from the United States. This foreign aid, which has increased in recent years, totaled approximately $3 billion in 1985.

Agriculture Agriculture in Israel cannot be discussed only in economic terms. The development of Jewish agricultural laborers was an important component of Zionism ever since the earliest Jewish settlements were established at the end of the nineteenth century. At the beginning of the twentieth century, unique forms of cooperative farming were created. Most of the agricultural farm units are organized on a cooperative basis, accounting

for two-thirds of the Jewish farmers. There are 267 kibbutzim (settlements based on complete collective ownership) and 405 moshavim (partial collective ownership) in Israel. The agricultural sector employs 6.5 percent of the labor force and contributes 6 percent to the GDP (1985).

The arable land is limited. Approximately half of Israel's land surface is desert, while in other areas there are problems of soil quality, limited water resources, and a topography that precludes modern farming methods. Despite these limitations, the cultivated area increased threefold between 1949 and 1979, covering 1 million acres. This increase was largely due to the transformation from dry-farming to irrigation. Since 1964, the irrigated areas have greatly benefited from the completion of the "National Water Carrier," which transports water from the Sea of Galilee in the north to the south of the country. In 1985, 940,000 acres were cultivated, 70 percent of which were irrigated.

The agricultural sector uses modern farming techniques, and new hybrid crops. Farmers also have access to advanced systems of planning, research, and marketing. These have resulted in a diversified crop structure and a significant increase in the agricultural output destined for export. Most of the cultivated area provides field crops (barley, wheat, and fodder) for the livestock economy. Other important crops are vegetables, citrus fruits, cotton, and flowers.

The livestock economy is among the most advanced in the world. Output is extremely high. Of particular importance are poultry, dairy farming, sheep, and cattle.

Despite the variety of agricultural produce, Israel is nevertheless obliged to import food, including seeds, sugar, and raw materials for the vegetable oil industry.

Minerals Israel is poor in mineral resources. The most important natural mineral resources are concentrated in the Dead Sea and the surrounding region. Potassium, bromine, manganese, and a variety of salts for the chemical industry are all procured from the Dead Sea. Southwest of the Dead Sea are phosphate deposits, which are mined at Oron. Until 1975, Israel also mined copper at Timna, north of Elat.

Commercially viable petroleum was discovered in 1955 at the Ḥeleẓ field in the southern coastal plain, supplying approximately 12,500 tons of crude oil per year (0.25 percent of domestic consumption). Most of the imported crude oil is processed at the refineries in Haifa, with an annual capacity of over 6 million tons.

Near the Dead Sea (at Rosh Zohar and Kidod) are natural gas fields, producing approximately 73 million cubic meters per year. Most of the gas is piped to the potassium production plant at Sedom and the phosphate plant at Oron.

Industry Israel's industrial sector was first developed by Jewish immigrants from Europe during the 1930s. During the first few years following the establishment of the state, the industrial sector underwent a period of rapid development. This was due to the influx of artisans and professional workers in all trades among the immigrants, the large amounts of capital brought into the country by the immigrants or from other external sources, and a government policy of encouraging industrial development. This led to the establishment of a diversified industrial structure, mostly based on the manufacture of finished goods.

During the early years of the state, most of the factories specialized in agricultural processing and the production of foodstuffs, beverages, vegetable

Land Use, 1985

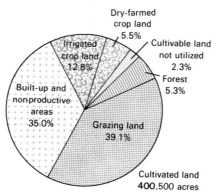

Dry-farmed
crop land
5.5%

Irrigated
crop land
12.8%

Cultivable land
not utilized
2.3%

Forest
5.3%

Built-up and
nonproductive
areas
35.0%

Grazing land
39.1%

Cultivated land
400,500 acres

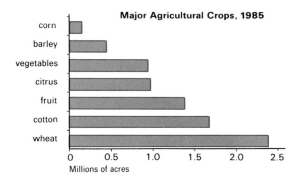

Major Agricultural Crops, 1985

(Bar chart showing, from top to bottom: corn, barley, vegetables, citrus, fruit, cotton, wheat)

Millions of acres
(x-axis: 0, 0.5, 1.0, 1.5, 2.0, 2.5)

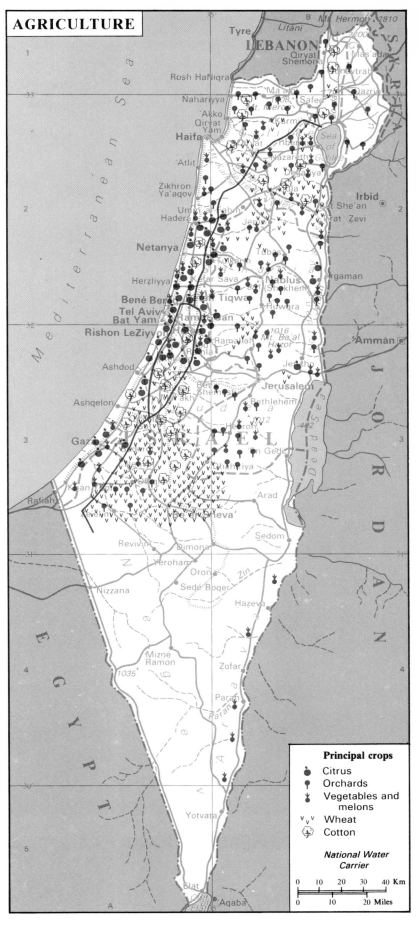

Principal crops

- Citrus
- Orchards
- Vegetables and melons
- Wheat
- Cotton

National Water Carrier

oils, and textiles. Much of the industrial products was destined for local consumption. The industrial base gradually became more diversified, expanding into metals, electrical goods, construction materials, wood, paper, and other consumer products.

As a result of the scarcity of local raw materials and because of the existence of a highly qualified technological work force, scientific and technological industries gradually surpassed the food, textiles, clothing, and construction sectors as the major components of the country's economy. Electronics, optics, and plastics were developed, as were chemicals, fertilizers, and pesticides, the latter two using the raw materials from the Dead Sea area.

The industrial sector, originally intended to serve the local market, now produces mostly for export. The value of Israel's industrial exports in 1950 was $18 million dollars; this increased to $5.2 billion by 1984. Prominent among the exports are polished diamonds, with an export value of $1.03 billion in 1984. In 1985, industry provided employment for 23 percent of the national work force and contributed 22 percent to the GDP.

Tourism Tourism is an important element in Israel's economy, especially as a source for foreign currency. Israel, known as the "Holy Land" because of its many biblical sites such as Jerusalem, Bethlehem, and Nazareth, attracts pilgrims from around the world. Jerusalem, one of the most unique cities in the world, is the center of the three great monotheistic religions — Judaism, Christianity, and Islam. Tourists are also attracted to Israel because of the unique character of the country as a Jewish state, the many archaeological digs and historical sites of importance, and a favorable climate throughout the year. In 1985, approximately 1.5 million tourists visited Israel, bringing in over $1 billion.

The Economy of Judea and Samaria Until 1967, the economy of this region was based on traditional agriculture, employing 40 percent of the labor force of Judea and Samaria and contributing approximately 25 percent to the GDP. Industry was only of marginal importance, providing employment for only 7 percent of the local labor force and contributing only 8 percent to the region's GDP. Most of the workers were employed in commerce and services. Following the transfer of these areas to Israeli control in 1967, a number of changes took place. Modern technology and general expertise were gradually introduced to the agricultural sector. As a result, agricultural yields increased substantially. At the same time, the number of workers employed in agriculture decreased to 22 percent by 1985. Nevertheless, commerce and services remained the principal economic sectors, employing 37 percent of the local labor force and contributing 56 percent to the GDP of the region in 1985. The industrial sector remained of limited proportions. A large

119

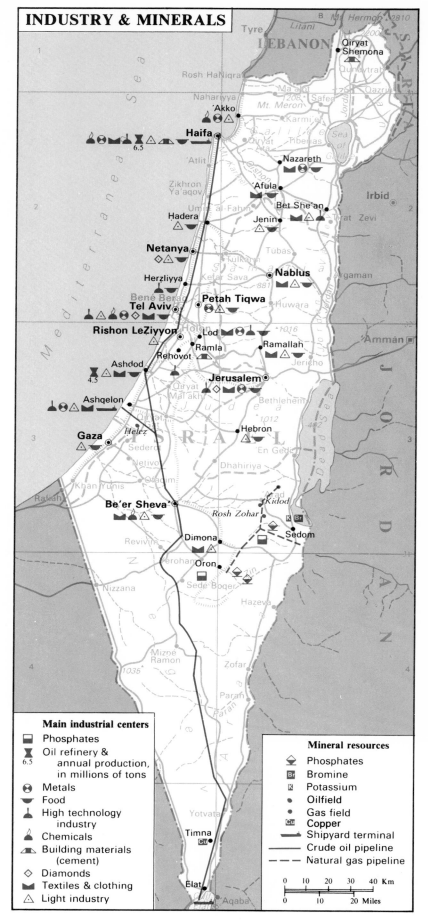

INDUSTRY & MINERALS

Main industrial centers

- ⊟ Phosphates
- ⧗ Oil refinery & annual production, in millions of tons
  6.5
- ⊗ Metals
- ⏝ Food
- ⚐ High technology industry
- 🜂 Chemicals
- ⛰ Building materials (cement)
- ◇ Diamonds
- ⛏ Textiles & clothing
- △ Light industry

Mineral resources

- ⬦ Phosphates
- Br Bromine
- K Potassium
- • Oilfield
- ⊘ Gas field
- Cu Copper
- ▬▬▬ Shipyard terminal
- ──── Crude oil pipeline
- ──── Natural gas pipeline

```
0   10   20   30   40 Km
0        10        20 Miles
```

number of the local labor force began to work inside Israel, especially in construction, industry, and services.

The cultivated area in Judea and Samaria totals 400,000 acres, nearly all of which (94 percent) is dry-farmed. Agricultural crops include orchards (approximately 250,000 acres, nearly all of which are olive trees), field crops (140,000 acres), vegetables, and melon crops.

The small amount of industry that does exist includes agricultural processing, foodstuffs, beverages, tobacco, clothing, and textiles.

The Economy of the Gaza Strip Agriculture is the principal economic sector, which employs approximately 20 percent of the labor force of the Gaza Strip. The industrial sector is small. Thirty-eight percent of the local labor force is employed in commerce and services, which contribute 52 percent to the GDP of the region. Some of the labor force is employed in Israel.

The cultivated area covers 45,000 acres — half of the total area of the Gaza Strip — of which approximately 40 percent is irrigated. The principal crops are citrus fruits, vegetables, and melons.

The factories are small and specialize in the manufacture of beverages, tobacco, textiles, clothing, and plastic goods.

History An independent Israelite nation existed in Palestine as long ago as 1300 BCE. Jewish sovereignty came to an end in the first century CE, following the Roman destruction of the nation and the exile of its inhabitants throughout the world. From then until the twentieth century, Palestine remained part of various empires, never regaining an independent status. Among the many conquerors of this region were the Byzantines, the Arabs, the Crusaders, the Mamluks, and the Ottomans.

Jewish settlement in Palestine was renewed toward the end of the nineteenth century. There was a desire among world Jewry to return to their historic birthplace and to renew their independent existence. During World War I, the British conquered Palestine from the Ottomans. In 1922, British sovereignty was recognized through the granting of a mandate by the League of Nations obliging the British to create conditions that would enable the ultimate establishment of an independent Jewish state. The Arab inhabitants of Palestine opposed the idea of an independent Jewish state. Sporadic acts of violence broke out between the Arab and Jewish inhabitants of the country. Despite this, both the Jewish and Arab population increased under British rule and the country's economy continued to develop.

The British did not fulfill the conditions laid down in the mandate and both the Jewish and the Arab inhabitants led separate struggles against British rule. In 1947, the Palestine problem was submitted to the United Nations assembly, which decided to terminate the British mandate and to partition Palestine into separate Jewish and Arab states. The Arabs refused to accept this partition proposal. Following the declaration of an independent Jewish state by David Ben-Gurion on May 15, 1948 (the day on which the British mandate terminated), the armies of Lebanon, Syria, Jordan, Iraq, and Egypt invaded Israel. Following a year of warfare, the Arab armies were repelled and a cease-fire agreement was signed. According to this agreement, approximately three-quarters of Western Palestine was included within the state of Israel. In the period immediately following the establishment of the state, Israel absorbed hundreds of thousands of Jews who immigrated from countries throughout the world. Large-scale settlement and economic development projects were implemented. Despite the cease-fire agreements, Israel was exposed to sporadic attacks from regular and irregular Arab forces. In 1956, with the objective of putting an end to the incursions from Egypt, Israel — in a joint military operation with Britain and France — captured the Sinai Peninsula. Superpower pressure from both the United States and the Soviet Union forced Israel to withdraw from this region a few months later. Tension between Israel and its neighbors continued, culminating in a further war between Israel and Syria, Jordan, and Egypt in June 1967. The Arab armies were completely defeated following six days of fighting. Israel conquered the Golan Heights from Syria, Judea and Samaria (the West Bank) from Jordan, and the Sinai Peninsula and Gaza Strip from Egypt.

In October 1973, Syria and Egypt attempted to retrieve the lost territories. Their sudden attack initially caught Israel unaware. Following eighteen days of battle, a cease-fire was obtained. Through American mediation during 1974, military disengagement agreements were reached with both Syria and Egypt. The war resulted in a political and social crisis in Israel, culminating in a victory for the right-wing Likud party headed by Menachem Begin in 1977. This electoral victory brought an end to thirty years of uninterrupted control by the left-wing parties, whose representatives had headed the government ever since the establishment of the state.

In November 1977, Egyptian President Anwar Sadat initiated an important change in policy when he recognized the existence of the state of Israel and paid a visit to Jerusalem. A peace treaty was signed between the two countries in March 1979, according to which Israel agreed to withdraw — in stages — from the Sinai Peninsula. The withdrawal was completed in 1982, bringing about a more relaxed situation on the southern border.

From the mid-1970s, terrorist operations originating in South Lebanon increased in intensity. In an effort to prevent these activities, Israel invaded Lebanon in March 1978, remaining in control of the area south of the river Litāni for three months. Following Israel's withdrawal, the terrorist activity recommenced.

In 1981, a cease-fire was reached. However, the terrorist military reinforcements continued to pose a threat to Israel. On June 6, 1982, Israel invaded Lebanon again in an attempt to completely destroy the terrorist infrastructure, conquering the whole of the area as far as the Beirut–Damascus highway. The Israeli army remained in Lebanon until June 1985.

Government and Politics   Israel is a parliamentary republic. The legislative assembly (the Knesset) comprises 120 representatives elected in proportional elections held every four years. The country is headed by a president who is chosen by the Knesset every five years. He has only representative duties and does not possess real power. Daily affairs of state are administered by a government put together by a member of the Knesset (usually the leader of the largest party) who is selected to do so by the president. The government is responsible to the Knesset, and its continued existence is dependent on support from a majority of the Knesset members.

In 1988, Chaim Herzog began his second term as president. Following the elections of 1984, a coalition government of both right- and left-wing parties was established. The coalition is supported by 80 percent of the Knesset members and is headed by Prime Minister Yitzhak Shamir (1987).

Israel's present borders, with the exception of the Egyptian border, were determined according to the military positions occupied at the end of

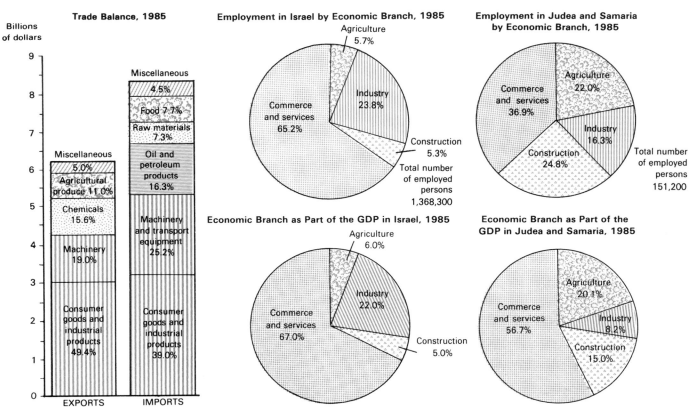

Population in Israel by Religion, 1985

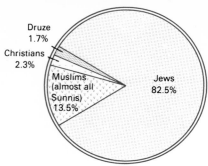

Druze 1.7%
Christians 2.3%
Muslims (almost all Sunnis) 13.5%
Jews 82.5%

Population in Israel by Age Group, 1985

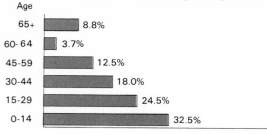

Age
65+   8.8%
60-64   3.7%
45-59   12.5%
30-44   18.0%
15-29   24.5%
0-14   32.5%

Population in Judea, Samaria and the Gaza Region by Age Group, 1984

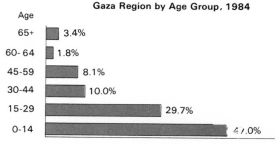

Age
65+   3.4%
60-64   1.8%
45-59   8.1%
30-44   10.0%
15-29   29.7%
0-14   41.0%

the various wars. The border with Lebanon is the agreed cease-fire line of 1949. The boundary with Syria is the disengagement line agreed to in 1974. The border with Jordan is the cease-fire line that was fixed at the end of the Six-Day War in 1967. The border with Egypt is the international boundary agreed to by Israel and Egypt in the 1979 peace agreement.

Since 1973, there has not been any direct fighting between Israel and Syria, Jordan, or Egypt. Along the Lebanese border, there have been continual clashes between the Israeli army and the Palestinian terrorists. Israel provides assistance to the Christian forces in South Lebanon. There are occasional acts of terrorism against Israeli military and civilian targets in Judea and Samaria and the Gaza Strip.

The state of Israel is isolated in its immediate region. With the exception of Egypt, with whom Israel has diplomatic relations, it has no formal ties with the majority of Middle Eastern countries.

The United States is Israel's most important ally. Since the end of the 1960s, the United States has been Israel's principal military and economic supporter. Since 1985, Israel has slowly expanded its links with the Eastern bloc countries, as well as countries in Africa and Asia.

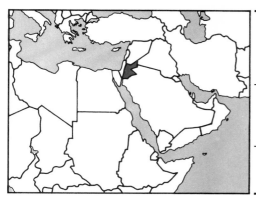

JORDAN

Area **34,442 sq. miles (89,206 sq.km)**
Population (1985 estimate) **2,800,000**
Capital city **'Ammān**
Gross domestic product (GDP) per capita (1984) **$1,506**

Population in main cities (1985 estimates)	'Ammān 777,000 Az-Zarqā' 290,000 Irbid 160,000	'Aqaba 40,000

Jordan shares borders with Syria to the north, Iraq to the northeast, Saudi Arabia to the east and south, and Israel to the west. An area of some 2,317 square miles (6,000 sq.km) to the west of the Jordan river (the West Bank), annexed by Jordan in 1948, has been under Israeli control since June 1967. Jordan has an outlet to the Red Sea, a short coastal section on the Gulf of 'Aqaba of 16 miles (26 km), and approximately half of the total area of the Dead Sea, some 193 sq. miles (500 sq.km).

Topography Jordan is made up of three geographical units, each of which stretches in a north–south direction: the valley region (consisting of the Jordan valley and Wādī al-'Arabah); the highlands; and the desert plateau.

1. The valley region, in the western part of the country, is part of the Syrian-African Rift valley. Most of this region in Jordan is below sea level. In the Jorden valley the Jordan river flows into the Dead Sea — the lowest point on earth (–1,319 ft [–402 meters]). The rift valley extends to the Gulf of 'Aqaba and varies in width from 2.5–10 miles (4–15 km).

2. The highlands rise steeply eastward from the rift valley and are divided into a number of blocks by deeply incised streams which dissect it in an east–west direction and which drain the region into the valleys. Only some of them carry water all the time. Some of the highland blocks are in fact plateaus (such as the Irbid and Moab Plateaus) while others are mountainous.

The average height of the northern section, which is built mostly of thick limestone beds, is 3,000 ft (700 meters). The southern section is higher, with peaks reaching more than 4,920 ft (1,500 meters), built of thick beds of sandstone and granite.

3. The desert plateau comprises about 80 percent of Jordan's territory. It is covered mainly by bare limestone and gravel. This is overlaid in the northwest of the plateau by large flows of volcanic rock, making the passage from Jordan to Iraq difficult. Sandstone beds are exposed in the south of the plateau. A large part of the area drains into the al-Jafr basin in the plateau's interior. The remainder of the area of the plateau drains eastward into Wādī Sirḥan in Saudi Arabia.

Climate A desert climate prevails over most of Jordan; only the western slopes of the highland region have a Mediterranean climate.

In the valley region, temperatures are high in summer and moderate in winter. The average temperature in August is 88° F. (31° C.) and 59° F. (15° C.) in January. The temperatures are comfortable in the highlands with an August average of 79° F. (29° C.) and a January average of 48° F. (9° C.). Throughout Jordan there is a wide diurnal range of some 50–54° F. (10–12° C.).

Rains fall only in the winter season, from November to April. The highest precipitation is in the highlands, chiefly on the western slopes, which are exposed to the winds bringing rain clouds from the Mediterranean Sea. In the north, the western slopes receive an average of 23–27.5 in (600–700 mm) per year. The amount of rain decreases to the south and east. The upper parts of the highlands, in the south, get an average of 16–24 in (400–500 mm), while most of the desert plateau receives less than 4 in (100 mm) per year. The hot valley is sheltered from the rain-bearing winds and receives on the average about 10 in (250 mm) per year in the north, decreasing to less than 2 in (50 mm) in the south. There are great fluctuations in the amount of precipitation in all regions from year to year.

Population Nearly 99 percent of Jordan's inhabitants are Arabs, of which the great majority are Sunni Muslims. About 110,000 are Christians (70,000 Greek Orthodox, 20,000 Greek Catholics, 4,000 Armenians, and a few hundred Protestants and Syrian Orthodox). There are also about 25,000 Circassians (Sunni Muslims) and 2,500 Chechens (Shiite Muslims) in the country. Over 50 percent of the population are Palestinians with Jordanian citizenship.

Nearly 60 percent of the population live in urban settlements, most of them in the 'Ammān and Irbid districts. The remainder live in villages, with the exception of a few thousand nomads and seminomads.

Economy Since its independence in 1946, Jordan's economy has been largely dependent on foreign aid. In the first years of independence, the country received financial aid from Britain and financial and military assistance from the United States. The wealthy oil states, especially Saudi Arabia and Kuwait, added an annual grant of about $1 billion. In 1982, aid from the oil-rich Arab states was cut in half.

In spite of the foreign aid, Jordan's economic situation was difficult until the mid-1970s. The main reasons for this were a shortage of land and water for agriculture, limited natural resources, and the absorption of over 700,000 refugees who fled to Jordan following the 1948 and 1967 wars with Israel. The 1967 war resulted in the loss of the West Bank, which had constituted an important agricultural hinterland for Jordan.

Since 1975, growth has taken place in all sectors of the economy. This was due mainly to internal political stabilization and the transfer of funds from Lebanese banks (in the wake of Lebanon's civil war) to banks in Jordan. Since 1983 this trend has been halted, chiefly on account of the oil crisis affecting oil-producing countries in the Persian Gulf. This has caused a reduction in financial aid from these countries, an increase in the number of unemployed Jordanians returning home from the Persian Gulf states, and a reduction in the amount of money transferred back home — about $1 billion annually — by Jordanian workers abroad.

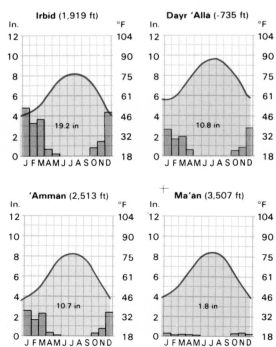

Climate
RAINFALL AND TEMPERATURE

Annual temperature

Average monthly rainfall

8.6 in   Total annual rainfall

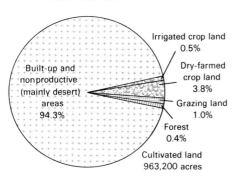

Irrigated crop land
0.5%

Dry-farmed
crop land
3.8%

Grazing land
1.0%

Forest
0.4%

Built-up and
nonproductive
(mainly desert)
areas
94.3%

Cultivated land
963,200 acres

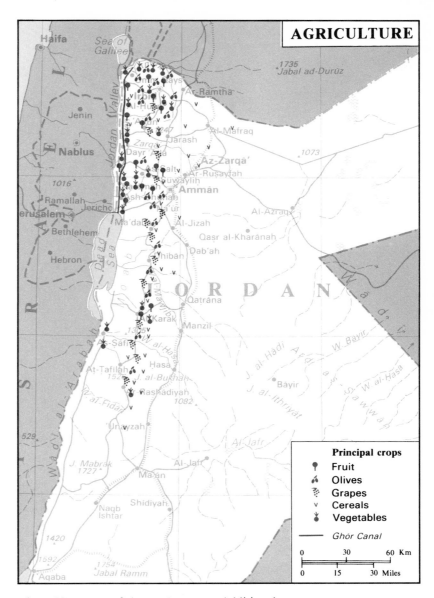

AGRICULTURE

Principal crops

♀ Fruit
🌿 Olives
🍇 Grapes
v Cereals
🌱 Vegetables

—— Ghor Canal

| 0 | 30 | 60 Km |
| 0 | 15 | 30 Miles |

Agriculture Until the mid-1970s, agriculture constituted the main branch of the economy, even though only about 1,408,500 acres — 6.3 percent of the total area — are suitable for cultivation. Almost the entire area was under dry-farming. In the highlands, particularly in the Irbid Plateau, non-irrigated fields consist of wheat and barley (about 420,000 acres) and fruit trees (about 95,000 acres). Irrigated agriculture in Jordan began to develop following the construction of the first section of the Ghor Canal (1966). The canal carries water south from the Yarmūk river, flowing parallel to the course of the river Jordan. Today the canal is 65 miles (105 km) long. The Jordan valley now grows some 70 percent of irrigated crops, particularly vegetables and subtropical fruits. Conditions here enable three crops a year. Side canals branch off from the main canal allowing irrigation for market gardening.

Since the crop yields depend on the amount of rain in 90 percent of the cultivated area, there are fluctuations in yield. As a result, it is necessary to import a substantial amount of basic food supplies in dry years.

Minerals Jordan has few mineral resources. Its main resource is phosphates, deposits of which are currently being mined at ar-Ruṣayfah, Wādī al-Ḥasā, and Wādī Abiyad. Additional rich deposits, as yet untapped, were discovered in the 1980s at Shīdiyah in the south. Phosphate production has risen from 1.16 million tons in 1968 to 4.7 million tons in 1985. The proven reserves are estimated at about 1.6 billion tons.

Another mineral source is the Dead Sea, where the waters are rich in natural minerals, particularly potassium. Commercial production of potassium in Jordan began in 1983. Production reached 485,000 tons in 1984.

Jordan has one commercial oilfield at al-Azraq, in the east. Since 1986, its three wells have been producing about 100,000 tons of oil per year. Most of the local demand for oil is supplied by Saudi Arabia by means of a pipeline which passes through Jordan on its way to Sidon in Lebanon. The oil is piped to the refineries at az-Zarqā', whose production capacity reached 4.2 million tons in 1985, of which 2.5 million tons were for local consumption.

Additional, economically nonviable minerals include copper, manganese, and iron ore.

Industry Despite the fact that two-thirds of Jordan's factories produce food and clothing, the greatest contribution to the GDP comes from heavy industry, petrochemicals, and construction. Production in 1983 was: phosphates, 4.7 million tons; potassium, 485,000 tons; petroleum products, 2.5 million tons; cement, 1.3 million tons; and fertilizers, 300,000 tons. Phosphate exports constitute 32 percent of the total exports. Additional plants produce iron and steel goods, medicines, and ceramic products. Most of the industrial plants are concentrated in the 'Ammān region, ar-Ruṣayfah, and az-Zarqā'.

History Transjordan was part of the Ottoman Empire until 1918, when the British occupied the region. From the end of World War I, Britain ruled over Transjordan under a League of Nations mandate. In 1921, the British transferred internal control to the Emir 'Abdullah, the second son of the Sharif of Mecca. The emir ruled the country under British suzerainty until the attainment of independence on March 22, 1946. On May 25, 1946, Emir 'Abdullah proclaimed himself king of the Hashemite Kingdom of Jordan. The borders of the kingdom were those determined by Britain and France during the mandate period.

Following the establishment of the state of Israel in May 1948, Jordan — together with Syria, Iraq, and Egypt — participated in the Arab military invasion of Mandatory Palestine. At the end of the war, an area to the west of the river Jordan — including East Jerusalem — remained under Jordanian rule. During 1948-1950, some 350,000 to 400,000 refugees emigrated from Palestine to Transjordan. Together with the residents of the

HIGH SCHOOL PUPILS (1983)
80,170

UNIVERSITY STUDENTS (1983)
16,140

LITERACY RATE (1983) 70%

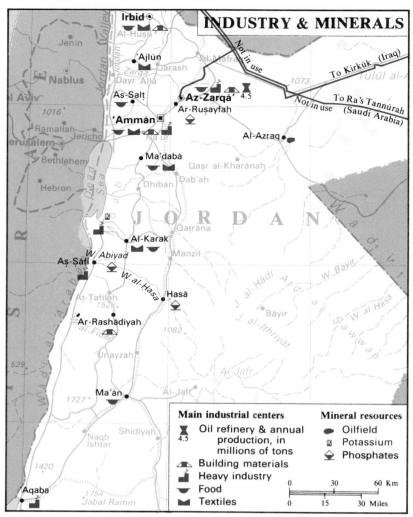

INDUSTRY & MINERALS

Main industrial centers

- ⚒ Oil refinery & annual production, in millions of tons
- ⛟ Building materials
- ▮ Heavy industry
- ◡ Food
- ⋈ Textiles

Mineral resources

- ● Oilfield
- ◪ Potassium
- ◈ Phosphates

0 — 30 — 60 Km
0 — 15 — 30 Miles

West Bank, which Jordan officially annexed in April 1950, the Palestinian Arabs tripled the country's population.

On July 20, 1951, King 'Abdullah was assassinated during a visit to East Jerusalem. His son Talal (who suffered from a mental illness) succeeded him for a short period, following which Talal's son, Hussein, ascended the throne in May 1953. Until June 1967, Hussein's rule was marked by a series of internal struggles, riots, and clashes between the regime's opponents, headed by the terrorist organizations concentrated mainly in the West Bank. The internal unrest was accompanied by deterioration in Jordan's relations with other Arab states, particularly Egypt and Syria.

In June 1967, during the course of another war with Israel, Jordan was cut off from the West Bank, the latter being captured by Israel. Some 250,000 additional refugees moved into Jordan from the West Bank, including activists from the underground organizations who established their military units within the country. They carried out actions against Israel, thus exposing Jordan to Israeli retaliatory measures. Within Jordan itself, they attempted to assassinate King Hussein and to topple his government. This situation eventually resulted in a civil war, during which many of the Palestinian terrorists were expelled, others were imprisoned, and the terrorist bases in Jordan were destroyed.

Jordan did not participate in the October 1973 war against Israel. Despite this, Jordan's ties with the Arab world strengthened after the war. This resulted in an increase in financial aid, enabling the implementation of economic development programs.

Since the Rabat Summit of 1974, at which the Arab states decided that the Palestine Liberation Organization (PLO) would be the exclusive representative of the West Bank population, there

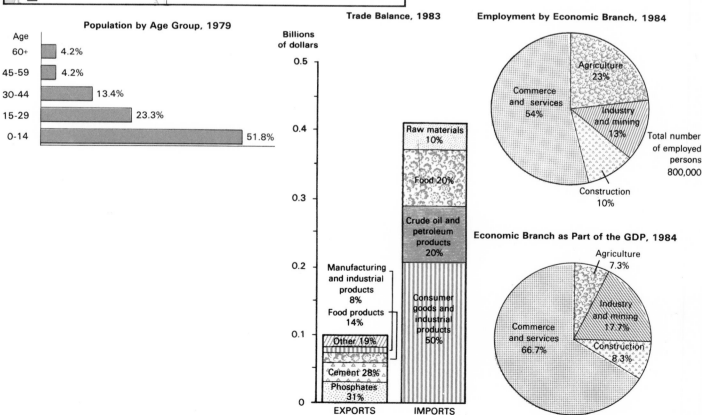

Population by Age Group, 1979

Age	
60+	4.2%
45-59	4.2%
30-44	13.4%
15-29	23.3%
0-14	51.8%

Trade Balance, 1983

Billions of dollars

EXPORTS
- Manufacturing and industrial products 8%
- Food products 14%
- Other 19%
- Cement 28%
- Phosphates 31%

IMPORTS
- Raw materials 10%
- Food 20%
- Crude oil and petroleum products 20%
- Consumer goods and industrial products 50%

Employment by Economic Branch, 1984

- Commerce and services 54%
- Agriculture 23%
- Industry and mining 13%
- Construction 10%

Total number of employed persons 800,000

Economic Branch as Part of the GDP, 1984

- Commerce and services 66.7%
- Agriculture 7.3%
- Industry and mining 17.7%
- Construction 8.3%

has been a rapprochement between King Hussein and the Palestinian organization headed by Yasir Arafat. In this context, there has been a growing degree of participation by Palestinian representatives in government institutions.

Government and Politics   Power in the country is in the hands of the king and is passed by inheritance within the Hashemite family. Hussein has ruled since ascending the throne in 1953 at the age of eighteen. The heir apparent is his brother, Hassan. Affairs of state are managed by a cabinet whose head is appointed by the king and whose composition requires his approval. Since April 1985, Zaid ar-Rifa'i has served as prime minister. Government decisions and state laws require the approval of a bicameral national assembly: a Senate (upper house) consisting of thirty representatives appointed by the king once every four years, and a House of Representatives in which there are sixty elected delegates (thirty from each bank of the Jordan). Between 1967 and 1984, no elections for the House of Representatives were held. In January 1984, the members of the House of Representatives elected seven representatives from among the West Bank population to replace representatives who had died in the interim period. In general elections held in March of that year,

eight representatives were chosen from among East Bank residents.

The country's borders were determined in a number of stages: the border with Syria was fixed by Britain and France when they held the mandates for this region; the border with Iraq was fixed in 1924–1925; and the border with Saudi Arabia was finally delineated in 1965. Jordan's border to the west, with Israel, has not been formally determined; the present boundary in the Dead Sea region and along the 'Arava valley was fixed by the 1949 cease-fire agreements, while the present border along the river Jordan is a result of the 1967 war.

Jordan's relations with Syria improved in 1986, after a long period of tension between the two countries. Jordan maintains close ties with Iraq and Saudi Arabia. No formal neighborly ties exist along the border with Israel, although limited commercial links and the passage of Jordanian citizens by way of the "open bridges" take place. During the Iran–Iraq war, the Jordanians have allowed the Iraqis use of the port of 'Aqaba, through which they transfer military and civilian supplies. When the oil pipeline (begun in 1985) from Iraq to 'Aqaba is completed the port will serve as the export point for some of Iraq's oil.

NATURAL INCREASE
(1980-1983)
3.6%

LIFE EXPECTANCY
(1980-1985)
male - **60.3** years
female - **64.2** years

DOCTORS
(1983)
6.6 per 10,000 inhabitants

HOSPITAL BEDS
(1983)
1.8 per 1,000 inhabitants

INFANT MORTALITY
(1982)
63.4 per 1,000 births

Bibliography

General

Beaumont P., H. Blake, and J. N. Wagstaff, *The Middle East*. London, 1976.
Clarke, J. I., and W. M. Fisher, *Population in the Middle East*. London, 1972.
Drysdale, A., and G. H. Blake, *The Middle East and North Africa: A Political Geography*. Oxford, 1985.
Economist Intelligence Unit, *Quarterly Economic Review of Egypt, Jordan, Iraq, Iran, Libya, Lebanon, Saudi Arabia, the Arabian Peninsula, Turkey, Sudan, Israel*. Annual Supplement 1986, London.
Economist Intelligence Unit, *Oil in the Middle East*. London, 1987.
Fisher, W. B., *The Middle East*. London, 1977.
Kanovsky, E., *Recent Economic Development in the Middle East*. Tel Aviv, 1977.
Longrigg, S. H., *Oil in the Middle East: Its Discovery and Development*, 3rd ed., London, 1968.
Meteorological Office, *Tables of Temperature and Precipitation for the World*, Part V, *Asia*. London, 1970.
The Middle East and North Africa, Europa Publication. London, 1987.
The Middle East Annual Review, 1980–1987. Essex, England.
Organization of Arab Petroleum Exporting Countries, *Annual Statistical Report, 1975–1985*. Kuwait, 1986.
Shell International Petroleum Company, *Oil and Gas in 1985*. London, 1986.

Atlases and Maps

Beckingham, C. F., *Atlas of the Arab World*. London, 1966.
Brawer, M., and Y. Karmon, *Atlas of the Middle East* (in Hebrew). Tel Aviv, 1980.
GEOprojects Arab World Map Library of Sheet Maps. London, 1980–1985.
Robinson, F., *Atlas of the Islamic World Since 1500*. New York, 1982.
The Times Atlas of the World, Comprehensive Edition. London, 1985.
Tübinger Atlas des Vorderen Orients. Wiesbaden, 1978.

Regional

Libya

Allan, J. A., K. S. Malachan, and E. T. Penrose, *Libya: Agriculture and Development*. London, 1973.
Area Handbook for Libya. Washington, 1980.
Hajjaji, S. A., *The New Libya*. Tripoli, 1967.

Egypt

Area Handbook for Egypt. Washington, 1985.
Little, T., *Modern Egypt*. London, 1967.
Vatikiotis, P. J., *The Modern History of Egypt*. London, 1969.

Sudan

Barbour, K. M., *The Republic of Sudan: A Regional Geography*. London, 1961.
Voll, J. O., and S. P. Voll, *The Sudan*. London, 1985.
Woodward, P. (ed.), *Sudan Since Nimeiri*. London, 1985.

The Arabian Peninsula

Area Handbook for Saudi Arabia. Washington, 1980.
Hawley, D. F., *The Trucial States*. London, 1970.
Litwak, R., *Security in the Persian Gulf (2): Sources of Inter-State Conflict*. London, 1981.
Mallakh, R., *Saudi Arabia: Rush to Development*. London, 1982.
Miles, F. B., *The Country and Tribes of the Persian Gulf*. London, 1982.
Stookey, R. W., *South Yemen*. London, 1982.

Iraq

Abdulghani, J. M., *Iraq: The Years of Crisis*. London, 1968.
Area Handbook for Iraq. Washington, 1979.
Kelidar, A. (ed.), *The Integration of Modern Iraq*. New York, 1979.
Niblock, T., *Iraq: The Contemporary State*. London, 1982.

Iran

Avery, P. W., *Modern Iran*. London, 1965.
Fisher, W. B. (ed.), *The Cambridge History of Iran*, Vol. I, *Land and People*. London, 1968.
Graham, R., *Iran: The Illusion of Power*. London, 1978.
Jacqz, J. W. (ed.), *Iran: Past, Present and Future*. New York, 1976.

Turkey

Area Handbook for Turkey. Washington, 1980.
Hale, W., *The Political and Economic Development of Modern Turkey*. London, 1981.
Newman, B., *Turkey and the Turks*. London, 1968.

Cyprus

Henderson, C., *Cyprus: The Country and Its People*. London, 1968.
Markides, K. C., *The Rise and Fall of the Cyprus Republic*. London, 1977.
Polyviou, P. G., *Conflict and Negotiation 1960–1980*. New York, 1980.

The Levant

Area Handbook for Lebanon. Washington, 1974.
Devlin, J. F., *Syria: Modern State in an Ancient Land*. London, 1983.
Frankel, W., *Israel Observed: An Anatomy of the State*. London, 1980.
Gordon, D. C., *Lebanon the Fragmented Nation*. London, 1980.
Gubser, P., *Jordan, Crossroad of Middle Eastern Events*. London, 1983.
Kanovsky, E., *Economic Development of Syria*. Tel Aviv, 1970.
Karmon, Y., *Israel* (in Hebrew). Tel Aviv, 1980.

Further Reading

prepared by Linda S. Vertrees

The Region *The First Cities* by Ruth Whitehouse (Phaidon, 1977) is a heavily illustrated archaeological study of the area around the Tigris and Euphrates rivers, the Indus valley, and the Nile River delta. This book explains what these early cities were like, and why they developed in these regions. *The Arab World* by Peter Mansfield (Crowell, 1976) offers insight into Arab society, discussing the divergent tribes and their unification under the teachings of Muhammad and the development of the Arab empire. An excellent general history of the Middle East is by Lois Aroian and Richard P. Mitchell, *The Modern Middle East and North Africa* (Macmillan, 1984). This book provides an appreciation of Middle Eastern and North African history, culture, and people. A biography of Shakib Arslan (1869–1946), *Islam Against the West*, by William L. Cleveland (University of Texas at Austin, 1985) tells the story of one of the leading writers and politicians of his day; the transition of the Arab world from the Ottoman Empire at the end of World War I; and his fight to preserve Islamic ideals. Edward Jablonski's *A Pictorial History of the Middle East* (Doubleday, 1984) presents a graphic record of the violent history of this area. In *The Arabs: Journey Beyond the Mirage* (Random House, 1987), David Lamb explains many of the contradictions in the Arab world (at least in Western eyes). *The Blood of Abraham* by Jimmy Carter (Houghton Mifflin, 1985) presents an overview of the current conflict against a background of biblical history and forty centuries of war and debate. For a good general introduction to the Persian Gulf, read John Bulloch's *The Persian Gulf Unveiled* (Congdon & Weed, 1984), a colorful and entertaining report on the desert countries surrounding the Persian Gulf.

Isaak Diqs wrote *A Bedouin Boyhood* (George Allen & Unwin, 1983) as a portrait of the simple good life with traditions, rituals, and customs unchanged for many generations. The creation of Israel led to the eventual dispursement of his tribe as refugees. For a personal account of traveling through Arabia, read *Arabia: A Journey Through the Labyrinth* by Jonathan Raban (Simon & Schuster, 1979). *Traveller Through Time* by Malise Ruthven (Viking, 1986) is an interesting biography of Freya Stark, who traveled alone from the 1920s through the 1970s through countries where few European men traveled.

The Arab Gulf and the West, edited by B. R. Pridham (St. Martin's Press, 1985), is a collection of essays on the economic, financial, and industrial importance of this area from Arab and international perspectives. Seth P. Tillman's *The United States in the Middle East* (Indiana University Press, 1982) identifies the domestic political environment in which American Middle Eastern policy is made. Wilber C. Eveland's *Ropes of Sand* (Norton, 1980) discusses many of the present crises from his perspective of thirty years of government service in the Middle East. For the importance of the area from the Soviet perspective, read Robert O. Freedman's *Soviet Policy Toward the Middle East Since 1970*, 3rd edition (Praeger, 1982). For an interesting and scholarly work on the origins and development of the Cold War in this area, see *The Origins of the Cold War in the Near East* by Bruce R. Kuniholm (Princeton University Press, 1980).

For a look into the future by international experts, see *Middle East Perspectives: The Next Twenty Years*, edited by George Wise and Charles Issawi (Darwin Press, 1981). The book analyzes the effect on the region of the Khomeini takeover of Iran and the Russian invasion of Afghanistan for the remainder of this century. The essays in *The Powers in the Middle East*, edited by Bernard Reich (Praeger, 1987), discuss the role of oil, the geopolitical importance of the region, and the impact of regional conflicts on international policies. Elias H. Tuma's *Economic and Political Change in the Middle East* (Pacific Books, 1987) is a technical study of the socioeconomic and political development of the area in recent years. *Technology Trade with the Middle East* by James Emery and others (Westview Press, 1986) discusses the large-scale importation of Western technology and its impact on the economies of the different Arab states.

W. Montgomery Watt's *Muhammad: Prophet and Statesman* (Oxford University Press, 1974) is considered a classic. It provides a short account of Muhammad's life and achievements, as well as an excellent introduction to one of the world's major religions. *Muhammad* by Maxime Rodinson (Pantheon Books, 1980) is another narrative of the prophet's life and the development of Islam. Two introductory books on Islam are Frithjof Schuon's *Understanding Islam* (Unwin Paperbacks, 1976) and *Know Your Islam* by Yousuf N. Lalljee (Tahrik-E-Tarsil-E-Quaran, 1977). Both explain the fundamental principles of Islam.

Holy War by Wilhelm Dietl (Macmillan, 1984) is an interesting look at the Muslim Brotherhood, the terrorists who keep the Middle East in turmoil. Emmanuel Sivan's *Radical Islam, Medieval Theology, and Modern Politics* (Yale University Press, 1985) analyzes numerous fundamentalist writings. It also discusses the intellectual differences between the Sunni and Shiite fundamentalists of Khomeini's Iran.

The PLO by Jillian Becker (St. Martin's Press, 1984) is based on interviews with representatives of the many sides of the PLO, providing an explanation of the structures, aims, tactics, and role of the PLO in world politics. For additional books on the Palestinians, see the Jordan and Lebanon entries.

Libya For an interesting look at Bedouin society, see Roy H. Behnke, Jr.'s *The Herders of Cyrenaica* (University of Illinois Press, 1980). A good contemporary history covering the period 1951–1980 is *Political Development and Social Change in Libya* by Omar I. El Fathaly and Monte Palmer (Lexington Books, 1980). Lillian C. Harris's *Libya* (Westview Press, 1986) is a comprehensive study of the social, cultural, political, and economic forces that shape Libya today.

Two excellent books on Muammar Qaddafi are: *Qaddafi: His Ideology in Theory and Practice* by Mohamed A. El-Khawas (Amana Books, 1986), a comprehensive study of his ideas and policies, and *Qaddafi and the Libyan Revolution* by David Blundy and Andrew Lycett (Little, Brown, 1987), which portrays the colonel in his own social and political environment. J. A. Allan's *Libya Since Independence* (Croom Helm, 1982) is a scholarly study of the socioeconomic and political changes experienced since 1951. Also by J. A. Allan is *Libya: The Experience of Oil* (Croom Helm, 1981), which examines the effect on the economy of the policies of the monarchy and the 1969 revolution.

Egypt An excellent introduction to ancient Egyptian history and culture is Margaret A. Murray's *The Splendour That Was Egypt* (Philosophical Library, 1961). This book also provides information on religion, arts and sciences, language and literature, and the social conditions of the ancient Egyptians. *The Civilization of Ancient Egypt* by Paul Johnson (Atheneum, 1978) is another good history of Egypt with many illustrations and maps. One of the best general histories available in English is P. J. Vatikiotis's *The History of Egypt*, 3rd edition (Johns Hopkins University Press, 1985). For a look at everyday life during the Roman occupation, see Naphtali Lewis's *Life in Egypt Under Roman Rule* (Clarendon Press, 1983). *The Origin of the Egyptians* by Augustus Le Plongeon (Philosophical Research Society, 1983) states that the Egyptians are from the lost continent of Atlantis. He bases this claim on identical characters in the written languages of ancient Egypt and the Mayan civilization.

Egyptian Art by Cyril Aldred (Oxford University Press, 1980) is an excellent overview of the art and history of Egypt. John Romer's *Valley of the Kings* (William Morrow, 1981) tells of the scholars who studied the royal tombs and of the tombs themselves. *The Pyramids of Egypt* by I. E. S. Edwards (Penguin Books, 1985) provides a chronology of the thirty-odd dynasties of Egyptian kings and many floor plans of the pyramids. Donald B. Redford's *Akhenaten, the Heretic King* (Princeton University Press, 1984) is a striking portrait of the sun worshipper and the best known king after Tut. *Tutankhamen* by Christine Desroches-Noblecourt (New York Graphic Society, 1963) is an exciting story of the discovery and excavation of King Tut's tomb. The book contains many photographs of the treasures found in the tomb. *X-Raying the Pharaohs* by James Harris and Kent R. Weeks (Charles Scribner's Sons, 1973) provides many pictures of the mummies and their x-rays.

Two interesting travel books are William Golding's *An Egyptian Journal* (Faber & Faber, 1985), an entertaining and humorous account of his family's trip through Egypt in 1983. Amelia B. Edwards, an English novelist, took a leisurely 1,000 mile trip up the Nile in 1873. Her story was originally published in 1891. The current edition of her book is *A Thousand Miles up the Nile* (J. P. Tarcher and Houghton Mifflin, 1983).

A Short History of Modern Egypt by Afaf Lutfi Sayyid-Marsot (Cambridge University Press, 1985) is an excellent history from the Arab conquest of Egypt in 639 to the present. Donald Neff's *Warriors at Suez* (Linden Press and Simon & Schuster, 1981) provides a good analysis of the Suez crisis in 1956. Another excellent book on the Suez crisis is *The Lion's Last Roar* by Chester L. Cooper (Harper & Row, 1978). *Egypt and Israel* by Howard M. Sachar (Richard Marek Publishers, 1981) is a broad chronological study of Egypt and Israel, culminating in the historic signing of the Egyptian–Israeli Peace Treaty.

Economic Aid and American Policy Toward Egypt, 1955–1981 by William J. Burns (State University of New York Press, 1985) analyzes the use of economic aid by the United States as a tool of foreign policy. *The Political Economy of Nasserism* by Mahmoud Abdul-Fadil (Cambridge University Press, 1980) discusses Nasser's form of socialism from ideology to actual practice. Khalid Ikram's *Egypt* (Johns Hopkins University Press, 1980) is a history of the management of the Egyptian economy since 1952.

The Last Pharaoh by Hugh McLeave (McCall Publishing Co., 1969) is an interesting biography of King Farouk. Anthony Nutting's *Nasser* (Dutton, 1972) is a biography of Gamal Abdel Nasser. *Man of Defiance: A Political Biography of Anwar Sadat* by Raphael Israeli (Barnes & Nobel Books, 1985) traces his life and character. Jehan Sadat's *A Woman of Egypt* (Simon & Schuster, 1987) is an excellent autobiography of an Egyptian patriot.

Sudan *The Sudan Crossroads of Africa* by Beshir Mohammed Said (The Bodley Head, 1965) is an interesting and informative history of the Sudan. It is the study of a nation with borders created artificially by colonial powers. R. S. O'Fahey and J. L. Spaulding's *Kingdoms of the Sudan* (Methuen & Co., 1974) discusses the economic and social patterns that are rooted in antiquity. *History of the Sudan: From the Coming of Islam to the Present Day*, 4th ed., by Peter M. Holt and M. W. Daly (Longman, 1988) is an excellent history of the Sudan. Cecil Eprile's *War and Peace in the Sudan 1955–1972* (David & Charles, 1974) is a balanced report of the conflict between the black Africans in the South and the Arabs in the North, with the Sudan as the battleground. It presents the Numeiri coup of 1969 in detail.

War on the Nile by Michael Barthorp (Blandford Press, 1984) tells of the epic defense of Khartoum by British General Charles Gordon. Philip Warner's *Dervish* (MacDonald, 1973), based on firsthand reports and diaries, describes the growth and strength of the Mahdist movement and the Dervish troops. *Omdurman* by Philip Ziegler (Knopf, 1974) is a skillful narration of the battle at Omdurman.

The White Nile by Alan Moorhead (Vintage Books and Random House, 1971) is the exciting story of two explorers and their overland journey from the east coast of Africa to discover the source of the Nile.

Yemen John Peterson's *Yemen: The Search for a Modern State* (Johns Hopkins University Press, 1982) traces the political history of Yemen from the 1930s to the 1980s. It examines how the traditional political structure has changed in recent years and how the country is coping with these changes. *The Yemen Arab Republic* by Robert D. Burrowes (Westview Press, 1987) is an excellent history of Yemen from 1962 to 1986.

The Economic Development of the Yemen Arab Republic by Ragael El Mallakh (Croom Helm, 1986) is an analysis of the economy beginning with the 1962 revolution.

There are many books that discuss both Yemen states. Robin Bidwell's *The Two Yemens* (Longman, 1983) is an excellent history of the Yemen people and their two countries. *Contemporary Yemen: Politics and Historical Background*, edited by B. R. Pridham (St. Martin's Press, 1984), is a collection of papers that discuss the internal and international politics of the two countries. The influence of the Soviet Union in South Yemen is also discussed. See the *South Yemen* entry for additional books.

South Yemen *South Yemen: A Marxist Republic in Arabia* by Robert W. Stookey (Westview Press, 1982) is a balanced introduction to the country and its people. Helen Lackner's *P. D. R. Yemen* (Ithaca Press, 1985) is a good history from the colonial period to today.

Saudi Arabia *The New Arabians* by Peter Mansfield (J. G. Ferguson and Doubleday, 1981) explores the historical background, culture, religion, and institutions of Saudi Arabia, Kuwait, Bahrain, Qatar, and the United Arab Emirates. Another interesting overview of the Arabian Peninsula is Mary Louise Clifford's *The Land and People of the Arabian Peninsula* (J. B. Lippincott, 1977). It explores the contemporary life and customs of the many peoples that live on the Arabian Peninsula. *State, Society and Economy in Saudi Arabia*, edited by Tim Niblock (St. Martin's Press, 1982), is a collection of essays that provide different insights into the particular aspects of politics, society, and economics in Saudi Arabia. Richard F. Nyrop's *Saudi Arabia: A Country Study* (United States Government Printing Office, 1984) is an excellent survey of the dominant historical, social, economic, and political aspects of contemporary life in Saudi Arabia. *Saudi Arabia: Forces of Modernization* by Bob Abdrabboh (Amana Books, 1984) introduces the reader to the culture and economy of Saudi Arabia. *Saudi Arabia: A Case Study in Development* by Fouad Al-Farsy (Stacey International, 1978) gives a concise history of the kingdom, its geography, the rise of Islam, foreign relations, and economy. *Medina, Saudi Arabia* by M. S. Makki (Avebury, 1982) analyzes the importance of the city's location and its impact on the city's growth and evolution.

The House of Saud by David Holden and Richard Johns (Holt, Rinehart & Winston, 1981) is an excellent history of the ruling house of Saudi Arabia.

John R. Presley's *A Guide to the Saudi Arabian Economy* (St. Martin's Press, 1984) focuses on the uses of oil and the revenues it produces. *The Saudi Arabian Economy* by Ali D. Johany and others (Johns Hopkins University Press, 1986) is an excellent introduction to the unprecedented changes in the Saudi Arabian economy over the past twenty years.

Oman Christine Osborne's *The Gulf States and Oman* (Croom Helm, 1977) includes sections on Bahrain, Kuwait, Qatar, United Arab Emirates, and Oman. It also discusses the plight of the Bedouin and the changing role for women of the Gulf countries. For

an excellent history, see *The Omans* by Liesl Graz (Longman, 1982). Another good history of Oman is F. A. Clements, *Oman the Reborn Land* (Longman, 1980). *The Imamate Tradition of Oman* by John C. Wilkinson (Cambridge University Press, 1987) is an excellent history of Oman. Calvin H. Allen Jr.'s *Oman: The Modernization of the Sultanate* (Westview Press, 1987) describes the political, economic, and social development of Oman and its relationships with the international community.

P. S. Alfree's *Warlords of Oman* (A. S. Barnes, 1967) is a personal account of a British soldier stationed in Oman. It is an interesting account of his experiences in Oman and his discovery of the Arabian Peninsula. *Dawn over Oman* by Pauline Searle (Allen & Unwin, 1979) is an interesting personal account of the author's activities as a correspondent from 1968–1977 in Oman. She describes the natural history of Oman and the indigenous arts and crafts of the people.

United Arab Emirates *The Trucial States* by Donald Hawley (Twayne Publications, 1970) is an informative history of this little known area. Rosemarie Said Zahlan's *The Origins of the United Arab Emirates* (St. Martin's Press, 1978) is a good general history of the Trucial States and their eventual formation into the United Arab Emirates. *From Trucial States to United Arab Emirates* by Frauke Heard-Bey (Longman, 1982) is a modern history of the United Arab Emirates (UAE). *The United Arab Emirates* by Malcolm C. Peck (Westview, 1986) discusses the close ties between the UAE and the United States, Japan, and Western European countries. *The Economic Development of the United Arab Emirates* by Ragael El Mallakh (St. Martin's Press, 1981) is a good general introduction to the economy of the area. K. G. Fenelon's *The United Arab Emirates* (Longman, 1973) discusses the economy and the social conditions of the seven sheikdoms.

Qatar An interesting and scholarly study of the archaeological excavations is *Qatar Archaeological Report*, edited by Beatrice DeCardi (Qatar National Museum and Oxford University Press, 1978), featuring illustrations, line drawings, and photographs. *Qatar*, published by the State of Qatar, is a beautiful picture book. The captions are in English, French, and German. There is a very short section on the history, geography, and customs of Qatar.

Zuhair Ahmed Nafi's *Economic and Social Development in Qatar* (Frances Pfinter, 1983) discusses the economy of Qatar since it became a sovereign state in 1971. *Qatar Energy & Development* by Ragael El Mallakh (Croom Helm, 1985) provides a different perspective on the economic development and rapid growth characterizing Qatar today.

Bahrain For an excellent illustrated introduction to the archaeology of Bahrain and the Arabian Gulf, see *Search for the Paradise Land* by Michael Rice (Longman, 1984). *Looking for Dilmun* by Geoffrey Bibby (Knopf, 1969) is a personal record of the archaeological search for Dilmun. Also by Michael Rice is *Dilmun*

Discovered (Longman, 1983), another interesting book on the ancient city on the trade routes between Mesopotamia and the Indus valley.

Emile A. Nakhleh's *Bahrain* (Lexington Books, 1976) is an analysis of the political developments in Bahrain as they relate to the people. An interesting and informative study of political authority is *Tribe and State in Bahrain* by Fuad I. Khuri (University of Chicago Press, 1980). It also discusses the socioeconomic changes from colonial to self-rule. Curtis E. Larsen's *Life and Land Use on the Bahrain Islands* (University of Chicago Press, 1983) is a technical study of land use over the last 4,000 years.

Kuwait *A Golden Dream* by Ralph Hewins (W. H. Allen, 1963) is an interesting and well-written, but dated, history of Kuwait. The Sabah ruling family is discussed in detail. H. V. F. Winstone and Zahra Freeth's *Kuwait: Prospect and Reality* (Allen & Unwin, 1972) presents Kuwait as a country with many contrasts. *Kuwait and the Gulf* by Hassan Ali Al-Ebraheem (Center for Contemporary Arab Studies and Croom Helm, 1984) is a short scholarly work focusing on the Gulf region and the small independent states in that area. *War in the Desert* by John B. Glubb (W. W. Norton, 1961) is an interesting narrative of the activities of the British Armed Forces as they attempted to establish peace in the area between the warring tribes.

Forty Years in Kuwait by Violet Dickson (Allen & Unwin, 1971) is an interesting account of the personal experiences of the wife of a high-ranking British diplomat from 1920 to 1959.

Y. S. F. Al-Sabah's *The Oil Economy of Kuwait* (Kegan Paul International, 1980) is a study of the impact of oil on the social and economic development of the country. *Marine Resources of Kuwait* by Fatimah H. Y. Al-Abdul-Razzak (KPI in association with Kuwait University, 1984) is a detailed and technical analysis of the Kuwaiti economy, as revenues generated by the oil industry are being used to develop other segments of the economy.

Iraq *History of Assyria* by A. T. Olmstead (University of Chicago Press, 1951) is the classic on the area now known as Iraq. *Iraq After the Muslim Conquest* by Michael G. Morony (Princeton University Press, 1984) is an excellent history of Iraq from the conquest in 740 CE. It also discusses the government, people, and religious communities. Christine Moss Helms's *Iraq: Eastern Flank of the Arab World* (Brookings Institution, 1984) examines the fundamental elements governing Iraqi policy and attempts to show the perspective from which the Iraqi government views its problems and chooses its priorities. *The Kurdish Question in Iraq* by Edmund Ghreeb (Syracuse University Press, 1981) discusses the problems of the Kurds. The focus is on the Iraqi government's attempts since 1968 to develop a political understanding with the Kurds in northern Iraq.

Lorenzo Kent Kimball's *The Changing Pattern of Political Power in Iraq, 1958 to 1971* (Robert Speller & Sons Publishers, 1972) is a short history of the political realities of Iraq. The social and economic development and the foreign policy of Iraq are discussed in Majid Khadduri's *Socialist Iraq* (Middle East Institute Press, 1978). The political history and re-evaluation of

the Arab socialist movement as it relates to Iraq is also presented. *Iraq in Transition*, edited by Frederick W. Axelgard (Westview Press, 1986), is a collection of essays that provide clear analyses of Iraq's emerging international policies and the implication for U.S. interests. *Iraq: The Contemporary State*, edited by Tim Niblock (St. Martin's Press, 1982), is a scholarly collection of essays that cover the economic structure, U.S.-Iraqi relations, relations with other Gulf states, oil policy, rural development, and industrial development.

Iran *History of the Persian Empire* by A. T. Olmstead (University of Chicago Press, 1948) is the classic work on the Persian Empire. Roger Stevens's *The Land of the Great Sophy* (Taplinger Publication Co., 1979) is another excellent introduction to the exotic history and traditions of Iran. A good general history ending with the conquest of Alexander the Great is *The Persian Empire* by J. M. Cook (Schocken Books, 1983). An interesting archaeological study is *Persia: An Archaeological Guide* by Sylvia A. Matheson.

Amin Saikal's *The Rise and Fall of the Shah* (Princeton University Press, 1980) is based on government documents and personal interviews. It critically reviews the domestic and foreign policy of the Shah and tells not only what happened, but how and why. The *Fall of the Peacock Throne* by William H. Forbes (Harper & Row, 1980) puts the fall of the Shah and the rise of the Ayatollah into perspective. *Paved with Good Intentions* by Barry Rubin (Oxford University Press, 1980) provides a dramatic and dispassionate narration of the American foreign policy in Iran from the first days of the Pahlevi dynasty (1925) to the fall of the Shah. Michael Ledeen and William Lewis's *Debacle: The American Failure in Iran* (Knopf, 1981) is a vivid account of the tumultuous months in Washington and Teheran before and right after the fall of the Shah. Anthony Parsons, the British ambassador to Iran from 1974 to 1979, in his book, *The Pride and the Fall: Iran 1974–1979* (Jonathan Cape, 1984) provides a personal account of the events leading up to the fall of the Shah. Gary Sick's *All Fall Down* (Random House, 1985) is a personal analysis of the U.S. failure in Iran. He was the principal White House aid to the National Security Council for Iran during this time.

Ruhollah Khomeini's *Islam and Revolution* (Mizan Press, 1981) is a detailed and reliable introduction to the ideas and pronouncements of the Imam Khomeini. A good biography of Khomeini is *The Spirit of Allah* by Amir Taheri (Adler & Adler, 1986). It tells the story of one man and his revolution. Hadi Khorsandi's *The Ayatollah and I* (Readers International and Persea Books, 1987) is an appealing collection of short articles on the current regime in Iran.

The Canadian Caper by Jean Pelletier and Claude Adams (William Morrow, 1981) is the story of the daring rescue of six Americans by the Canadian ambassador and his staff and their escape from Iran. Paul B. Ryan's *The Iranian Rescue Mission* (Naval Institute Press, 1985) presents the facts of the failed rescue mission. Two interesting and well-written books about the hostages are Kathryn Koob's *Guest of the Revolution* (Thomas Nelson Publishers, 1982), and Moorhead Kennedy's *The Ayatollah in the Cathedral* (Hill & Wang, 1986).

Turkey *Turkey in Pictures* by James Nach (Sterling Publishing Co., 1976) has a short basic essay on the land, history, people, government, and economy to accompany the many black and white photographs. Roland and Sabrina Michaud's *Turkey* (Thames & Hudson, 1986) is a beautiful picture book of Turkey, with a short description of Turkey today. For a short introduction to the many peoples who have inhabited Turkey, see Gwyn Williams's *Eastern Turkey: A Guide and History* (Faber & Faber, 1972). *Scotch and Holy Water* by John D. Tumpane (St. Giles Press, 1981) tells of the amusing experiences of an American living, working, and traveling in Turkey.

Two books by Noel Barber are *The Sultans* (Simon & Schuster, 1973), an illustrated history of the rulers of Turkey from the mid-sixteenth century to 1938, and *The Lords of the Golden Horn* (Macmillan, 1973), a collection of biographies of the Turkish rulers from Suleiman the Magnificent to Kemal Atatürk. *The Last Crusade* by William B. Munson (William C. Brown Book Co., 1969) is a scholarly presentation of the last crusade (1683–1699). Zeine N. Zeine's *The Emergence of Arab Nationalism*, 3rd ed. (Caravan Books, 1973) is an excellent history of the Ottomans and the conquest of the Middle East. Some of the misunderstandings of the East by the West are discussed. An interesting selection of papers is *The Ottoman Empire: Conquest, Organization and Economy*, edited by Halil Inalcik (Varcorum Reprints, 1978). These papers are based on the refound Ottoman archives, which provide information on the political, socioeconomic, and demographic history of the entire Middle East. *The Immortal Atatürk* by Vamik D. Vockan and Norman Itzkowitz (University of Chicago Press, 1984) is an excellent biography of the founder of modern Turkey.

Bridge Across the Bosporus by Ferenc A. Vali (Johns Hopkins University Press, 1971) deals with the foreign policy of Turkey. The book discusses the transformation of Turkey from a traditional Islamic country to a modern nation. George S. Harris's *Troubled Alliance* (AEI Hoover Policy Study, 1972) is a scholarly study of Turkish–American relations from 1945 to 1971. *The United States, Greece, and Turkey* by Theodore A. Couloumbis (Praeger, 1983) is a thought-provoking study of the relations between Turkey and Greece over Cyprus.

Cyprus Three excellent books on the archaeology of Cyprus are by Vassos Karageorghis, the director of antiquities in Cyprus for many years: *View from the Bronze Age* (E. P. Dutton, 1976), which describes and illustrates the archaeological excavations at Kition; *Cyprus from the Stone Age to the Romans* (Thames & Hudson, 1982), which has detailed maps of archaeological digs; and *Ancient Cyprus: 7,000 Years of Art and Archaeology* (Louisiana State University Press, 1981), which covers the time from Neolithic I (7000 BCE) to Roman III (250 CE). The latter is the best of the three for illustrations and coverage of the subject.

A good general history of Cyprus is the heavily illustrated *Footprints in Cyprus* by David Hunt (Trigraph, 1982). He also includes a chronological table of events. Charles Foley and W. I. Scobie wrote *The Struggle for Cyprus* (Hoover Institution Press, Stanford University, 1975), which covers the revolution from 1955–1960 and its aftermath. *Cyprus* by Christopher Hitchens (Quartet Books, 1984) is a case study of a long-suffering people. *Makarios: A Biography* by Stanley Mayes (St. Martin's Press, 1981) is an excellent biography of Archbishop Makarios III, the first president of Cyprus.

Syria *Ebla: An Empire Rediscovered* by Paolo Matthiae (Doubleday, 1981) is an excellent archaeological study. The discovery of the Royal Library containing over 15,000 clay tablets is recounted in Giovanni Pettinato's *The Archives of Ebla* (Doubleday, 1981). Both books are heavily illustrated with black and white photographs, line drawings, and examples of the cuneiform texts. *Syria, Lebanon, Jordan* by John B. Glubb (Thames & Hudson, 1967) deals with the early human history of the area covered by these three countries. Kamal S. Salibi's *Syria Under Islam* (Caravan Books, 1977) is an interesting history of the early Islamic rulers from 634 to 1097.

A good modern history of Syria is *The Islamic Struggle in Syria* by Umar F. Abd-Allah (Mizan Press, 1983). *The Syrian Arab Republic,* edited by Anne Sinai and Allen Pollack (American Academic Association for Peace in the Middle East, 1976), is a collection of papers that analyze many of the problems confronting Syria. Another, more current, collection of essays on Syrian power, relations with neighboring states, and superpowers is *Syria Under Assad,* edited by Moshe Ma'oz and Avner Yaniv (St. Martin's Press, 1986).

Syria and the Lebanese Crisis by Adeed I. Dawisha (St. Martin's Press, 1980) is a short description of the military, economic, and political setting before the crisis. Naomi Joy Weinberger's *Syrian Intervention in Lebanon* (Oxford University Press, 1986) is an excellent analysis of Syria's actions in Lebanon in 1975 and 1976 and of Syria's goal of greater influence in the whole area.

Lebanon An interesting study of the early history of Lebanon is *The World of the Phoenicians* by Sabatino Moscati (Weidenfeld & Nicolson, 1965). One of the most important cities in Phoenicia is discussed in *Tyre Through the Ages* by Nina Jidejian (Dar El-Mashreq, 1969). Tyre was the meeting place for merchants and travelers from the East and the West. Another archaeological study with many illustrations is *Baalbek* by Friedrich Ragette (Noyes Press, 1980).

The Mountain Arabs by John Sykes (Hutchinson of London, 1968) is about Lebanese society in 1967 before and after the Six-Day War with Israel. Jonathan Randal's *Going All the Way* (Viking Press, 1983) is an interesting personal account of a foreign correspondent's experiences in Lebanon.

David C. Gordon's *The Republic of Lebanon* (Westview Press, 1983) is an excellent short history of modern Lebanon since independence in 1943. *Lebanon in Crisis,* edited by P. Edward Haley and Lewis W. Snider (Syracuse University Press, 1979), is a collection of essays on the Lebanese war, the Middle East, and the international implications of the war. David Gilmore's *Lebanon: The Fractured Country* (St. Martin's Press, 1983) is a balanced account of the civil war and the tensions that have existed in Lebanon since the turn of the century. *The Struggle over Lebanon* by

Tabitha Petran (Monthly Review Press, 1987) shows how the present tension dates from the sixteenth century and is caused by Lebanon's many different religions, feudal governments, and cultures.

For an interesting discussion of Syrian and Israeli policies in Lebanon, see Yair Evron's *War and Intervention in Lebanon* (Johns Hopkins University Press, 1987). *Error and Betrayal in Lebanon* by George W. Ball (Foundation for Middle East Peace, 1984) provides an analysis of Israel's invasion of Lebanon and the implications this holds for United States–Israeli relations. *Dilemmas of Security* by Avner Yaniv (Oxford University Press, 1987) is a comprehensive study of the 1982 Israeli invasion of Lebanon. Dan Bavly and Eliahu Salpeter's *Fire in Beirut* (Stein & Day, 1984) discusses how Syria and the PLO took control of large areas during the warfare in Lebanon. *Peacekeepers at War* by Michael Petit (Faber & Faber, 1986) is a personal account of the frustrations of members of a multinational force trying to "keep the peace" during a civil war.

Israel *The History of Ancient Israel* by Michael Grant (Charles Scribner's, 1984) traces the evolution of the Israelites from the earliest permanent settlements in Canaan to the destruction of Jerusalem and the second temple in 70 CE. This book recreates the social, economic, political, and religious life of the times, placing Israel in the larger context of the Middle East.

Highly recommended is the two-volume work, *History of Israel,* by Howard M. Sachar: *From the Rise of Zionism to Our Time* (Oxford University Press, 1979) and *From the Aftermath of the Yom Kippur War* (Oxford University Press, 1987).

Israel: The First Forty Years (Charles Scribner's, 1984) presents 184 photographs to tell its story, with an introduction by Abba Eban.

Atlas of Israel (Macmillan, 1985) is the third edition of the official atlas of the state of Israel. It contains forty lavish, double-page spreads in full color in a very large format. The maps cover geology, climate, urban geography, and many aspects of socioeconomic life. The text in the back of the book contains bibliographies.

Carta's Historical Atlas of Israel: A Survey of the Past & Review of the Present (Carta, 1983) is concise and indispensable. Also see Martin Gilbert's *Jerusalem History Atlas* (Macmillan, 1977) and *Atlas of the Arab–Israeli Conflict* (Macmillan, 1974).

Political Dictionary of the State of Israel (Macmillan, 1987) is a very useful reference work with 500 entries on all aspects of Israeli politics.

Robert Goldstron's *Next Year in Jerusalem: A Short History of Zionism* (Little, Brown, 1978) is brief and readable. *If I Forget Thee O Jerusalem: American Jews and the State of Israel* (William Morrow, 1970) is lively and enthusiastic. Walter Laqueur's *A History of Zionism* (Schocken Books, 1976) is a classic work on the subject. Also see *The Making of Modern Zionism: The Intellectual Origins of the Jewish State* by Shlomo Avineri (Basic Books, 1981).

The epic drama of 1948 has never been told better than in *O Jerusalem!* (Simon & Schuster, 1972) by Larry Collins and Dominique Lapierre, the authors of *Is Paris Burning?*

An eyewitness account of the Six-Day War is given in *The Tanks of Tammuz* (Viking Press, 1968) by Shabtai Teveth. Another

forceful, factual record is *The Six Day War* by Randolph S. Churchill and Winston S. Churchill (Houghton Mifflin, 1967).

The 1973 war is told by the Insight Team of the London Sunday *Times* in *The Yom Kippur War* (Doubleday, 1974). *Duel for the Golan* (William Morrow, 1987) by Jerry Asher with Eric Hammel is the story of "the 100-hour battle that saved Israel."

A fresh look at the implacable hatred of the Palestinians and the Palestinian refugees is presented by David Grossman, a liberal Israeli journalist, in *The Yellow Wind,* translated by Haim Watzman (Farrar, Straus & Giroux, 1988). A collection of essays and book reviews sympathetic to the Palestinians is *Blaming the Victims: Spurious Scholarship and the Palestinian Question* (Methuen, 1987), edited by Edward Said and Christopher Hitchens.

Jerusalem is captured in original color pictures by Shlomo S. Gafni and Anthony van der Heyden in *The Glory of Jerusalem* (Cambridge University Press, 1982). Equally fascinating are *The Glory of the Holy Land* by the same authors; *The Glory of Bethlehem* by Bargil Pixner, George Hinthian, and Anthony van der Heyden; and *The Glory of Masada* by Raphael Posner and Anthony van der Heyden.

A presentation, in text and pictures, of the many diverse peoples that make up the modern State of Israel is given in *The Peoples of Israel* (Peebles Press, 1977).

A comprehensive independent biography of Menachem Begin is given in *Begin: The Haunted Prophet* by Eric Silver (Random House, 1984).

B-G: Fighter of Goliaths is the story of David Ben-Gurion (new revised edition, 1974, Thomas Y. Crowell Company). Ben-Gurion also edited *The Jews in Their Land* (Doubleday, 1974). *Ben-Gurion: The Burning Ground, 1886–1948* (Houghton Mifflin, 1987) is the first large installment in a multivolume life.

My Father, His Daughter (Farrar, Straus & Giroux, 1985) is the sensitive and loving story of Israel's foremost military leader, Moshe Dayan, by his daughter, Yaël Dayan. Also see Dayan's *Story of My Life* (William Morrow, 1976).

An Autobiography (Random House, 1977) by Abba Eban is also a diplomatic history of Israel. *My People* (Random House, 1968) and *My Country* (Random House, 1972) are also by Eban.

The well-known and irrepressible Mayor of Jerusalem, Teddy Kollek, has written two illustrated books with Moshe Pearlman, *Jerusalem* (revised edition, Steimatzky, 1985) and *Pilgrims to the Holy Land* (Weidenfeld & Nicolson, 1970) as well as a fascinating work that weaves together his own full life with that of the most fascinating city in the world, *For Jerusalem, A Life* by Teddy Kollek, with his son, Amos Kollek (Random House, 1978).

The Golda Meir Story by Margaret Davidson is brief and accessible to younger readers (Scribner's, 1976). Not to be missed is *My Life* by Golda Meir (Weidenfeld & Nicolson, 1975).

Shimon Peres recalls seven men (David Ben-Gurion, Levi Eshkol, Berl Katznelson, Nathan Alterman, Ernst David Bergmann, Moshe Haviv, and Yonathan Netanyahu) whom he knew in *From These Men: Seven Founders of the State of Israel* (Wyndham Books, a Division of Simon & Schuster, 1979).

Chaim Weizman published his autobiography, *Trial and Error,* in 1949 and Greenwood Press reissued it in 1972.

Also see *Chaim Weizman: The Making of a Zionist Leader* by Jehuda Reinharz (Oxford University Press, 1985) and *Chaim Weizman: A Biography* by Norman Rose (Viking, 1986).

Jordan *Roman Arabia* by G. W. Bowersock (Harvard University Press, 1983) discusses the Roman occupation of the Nabatean Kingdom, and concludes with the reign of Constantine. For an excellent history of the Nabatean society and the city of Petra, see Avraham Negev's *Nabatean Archaeology Today* (New York University Press, 1986). *Studies in the History and Archaeology of Jordan*, edited by Adnan Hadidi (Routledge & Kegan Paul, 1985, 2 volumes), is an excellent overview of Jordanian archaeology from earliest prehistoric times to the end of the Ottoman Empire.

Edward Nevins and Theon Wright's *World Without Time: The Bedouin* (John Day Co., 1969) is a personal account of Edward Nevins's journey following T. E. Lawrence's trail. *Jordan* by Peter Gubser (Westview Press, 1983) is a history from the end of the Ottoman Empire, emphasizing the role of King Hussein. Paul A. Jureidini and R. D. McLaurin's *Jordan* (Praeger, 1984) deals with the political impact of social change and the stability of Jordan's government under King Hussein. For a study of the political development and external factors on the economy and social structure, see Naseer H. Aruri's *Jordan: A Study in Political Development (1921–1965)* (Martinus Nijhoff, 1972). Michael P. Mazur's *Economic Growth and Development in Jordan* (Westview Press, 1979) is a technical analysis of the Jordanian economy during the years from 1948 to 1978.

Three books on the Palestinians in Jordan are *West Bank/East Bank* by Shaul Mishal (Yale University Press, 1978); *The Palestinian Refugees in Jordan 1948–1957* by Avi Plascov (Frank Cass, 1981); and Clinton Bailey's *Jordan's Palestinian Challenge, 1948–1983* (Westview Press, 1984).

Index

The index consists of geographical names and persons. The figure after each entry refers to the page number. A grid reference is added for geographical names, found in the main map of each country. With few exceptions, only one reference is given for place names.

The Arabic definite articles — al-, ar-, as-, etc. — are disregarded in the alphabetical listing.

136

Saqqez (Iran) 86 B1
Sarāb (Iran) 86 B1
Sarafand (Lebanon) 112 A4
Sarakhs (Iran) 86 E1
Saravan (Iran) 86 E3
Sārī (Iran) 86 C1
Sarıkamış (Turkey) 94 E1
as-Sarir (Libya) 29 C3
Sarir Tibesti (Libya) 29 C4
Saros Bay (Turkey) 94 A1
Sa'ud Ibn 'Abd-ul-'Aziz 58
Sāveh (Iran) 86 C1
Sawākin (Sudan) 41 E2
Sawdiri (Sudan) 41 C3
Sayda see Sidon
Sayhūt (S. Yemen) 51 E3
Say'ūn (S. Yemen) 51 D3
Şebinkarahisar (Turkey) 94 D1
Sedé Boqer (Israel) 117 A4
Sederot (Israel) 117 A3
Sedom (Israel) 117 B3
Semnān (Iran) 86 C1
Serakhis, River (Cyprus) 101 A1
Seydişehir (Turkey) 94 B2
Seyhan, River (Turkey) 94 C2
Sha'am (UAE) 67 D1
ash-Sha'bi, Qahtan 53
Shabwah (S. Yemen) 51 C3
Shadādī (Syria) 105 D1
Shadwān Island (Egypt) 33 C2
Shah (UAE) 67 B3
ash-Shahanīyah (Qatar) 70 B2
Shahr-e Bābāk (Iran) 86 D2
Shahr-e Kord (Iran) 86 C2
Shahrūd see Emāmrūd
Shahsavār (Iran) 86 C1
Shamir, Yitzhak 121
ash-Shāmiyah (Syria) 105 B2
Shammar (Saudi Arabia) 55 B2
Shandī (Sudan) 41 D2
ash-Shaqiq (Kuwait) 77 B3
Shaqrā' (Saudi Arabia) 55 C2
Sharawrah (Saudi Arabia) 55 C4
Sharjah (UAE) 67 C2
ash-Sharqāt (Iraq) 81 C2
ash-Shatrah (Iraq) 81 E4
Shatt al-'Arab (Iraq, Iran) 81 E4; 86 B2
ash-Shawal (Sudan) 41 D3
Shaykh 'Uthmān (S. Yemen) 51 B4
Shekhem see Nablus
Shekkā (Lebanon) 112 B2
Shetawrā (Lebanon) 112 B3
Shibām (S. Yemen) 51 D3
Shibin al-Kom (Egypt) 33 B1
Shīdiyah (Jordan) 123 B5
Shihab, Fu'ad 114
ash-Shihr (S. Yemen) 51 D3
Shinās (Oman) 62 D2
Shiqqat Ibn Suqayh (Kuwait) 77 B2
Shīrāz (Iran) 86 C3
ash-Shishakli, Adib 110
Shu'aybah (Kuwait) 77 C2
ash-Shūnah (Jordan) 123 B3
Shuqrā' (S. Yemen) 51 B4
ash-Shurayf see Khaybar
Shūsh (Iran) 86 B2
Shushtar (Iran) 86 B2
ash-Shuwayrif (Libya) 29 B2
as-Sidārah (S. Yemen) 51 C3
Sidon (Lebanon) 112 A3
as-Sidrah (Libya) 29 C2
Sih Za'bah (UAE) 67 C3
Siirt (Turkey) 94 E2
Sila (UAE) 67 A2
Silifke (Turkey) 94 B2

Simav (Turkey) 94 A1
—, River 94 A1
Sinai (Egypt) 33 C1
Sinjah (Sudan) 41 D3
Sinjār (Iraq) 81 B1
Sinkāt (Sudan) 41 E2
Sinop (Turkey) 94 C1
Şir Abū Nu'âyr, Island (UAE) 67 C2
Şir ad-Daniyah (Lebanon) 112 C2
Şir Bani Yās, Island (UAE) 67 B2
Şirnak (Turkey) 94 E2
Sirri, Island (Iran) 86 C3
Sirte (Libya) 29 C2
— Desert 29 C2
—, Gulf of 29 C2
Sistan (Iran) 86 D2
Sitrah, Island (Bahrain) 73 C2
Sivas (Turkey) 94 C1
Siverek (Turkey) 94 D2
Sivrihisar (Turkey) 94 B1
Siwah (Egypt) 33 A1
— Oasis 33 A1
Siwar-al-Dhahab 45
Sobat, River (Sudan) 41 D4
Socotra, Island (S. Yemen) 51 F4
Sôhâg (Egypt) 33 B2
Söke (Turkey) 94 A2
Stavros (Cyprus) 101 A1
aş-Şubayhiyah (Kuwait) 77 B3
as-Sudd (Sudan) 41 C5
Sudr (Egypt) 33 C1
Sue (Sudan) 41 B5
Suez (Egypt) 33 C1
—, Gulf of 33 C1
Şuhār (Oman) 62 D2
Sulaymānīyah (Iraq) 81 D2
as-Sulayyil (Saudi Arabia) 55 C3
al-Sulh, Riyad 114
Sulūq (Libya) 29 D2
Sumaysmah (Qatar) 70 B2
Süphan, Mt. (Turkey) 94 E1
as-Sūq (Saudi Arabia) 55 B3
Sūq ash-Shuyūkh (Iraq) 81 E4
Şūqrah Bay (Oman) 62 D5
Suqutrā see Socotra
Şūr (Oman) 62 E3
Şūr see Tyre
Sūsah (Libya) 29 D2
Sūsangerd (Iran) 86 B2
Şuwār (Syria) 105 D2
as-Suwaydā' (Syria) 105 B3
Şuwaylih (Jordan) 123 B3
aş-Şuwayrah (Iraq) 81 D3
as-Süways see Suez
Syrian Desert 81 A2; 105 C3; 123 D2

T
Ţa'âm (Yemen) 46 B1
aţ-Ţabaqah (Syria) 105 C2
Ţabas (Iran) 86 D2
Tabriz (Iran) 86 B1
Tabūk (Saudi Arabia) 55 A2
aţ-Ţafīlah (Jordan) 123 B4
Taḥtā (Egypt) 33 B2
aţ-Ţā'if (Saudi Arabia) 55 B3
Ta'izz (Yemen) 46 B3
Tajarhi (Libya) 29 B4
Tājūrā' (Libya) 29 B2
Talal Ibn 'Abdullah 126
Tal'at Musa (Syria) 105 A3
Talawdi (Sudan) 41 C4
Talibani, Jalal 85
Tall Abyaḍ (Syria) 105 C1
Tall 'Afar (Iraq) 81 C1
Tall Kalakh (Syria) 105 B2

Tall Kūshik (Syria) 105 E1
Tambura (Sudan) 41 B5
Ţanţā (Egypt) 33 B1
Ţaqar, Mt. (Yemen) 46 B3
Ţarâbulus see Tripoli
Tarhūnah (Libya) 29 B2
Tarif (UAE) 67 B2
Tarim (S. Yemen) 51 D2
Ţārom (Iran) 86 D3
Tarso Ouri, Mt. 29 C4
Tarsus (Turkey) 94 C2
Ţarţūs (Syria) 105 A2
Tathlith (Saudi Arabia) 55 B4
Tatvan (Turkey) 94 E1
Taurus Mts. (Turkey) 94 B2
Ţawkar (Sudan) 41 E2
Taymā' (Saudi Arabia) 55 A2
Tâzirbū (Libya) 29 D3
Tefenni (Turkey) 94 A2
Tehrān (Iran) 86 C1
Tekirdağ (Turkey) 94 A1
Tel Aviv (Israel) 117 A2
Tendelti (Sudan) 41 C3
Thamarit (Oman) 62 C6
Thamūd (S. Yemen) 51 E2
al-Thani 71, 72
Tiberias (Israel) 117 B2
Tibnī (Syria) 105 C2
Tibnīn (Lebanon) 112 A4
Tibesti 29 C4
Tigris, River 81 C2 E3; 94 D2; 105 E1
at-Tīh (Egypt) 33 C1
Tihāmah (Yemen, Saudi Arabia) 46 A1; 55 B3
Tikrit (Iraq) 81 C2
Timi (Cyprus) 101 A2
Tirat Zevi (Israel) 117 B2
Tire (Turkey) 94 A1
Tirebolu (Turkey) 94 D1
Tmassah (Libya) 29 C3
Tokat (Turkey) 94 C1
Tombe (Sudan) 41 C5
Tonga (Sudan) 41 C4
Tonj (Sudan) 41 C5
Torbat-e Heydariyeh (Iran) 86 D1
Torbat-e Jām (Iran) 86 E1
Torit (Sudan) 41 D5
Ţorūd (Iran) 86 D1
Tosya (Turkey) 94 C1
Toummo (Libya) 29 B4
Trabzon (Turkey) 94 D1
Traina Garden (Qatar) 70 B3
Trikomo (Cyprus) 101 B1
Tripoli (Lebanon) 112 B2
Tripoli (Libya) 29 B2
Tripolitania (Libya) 29 B2
Troödos Mts. (Cyprus) 101 A2
Trucial Coast (UAE) 67 B2
Tsadha (Cyprus) 101 A2
Tūbās (Israel) 117 B2
Ţubruq (Libya) 29 D2
Tudho (Oman) 62 B6
Tudmur (Syria) 105 C2
Tūkh (Egypt) 33 B1
Tūlkarm 117 B2
Tulūl al-Ashāqif (Jordan) 123 D2
Ţunb Islands (Iran) 86 D3
Tunceli (Turkey) 94 D1
aţ-Ţūr (Egypt) 33 C1
Turabah (Saudi Arabia) 55 B3
at-Turbah (S. Yemen) 51 A4
at-Turbah (Yemen) 46 B3
Turgutlu (Turkey) 94 A1
Turhal (Turkey) 94 C1
aţ-Ţuwayshah (Sudan) 41 B3

Ţuz Khūrmatū (Iraq) 81 D2
Tyre (Lebanon) 112 A4

U
al-Ubayyiḍ (Sudan) 41 C3
al-'Udayd (UAE) 67 A2
al-Udayyah (Sudan) 41 C3
al-'Ulā (Saudi Arabia) 55 A2
Umm al-Arānib (Libya) 29 B3
Umm al-Faḥm (Israel) 117 B2
Umm al-Madāfi' (Kuwait) 77 B2
Umm al-Qaywayn (UAE) 67 C2
Umm as-Samim (Oman) 62 C4
Umm Bāb (Qatar) 70 A2
Umm Kaddādah (Sudan) 41 B3
Umm Lajj (Saudi Arabia) 55 A2
Umm Na'sān, Island (Bahrain) 73 B2
Umm Qaşr (Iraq) 81 E4
Umm Qays (Jordan) 123 B2
Umm Rusays (Oman) 62 E4
Umm Ruwābah (Sudan) 41 C3
Umm Said (Qatar) 70 B2
Umm Silal 'Ali (Qatar) 70 B2
Umm Silal Muḥammad (Qatar) 70 B2
'Unayzah (Jordan) 123 B4
'Unayzah (Saudi Arabia) 55 B2
Ünye (Turkey) 94 C1
Urfa (Turkey) 94 D2
Urmia (Iran) 86 B1
Uşak (Turkey) 94 A1
Üsküdar (Turkey) 94 A1
Uwayl (Sudan) 41 B4
Uzaym, River (Iraq) 81 D2

V
Van (Turkey) 94 E1
Vasht see Khāsh
Vasilikos (Cyprus) 101 B2
Vassiliou, Georgios 104
Vatili (Cyprus) 101 B1
Viranşehir (Turkey) 94 D2
Vroisha (Cyprus) 101 A1

W
Wad Bandah (Sudan) 41 B3
Waddān (Libya) 29 C3
Wad Hāmid (Sudan) 41 D2
Wādī Abrād (Yemen) 46 B2
Wādī 'Aḍānah (Yemen) 46 B2
Wādī ad-Dawāsir (Saudi Arabia) 55 B3
Wādī al-Aqiq (Saudi Arabia) 55 B3
Wādī al-'Arabah (Jordan) 123 B4
see also 'Arava
Wādī al-'Ayn (Oman) 62 D3
Wādī al-Bāţin 55 C2; 77 A2; 81 E5
Wādī al-Fidān (Jordan) 123 B4
Wādī al-Ḥamḍ (Saudi Arabia) 55 A2
Wādī al-Ḥasā (Jordan) 123 B4
Wādī al-Ḥasā (Jordan) 123 D4
Wādī al-Jawf (Yemen) 46 B1
Wādī 'Allaqi (Egypt) 33 C3
Wādī al-Malik (Sudan) 41 C2
Wādī al- Mawjib (Jordan) 123 B3
Wādī al-Miyāh (Syria) 105 C3
Wādī al-Ubayyiḍ (Iraq) 81 C3
Wādī al-'Unnāb (Jordan) 123 C4
Wādī Amūr (Sudan) 41 D2
Wādī Armāḥ (S. Yemen) 51 E2
Wādī ar-Rimah (Saudi Arabia) 55 B2
Wādī ar-Ruwayshid (Jordan) 123 E2
Wādī ash-Shāti (Libya) 29 B3
Wādī 'Atfayn (Yemen) 46 B1
Wādī ath-Tharthār (Iraq) 81 C2

139